Himalayan Environment and Tourism
Development and Potential

ARUN PRATAP SINGH

Foreword by
Prof. R. P. Misra
Ex-Vice Chancellor
University of Allahabad, Allahabad-India

CHUGH PUBLICATIONS
ALLAHABAD—INDIA

Published by :
Chugh Publications
2, Strachey Road
Civil Lines, Allahabad, (India)

Telephone : 3012

First Edition : 1989

ISBN 81-85076-71-5

© Author

Printed at :
Prasad Mudranalaya
7, Beli Avenue, Allahabad.

HIMALAYAN ENVIRONMENT AND TOURISM
Development and Potential

*Dedicated to
my
Loving Parents*

Knowledge advances by steps, not by leap.

आस्ते भग आसीनस्योर्ध्वंस्तिष्ठति तिष्ठतः ।
शेते निपद्यमानस्य चराति चरतो भगः ॥   चरैवेति ।

कलिः शयानो भवति संजिहानस्तु द्वापरः ।
उत्तिष्ठंस्त्रेता भवति कृतं सम्पद्यते चरन् ॥   चरैवेति ।

चरन् वै मधु विन्दति चरन्स्वादुमुहुम्बरम् ।
सूर्यंस्त पश्य श्रेमाणं यो न तन्द्रयते चरन् ॥   चरैवेति ।

—ऐतरेय ब्राह्मणम् पंचिका 7, अध्याय : **3**.

Foreword

Spatial analysis of recreation and tourism is one of the newer facts of Geography having considerable potential for both theoretical and policy implications. Curiosity to know the unknown has been the prime mover for scientific development, and discoveries leading ultimately to a single united world and humanity. The earth, at least in physical terms, has become a global village.

This globalisation has opened up new opportunities for unity of the human race and the ultimately to *Vasudhaiva Kutumbkam* (the whole creation as a single family). It has also, however, released tendencies which can destroy the world, and make human being incapable of realising these potentialities. The stresses and strains generated by the mechanistic view of the world and driving the people to insanity and destroying the very earth and its elements which not only gave rise to all that is living but also sustain them. Environmental degradation in reaching a point of no return and human relations which constitute the foundation rock of progress of man are on the verge of collapse.

Why are such things happening ? There are those who would say that the human being have not changed much in matters of thinking and their attitude to the physical and non-physical environment around them. But their potentialities for destruction or construction, because of the scientific and technological progress has increased beyond limits. Others will say that the value system which once governed human relations and man's attitude to nature have undergone so drastic a change that the consequences can't be healthy and generative. There is some truth in these and similar other assertions. Each generation of men and women reap the crop, sown by those who have become a part of history. What we are reaping today is that which has been done during the last 50 years or so and what we are sowing today will be crop that our children will reap tomorrow.

Wanton destruction of nature has led us to the depletion of ozone layer, and pollution of water, air, and food. And equally wanton destruction of community relations has generated forces which divide people more than they unite. So we see today, two simultaneous forces working around us—one trying to unite and the other trying to divide. One giving the impression that the Mother Earth belongs to all and the other forcing us to succumb to narrow loyalties of caste, creed, nationality, etc. It is the second one which is now ruling the world. As a result the Earth is sick; the human beings—its children, are going crazy.

If the Earth has to be saved from destruction, and the humanity has to be saved from insanity and extinction, nature has to be preserved and man must realize that he is as much a natural being as a social being. He must try to rebuild the community it destroyed in the wake of Industrial Revolution. He must slow down the speed with which he is trying to move through mechanical means and make a rediscovery of himself sooner than later. He must match mechanical progress with spiritual progress.

When seen in this perspective of the things, recreation and tourism have a vital role to play. Nothing is more recreative than nature but this great resource can be accessible to us only if we unerstand its nuances and the intricacies of its evolution and re-generation, We must preserve the nature and evolve policies and programmes wherein conservation and development become two sides of a single coin.

Tourism brings peoples in contact with others and thus generate s feeling of brotherhood. Hundreds and thousands of people in ancient and medieval times moved from one place to another on foot. The guiding force might have been religion or something else. But the end result was tourism. Pilgrimage is also a tour. Since they went on foot they had to mix with people of other races, religions and languages. As they moved, they left behind something of themselves and carried something of the place and people they saw and met. It was through this means that the concept of Bharat as a *Rashtra* was created. It was through this means that the teaching of *Buddha, Christ, Shankaracharya Mohammad,* and *Mahatma Gandhi* reached long distance, Gandhi was a great communicator. He walked, for he wanted to know the people and impress on them the message he had for them.

Modern tourism has however generated many side-effects which I do not want to mention here. It Ras even helped the destruction of nature in many places and created ill-feeling among peoples. But its potentialities for generating a movement for conservation of nature and unity of man are great indeed.

Mountains and Hills have always soothed the mind and created an environment of peace and brotherhood. Such areas which about in natural bounties must be preserved and conserved. They must be developed keeping in view the delicate ecological balance that keeps the nature and man interaction dynamic and generative. India fortunately is rich in Mountain environment. The Great Himalaya have always inspired the people of the land to reach new heights in thought and action. Development of tourism in these regions on scientific basis will help people refresh themselves, understand themselves and their neighbours and above all understand the delicate relationship that binds man to nature.

I am glad, that Dr. Arun Pratap Singh has studied the U.P. Himalayas from geographical perspectives. This volume is the result of a very painstaking effort he has made. As I went through the volume, I could see how difficult must it have been to collect the relevant data and to subject it to analysis of the type he has attempted to derive useful results. I am confident that the volume will add to the growing literature on Recreation and Tourism Geography and find a place in public and educational libraries apart from being useful to tourism development and planning.

R. P. Misra
Ex-Vice-Chancellor
University of Allahabad
Allahabad—U.P (India)

Preface

"God's earth in all its fullness and beauty is for the people."
Thomas Cook

    The theme underlying the present work arises out of the author's keen interest in studying mountainous environment of the Himalayan region—a region of unique geographic personality and development and potential of tourism in such milieu. Lust for wandering and treading the maiden territory and environment has ever been haunting my mind from early childhood and the project I have embarked upon is the natural outcome of the same urge in me. Further, if the movement or circulation has been the moving spirit behind geography, the field of tourism constitutes the epitome of the same spirit. Tourism begins with the age-old dictum-no movement, no life and the process is an unending one. From wanderer, explorer, crusader, conquerer and pilgrim man has ultimately decided to turn a tourist in the modern sense to be added and welcome as an old-turned new phenomenon to the field of geography. Geography indeed has been benefitted a lot by travel, travellers and travelogues. Tourism, is one of the most popular elements in the shaping of 'one world'-the basic objective of geography as an integrating discipline. Interest in tourist and recreation seems suddenly to have exploded upon the geographical scene and geographers are now turning their attention to it. The present work is a humble effort in the same direction.

The region and the environment I chose for tourism study hardly needs any introduction or elaboration. Physically varied and panoramic naturally this is profusely rich in all the components of tourism. If Himalayas are the crown of India being repository of all the country stands for (religion, philosophy, culture, art, nature, aesthetics), the U. P. Himalaya (Hill Region of Uttar Pradesh) is decidedly the most pious, precious and bright jewel in the entire Himalayan crown.

U. P. Himalaya consists of Kumaun and Garhwal Divisions. Garhwal with sacred 'double twins'-Gangotri-Yamunotri, Kedarnath Badrinath-is studded with numberless spots filled with religious fervour and spirit. Every bit of land here throbs with spiritual pulse and the whole of Garhwal is 'sanctum sanctorum' of Indian culture-and the Indology would be missing heavily without the same. Besides this spiritual and heavenly boon, the region is also rich in physical-natural wealth. Nature has embroidered the total land canvas in such a fashion that its varigated scenario pours in immense pleasure. Kumaun region is the best testimony to it. Religious spirit conjugated with scenic beauty and aesthetics lies at the core of the Hill Region of Uttar Pradesh-that constitutes our region.

Though the wide spreading mountain ranges, lofty peaks, valleys, gorges, cliffs, varigated geological formations, rivers, waterfalls, lakes, springs, geysers, mineral waters, flora, fauna, folk and culture-all together make fascinating ground for tourism studies, the main thrust of study here has, however, been the urban scenario-townscape and towns scattered all over the region located and spread in varying styles in different situations. Out of 56 towns of all size and ranks, only eight have been taken for some detailed studies being important from tourism point of view. Hardwar-the gateway to God (and Himalaya) lying at the meeting point of Ganga plain and high hills has also been taken for detailed study, though the town lies in Saharanpur District of Meerut Division of Uttar Pradesh (outside the two Divisions of Kumaun and Garhwal). As the *raison'd etre* of Hardwar to be a hill station is beyond questioning, it is rightly included through in our regional analysis (Chapter Two) the district of Saharanpur has totally been left out. The treatment of Hardwar has been incorporated in the Garhwal region itself because of its physical proximity and affinity. In short, eight districts of U. P. Himalaya has been accepted as a complete territorial frame-work for our study.

The main objective of the study is to present some of the basic components, character and dynamics of geography of tourism in the urban spatial context of the hill region of Uttar Pradesh, as very few studies have appeared so far for sizeable areas. Tourism studies are mostly taken by those engaged in making policies, planning and executing programmes at different administrative levels, or by those in hotel managements and travel agencies, or by some lust wanderers themselves. Such studies are either an overview of some of the aspects of tourism at national level (all India level-macro) or case studies of some particular tourist resort (micro-level). Some vivid travel accounts and picturesque descriptions of tourist places also appear from time to time. Some students of economics, commerce and management have also worked on tourism to evaluate its contribution to local-regional market and economy. The exchange potential of international tourism in the national context is a much talked of theme among them. The realization of importance of tourist industry at the regional level and its relevance for socio-economic development in the hill region of Uttar Pradesh prompted the author to take up this research work.

No study whether descriptive, explanatory or normative can proceed without sufficient source material and informations. Data constitute the basic ingredients of any scientific enquiry. Tourism data whatsoever available are only for the foreign tourists coming and making visits to some of internationally known Indian resorts. Data are seldom available in the case of 'Indian tourists' in India. Tourism in Himalayan region barring exceptions come in the latter category for which the study has to be based completely on primary sources. As such informations were mostly collected through the field study and survey conducted by the author himself and alone. The selection of tourist places for detailed studies and the survey for data collection about them followed a systamatic methodology (See Cha. 4.2).

Efforts were made to go through the available literature on tourism as geographic phenomenon and consult the major contributions. However, references to hotel catering, business management, economics have mostly been ommitted. Attempt has always been there to justify tourism as an appropriate geographic study. Sufficient number of suitable illustrations have been given to clarify and analyse the key problems. Cartographic methods have been used to explain the trends of tourist behaviour. Mostly transferred data (recorded as percentage) have been used due to their increased comparableness and easy apprehension. A number of maps specially of towns and photographs of religious and scenic spots have been inserted to illustrate the basic traits of tourism in the region.

For a number of reasons the dissertation has its own limitations. The spirit of quality may ever be there but it lacks in the quantity of data as it was not possible to make any more intensive survey of such a vast area with no resources at the disposal. It does not claim to represent the character of foreign tourists as they constituted only a small fraction of the total tourist arrivals in the region. It was observed that domestic tourists were not frank enough to comment upon difficulties they encountered. Sometimes they needed a lot of pursuation to come to the point. Unfortunately the response was inadequate to justify a detailed analysis of their performance.

The present study has been carried out under six chapters. Chapter one deals with the conceptual background of geography of tourism and recreation. Analysing tourism as geographic phenomenon, effort has been made to trace its history and growth in successive periods of time. Some significant contributicnt to this emerging field have also been touched upon. The physical and cultural setting of the region of U. P. Himalaya constitutes the subject matter of Chapter Two. The regional setting has been dealt with at length with a view to make a base for town-tourism study. Tourism has always been the main focus in regional treatment. The origin and evolution of tourism in the hill region of Uttar Pradesh from the earliest period of history upto date is fully discussed in Chapter Three. Chapter Four and Five constitute the main planks of the work. Chapter Four relates with tourism in Kumaun region of Himalaya. After showing town and tourism relationship, the origin, structural growth and functional morphology of some selected towns have been fully exposed in the background of their history and physical-natural setting. Some of the basic tenets of tourist behaviour are also discussed with the data available through field survey. Nainital, Almora, Ranikhet and Corbett National Park have been incorporated in this chapter. Chapter Five is concerned with case studies of tourism in Garhwal region. Dehra Dun, Mussoorie, Hardwar, Rishikesh, Badrinath, Kedarnath, Gangotri, Yamunotri, Hemkund and Valley of Flowers have been elaborated in this chapter.

The last and the Sixth Chapter is an effort of evaluation of tourism as a potential multiplier of regional development. Economic, social and ecological impacts in the hill region of Uttar Pradesh have been discussed. After taking an overview of the tourism in the region, effort has been made to comprehend some of its related problems to suggest suitable planning measures and to say finally about its prospects.

The main heading, figures and tables all bear chapter numbers for their distinction. References have been arranged alphabetically finally at the end of the book. The book concludes with some appendices.

Makar Sankranti, 1989   Arun Pratap Singh
  Allahabad-India

Acknowledgement

Few authors ever dare scribble with pen in their hands without the help and aid of their elders-and I am no exception.

First of all, I must express my heartfelt sense of gratitude to Dr. R. N. Singh, Reader in Geography in the University of Allahabad, who in more ways than one made it possible for me to write this book. He not only took scrupulous pains in rendering advice on concepts, contents and organization of the entire work but also gave continuous encouragement. No words can adequately express the gratitude I owe to him for his affection, guidance and help. I also express my sincere thanks to Prof. Dr. R. N. Tiwari, Head of the Department of Geography, University of Allahabad, and Dr. S. Singh, Reader in Geography, University of Allahabad for their encouragement to me throughout.

Dr. T. V. Singh, Director, Institute of Himalayan Studies and Regional Development, Garhwal University, Srinagar has benefitted me a lot by throwing light on some aspects of tourism. I take this opportunity to express my sincere gratitude to him. I also thank Miss Ranjana Das for giving her suggestion from time to time.

I received all sorts of help and co-operation in collecting informations and data from the staff of the Directorate of Tourism, Lucknow ; Hill Development Corporation, Lucknow ; Kumaun Mandal Vikas Nigam Ltd., Nainital ; Garhwal Mandal Vikas Nigam Ltd., Dehra Dun ; Regional Tourist Office, Dehra

Dun ; Regional Tourist Office, Nainital ; Tourist Office, Badrinath. I extend my thanks to them. Thanks are also due to the Librarians and Library staff of Allahabad University, Banaras Hindu University and India Tourism Development Corporation Ltd., New Delhi for allowing me to have an access to the key source materials on the subject there.

My feelings of gratitude go to all hotel managements, tourist guides and municipal staff in the hill region of Uttar Pradesh who inspite of their busy schedule spared some time to furnish me with necessary informations. I indeed owe more than thanks to those Himalayan pilgrims and tourist who eagerly or sometimes even hesitatingly agreed to answer my questions parting some of their leisure and recreational time-so dear to them. I am really beholden to those Himalayan wanderers !

Now I would like to extend special thanks to my brother Ravindra Pratap Singh who often accompanied me in my field survey. I also extend my thank to Sri Ram Bachan for giving his helping hands and advice in preparing some of the maps.

Finally, I recognize that this effort has not been stimulated by the positive sets of values for education held by my parents and my wife Smt. Uma Singh. My gratitude to them accompanies this realization.

ARUN PRATAP SINGH

Abbreviations

B. K. T. C.	:	Badrinath Kedarnath Temple Committee
G. M. O. U. Ltd.	:	Garhwal Motors Owners Union Limited
G. M. V. N. Ltd.	:	Garhwal Mandal Vikas Nigam Limited
I. C. A. O.	:	International Civil Aviation Organization
I. T. D. C.	:	India Tourism Development Corporation
I. U. O. T. P. O.	:	International Union of Tourist Propaganda Organization
I. U. O. T. O.	:	International Union of Official Tourist Organization
K. M. O. U. Ltd.	:	Kumaun Motors Owners Union Limited
K. M. V. N. Ltd.	:	Kumaun Mandal Vikas Nigam Limited
N. T. O.	:	National Tourism Organization
O. E. C. D.	:	Organization for Economic Co-operation and Development
P. A. T. A.	:	Pacific Area Travel Association
R. T. O.	:	Regional Tourist Office
U. N.	:	United Nations
U. N. C. T. A. D.	:	United Nations Conference on Trade and Development
W. H. O.	:	World Health Organization
W. T. O.	:	World Tourism Organization

Content

	Pages
Foreword	ix
Preface	xiii
Abbreviations	xxi
Acknowledgement	xix

Chapter One ... 1

The Growth and Phenomenon of Tourism

    Introduction
    Tourist : Meaning and Definition
    Concept and Nature of Tourism
    Tourist Behaviour : Aims and Objectives
    Elements of Tourism
    Tourism as a Field of Geography
    Evolution of Tourism
    Role of Organization in the Development of Tourism
    Tourism Development in India
    Major Contributions

Chapter Two ... 39

Hill Region of Uttar Pradesh : Physical and Cultural Setting

    Location, Extent and Administrative Divisions
    Physiography
    Climate and Climatic Zones
    Flora and Fauna

Soils and Minerals
Power and Industry
Transport and Communication
Population
Urbanization and Urban Centres

Chapter Three ... **88**

Development of Tourism in Hill Region of Uttar Pradesh

Introduction
Growth of Tourism : Historical and
Spatial Perspectives
Recreational Resources in U. P. Himalaya
Potential Recreational Areas
Tourism Organization in Uttar Pradesh

Chapter Four ... **118**

Tourism in Kumaun Region : Case Profiles and Studies

Tourism and Town
Methodology
Nainital
Almora
Ranikhet
Corbett National Park

Chapter Five ... **179**

Tourism in Garhwal Region : Case Profiles and Studies

Introduction
Dehra Dun
Mussoorie-'Queen of the Hills'
Hardwar
Rishikesh
Badrinath
Kedarnath
Other Pilgrimage/Recreational Areas

Chapter Six ... **256**

    Impact of Tourism, its Problems and Planning

    Tourism as a Multidimensional Process of Development and Change

    Tourism in the Hill-Retrospect and Prospect

    References ... 281

    Appendices ... 288

1

The Growth and Phenomenon of Tourism

INTRODUCTION

Travel, from the very beginning of history, has had a fascination for man. The urge to know the unknown, to discover new and strange places, to seek change of environment and to achieve new experiences, inspired mankind to move from one place to another. Most of the travels in the past was almost unplanned, having not much significance, but as civilization developed and moved further, conscious travels began to invade the world. In fact, the history of civilization is a rather chronological account of tribes and clans leaving the land of their fore-fathers and going in search of new horizon.

Though the concept of travel is very old, the term 'Tourism' as we know or mean it today is of relatively modern origin, just five or six decades old. Since the world began to settle down after the long period of re-adjustment, there has been a surprising increase in both domestic and international tourism because of many factors such as increased leisure, higher standard of living and improved education etc. But the thing which gave it the real boost is means of speedy transport and communication. Such remarkable improvements have been made in transport during the last 20 or 25 years that it has made it possible for millions of people to move throughout the world easily and rapidly.

Tourism is developing fastly all over the world and is having its impacts on social, cultural and economic set-up of different countries. As tourism has assumed a new dimension, it becomes essential to make an in-depth study of the various aspects related with it.

Before dealing with tourism as phenomenon in detail it is necessary to throw some light on the meaning and definition of the tourist itself. How a man becomes a tourist ? How should a tourist be defined ? These questions are first to be reckoned with as they are the real source and soul of tourism.

TOURIST : MEANING AND DEFINITION

The word 'tourist' has come from the word 'tour' a derivation of the latin word 'tornus' meaning a tool for describing a circle or a turner's wheel. Almost in the entire 17th century, the term was used for travelling from one place to another for any purpose. Later on the '19th Century Dictionary' defines tourist as 'a person who travels for pleasure of travelling, out of curiosity and because he has nothing better to do'.

According to Dictionnaire Universal, 'the tourist is a person who makes a journey for the sake of curiousity, for the fun of travelling, or just to tell others that he has travelled'. But today the term 'tourist' is mostly used in the sense of a pleasure tour. Although the definitions given by several organizations are not very satisfactory, yet we should go through some of them to arrive at certain conclusions.

(i) Definition by the League of Nations

In the year of 1937, a committee of statistical experts of the League of Nations defined the tourist as any person visiting a

Growth of Tourism

country other than that in which he usually resides for a period of at least 24 hours. It considered only those persons as tourists whose travel involved some of the following purposes :

(a) travelling for pleasure and domestic reasons including health,

(b) travelling to attend international meetings,

(c) trvelling for business purposes,

(d) travelling in the course of a sea cruise even though the stay may be less than twenty-four hours.

The following persons should not be regarded as tourists according to this committee :

(a) those persons who arrive in a foreign country to establish a residence,

(b) those persons entering a country to take up an occupation,

(c) students and young persons in boarding schools,

(d) persons who live permanently in the frontier zone of one country but work in an adjacent foreign country,

(e) travellers passing through a country without stopping even though the journey takes time more than 24 hours.

(ii) **United Nations—Rome Conference**

In 1963, the United Nations Conference on International Travel and Tourism was held in Rome and after consideration, a revised definition was prepared by the International Union of Official Tourist Organization and adopted by many countries for the compilation of travel statistics.

The term visitor describes 'any person visiting a country other than that in which he has his usual place of residence, for any reason other than following an occupation remunerated from within the country visited'.

This definition covered two categories :

(a) tourists-temporary visitors who stay at least 24 hours in the country visited and the purpose of whose journey must be one of the following groups :

    (1) leisure, recreation, holiday, sport, health, study, religion.

    (2) business, family, friends, meetings, mission.

(b) excursionists-temporary visitors who stay less than 24 hours in the country visited, including cruise passengers.

The Tourism Committee of O. E. C. D. (Organisation for Economic Co-operation and Development) also adopted this definition with appropriate modification in 1970. Earlier in 1963 a vain attempt was made by the United Nations Statistical Commission to define the terms 'tourist' and 'visitor' separately. Peters comments-"the U. N. Commission considered the difficulty of collecting statistical data on tourism but omitted to define the methods of collection or, indeed, to improve the present unsatisfactory definition of a tourist" (Peters, M., 1969, p. 16). Some recent studies published by the World Tourism Organisation indicate that these definitions are gaining popularity day by day, and nearly 70 per cent of the countries use these definitions in the collection of international travel statistics.

In India, the department of tourism follows the definition of that conference on International Travel and Tourism organized by the United Nations at Rome in 1963. A foreign tourist is a person visiting India on a foreign passport, staying at least twenty four hours in India and the purpose of whose journey can be classified under one of the following headings :

(1) Leisure (recreation, holiday, health, study, religion and sports),

(2) Business, family, mission, meeting.

Growth of Tourism

The following categories are not regarded as Foreign Tourists :

(1) Persons arriving, with or without a contract, to take up an occupation or engage in activities remunerated from within the country,

(2) Persons coming to establish residence in the country,

(3) 'Excursionists', i. e. temporary visitors staying less than twenty-four hours in the country (including travellers on cruises).

However, statistics do not include the following as tourists :

(1) Nationals of Pakistan and Bangladesh,

(2) Nationals of Nepal entering India through land routes,

(3) All foreigners entering India from Bhutan by land.

CONCEPT AND NATURE OF TOURISM

As mentioned earlier, the term 'Tourism' as we understand today is a newly developed phenomenon. Industrialisation, urbanization and modernization have created great pressures in present human life; speed, stress and strain have made it more necessary for people to relax and refresh their body and mind. Speedy means of transport and communication have made travel an easy affair. Prosperity, leisure, improved education, technological and scientific advancement coupled with the quest for pleasure and recreation are major motivator/factors. Today in advanced countries, a large majority of people can afford an annual holiday.

The whole concept of pleasure travel has changed quite drastically during the past thirty years. Foreign travel in pre-war days was only for more affluent, leisured and well-educated people who were content to enjoy scenery, art, culture and flavour of foreign lands. This concept was however replaced by tourism-something totally different from earlier concept. Today, tourists have very different ideas about travel. He comes from a wider social set-up and his tastes, desires are much more varied; his leisure time is limited so he wishes to pack into it as much as possible. As such a clear, scientific and more precise definition of tourism is necessary to describe the term systematically.

The first logical and technical definition of tourism was given by Hunziker and Krapf in the year 1942. "Tourism is the totality of the relationship and phenomenon arising from the travel and stay of strangers, provided the stay does not imply the establishment of a permanent residence and is not connected with a remunerated activity". This definition clears three distinct elements of tourism :

(1) involvement of travel by non-residents,

(2) stay of temporary nature in the area visited,

(3) stay not connected with any activity involving earning.

This definition was adopted by the International Association of Scientific Experts in Tourism (AIEST). Tourism is a composite phenomenon. It is a human activity of great economic, socio-cultural, educational and political significance.

TOURIST BEHAVIOUR : AIMS AND OBJECTIVES

Now the question arises why do people engage in tourism ? Why do some people travel and not others ? Why in a particular country do more people engage in tourism than in another ? We have to clear all these questions in further discussion.

A study of tourist psychology and motivation discloses that tourism is the outcome of a combination of motivations in general. The question is what motivates the tourists ? There is a variety of reasons, many of which may operate at the same time, although man takes a holiday for particular reason. Those who can afford the time and money goes to enjoy some winter sports such as skiing, skating and tobogganing. Thousands of Britons rush towards Mediterranean lands only to enjoy abundant sunshine, blue skies and warm seas. Numerous Americans visit Europe just to look at the 'old home-land' and at such historic centres as London, Amesterdam, Heldelberg, Rome and Venice. However, basic travel motivators may be grouped into four categories (McIntosh, R. W., 1972, p. 52):

(a) *Physical motivators*, which are related to physical relaxation and rest, such as different sports and specific medical treatment, all are related with the individual's bodily health and well being.

(b) *Cultural motivators*, which mostly depend on individual desire to travel foreign country in order to learn about their people and cultural heritage expressed in their traditional art, literature, folklore.

(c) *Interpersonal motivators*, which are related to individual's desire to visit relatives or friends, or to meet new people and to seek new friendships, or simply to escape from the routine of daily life.

(d) *Status and prestige motivators*, which are identified with needs of personal esteem and personal development through travel for business or professional interests and education.

If we elaborate these basic motivations and analyse them, we can say that people engage in tourism mostly for eight reasons:

(1) *Pleasure*: It is necessary for every human being having some kind of fun, excitement and recreation in their heavy and tiring daily routine. The individual's desire and need for pure pleasure is very strong indeed. Of course travel and holiday making is the easiest way of having it.

(2) *Relaxation, rest and recreation*: Life is not easy in today's fast moving world. Rapid growing pupulation, industrialisation, urbanization have created enough pressure on man. Every human mind as well as body needs relaxation and rest. For this man looks towards clam and open space far from the hustle and bustle of city.

(3) *Health* : Today environmental pollution is a major problem all over the world. People must need fresh air, sun shine, often winter warmth to maintain their good health. That's why they travel in search of an unpolluted healthy atmosphere, some times for special kind of medical treatment.

(4) *Participation in sports* : In modern life of today people take wide interest in large number of sporting activities. The 'commercialisation' of many hobbies such as riding, boating, shooting has made them available to the ordinary man who is interested. Large number of people in developed countries are now going abroad to participate in more exciting games like mountaineering, water-skiing, under water swimming, pony-trekking etc.

(5) *Curiosity and culture* : There has always been curiosity in man about 'foreign land' specially those places having important historical or cultural association with the ancient past. International events like Olympic games, national celebration, exhibition, art or music festivals etc. attract thousands of tourists.

(6) *Ethnic and family* : Number of people make travel for impersonal reasons which include visiting one's relations and friends, meeting new people and seek new friendship.

(7) *Spiritual and religious* : Visiting religious places for spiritual purposes has been one of the earliest motivators of travel. Millions of people have been making pilgrimage to sacred religious or holy places all over the world. Hindus, Muslims, Christians Sikhs, Zorastrians, Buddhists and Jainis etc. all have their own places of worship and pilgrimage.

(8) *Professional or business* : Many people travel for their professions and business-attending conventions, conferences, business meeting, seminars related with it.

We have discussed enough about various motivators of tourism. In conclusion it will be useful to look at the factors why some people do not travel extensively or fail to travel at all. Lansing and Blood have made a detailed study of these barriers and grouped them into some broad categories : (i) expense, (ii) lack of time, (iii) physical limitations, (iv) family circumstances, (v) lack of interest, and (vi) psychological deterrents (Braun-Brumfield, 1964, p. 11).

ELEMENTS OF TOURISM

Tourism does not exist by itself alone. There are certain components, three of which may be considered as basic : Transport, Locale and Accommodation. The term 'Locale' reveals the holiday destination and what if offers to the tourist, natural attraction like bright sun-shine, scenic beauty or sporting facilities. In order to get his destination, the tourist has to travel and therefore he needs some mode of transportation. Finally having reached his destination he must have some kind of accommodation which provides him food and sleep.

TABLE 1.1

Peters' Inventory of Tourist Attractions

1.	Cultural	: Sites and areas of archaeological interest
		Historical buildings and monuments
		Places of historical significance
		Museums
		Modern culture
		Political and educational institutions
		Religion
2.	Traditions	: National festivals
		Arts and handicrafts
		Music
		Folk-lore
		Native life and customs.

3. Scenic : Outstanding panoramas and areas of natural beauty.
National parks
Wild life
Flora and fauna
Beach resorts
Mountain resorts.

4. Entertainments : Participation and viewing sports
Amusement and recreation parks
Zoos and oceanariums
Cinemas and theatres
Night life
Cuisine.

5. Other attractions : Climate
Health resorts or spas
Unique attractions not available elsewhere.

Among these basic components, locale with attraction and amenities is the most important. However, since interest and taste of tourist varies widely, the attraction of one place to some people may be anathema to others. Tourist demands are very affected with the change in fashion. Tourist may decide to visit somewhere else only due to change in fashion. Peters (1969, pp. 148-49) has made an inventory of various attractions which are of significance in tourism. His five categories are given in the above Table 1.1:

According to Robinson (1976, p. 42), the attractions of tourism are, to a large extent geographical in their character. He has tried to summarise all of them in the Table 1.2 :

After the careful study of the components of tourism as proposed by Peters and Robinson, we may conclude that transport, locale and accommodation are the three basic ingredients of tourism. Other writers on the subject have also hammered on these basic themes. However, there are certain other elements too, that play major role in the promotion of tourism. They need some elaboration :

TABLE 1.2
Geographical Components of Tourism

1.	Accessibility and location	
2.	Space	
3.	Scenery :	(a) Land forms, e.g. mountains, canyons, cliffs, volcanic phenomena, coral reefs.
		(b) Water, e.g. rivers, lakes, waterfalls, geysers, glaciers, the sea.
		(c) Vegetation, e.g. forests, grass land, moors, heaths, deserts.
4.	Climate :	sunshine and cloud, temperature conditions, rains and snow.
5.	Animal life :	(a) Wild life, e.g. birds, game reservations, Zoos.
		(b) Hunting and fishing.
6.	Settlement features:	(a) Towns, cities, villages.
		(b) Historical remains and monuments.
		(c) Archaeological remains.
7.	Culture :	ways of life, traditions, folk-lore, arts and crafts, etc.

(i) Pleasant Wheather

Pleasant weather with warmth and bright sunshine is one of the most important attractions of a tourist centre. In fact weather can make or mar a holiday. Millions of people from countries of extreme weather conditions visit sea beaches for having clear sky and bright sunshine. Particularly in United Kingdom weather is notoriously fickle and there is aweful lack of sunshine. Therefore millions of Britons are enticed to the Mediterranean coasts by the attraction of nothing other than the promise of few days of bright sunshine. Countries like Italy, Spain and Greece in Europe and California, Florida and Hawaian Islands in the United States attract a number of tourists only because of their pleasant weather in summer. Beautiful sea beaches in India, Sri Lanka, Thailand, Indonesia and Australia are the examples what good weather can do to tourism.

Areas with attractive winter climate-winter warmth and sun shine are also important centres of tourist attraction. Around these winter resorts variety of winter sports facilities such as skiing, ice hockey have made these centres more important to tourists. In countries with tropical climate, many up-land cool areas have been developed as 'Hill Station Resorts' such as Simla, Mussoorie, Nainital etc. in India. Climate, then, is of particular significance to tourism and there are many areas which because of their fine exhilarating climates are potential tourist centres.

(ii) **Scenic Attraction**

Scenic attractions are, perhaps, the second most important factor in tourism. Beautiful landscape with mountains, lakes, waterfalls, glaciers, forest, desert etc. always attract tourists. The magnificent mountain ranges with their snow-clad peaks provide calm and tranquil atmosphere. Tourists visiting Alps, Pyrenees or Himalayas are charmed by their physical grandeur. Great natural wonders such as Grand Canyon in United States, the Gaints' Causeway of Northern Ireland, the Niagara falls, the geysers of Iceland, glaciers of Alps, forest of Africa, the mighty rivers, lakes and deserts are a source of great interest to many tourists and have become the key source for tourist industry.

(iii) **Historical and Cultural Factors**

Historical and cultural features seem to be powerful attractions for many tourists. Startford-on-Avon draws a number of people because of its association with Shakespeare. Similarly Taj Mahal in India, Leaning Tower of Pisa in Italy and Pyramids of Egypt attract millions of tourists. Antiquities, famous ruins, castles and cathedrals, temples, art gallaries, all claim their pilgrims. Anything which had historic past, whether it is glorious or not have a strange fascination for man. Thousands of Americans and Canadians visit Europe not only to enjoy their holidays in its beautiful sea beaches or because of its long historical heritage but they view Europe as their original homeland and have a sentimental attachment. Cities of London, Rome, Venice, Paris, Moscow, Delhi, Calcutta, Agra, Varanasi are famous for their long historical background. Many countries which are still developing tourist industries are using the legacy of their historical past as their major tourist attractions. For example the world famous caves of Ajanta and Ellora in India draw thousands of tourists both from India and abroad every year.

(iv) Accessibility and Transport

Accessibility plays a very very crucial role in the development of tourism. Tourist attractions of whatever kind would be of little worth if location were inaccessible by normal means of transport. Physical isolation and inadequate transport facilities are clearly handicaps to tourism. The distance factor also plays an important role in determining a tourist's choice of destination. Longer distance costs much as compared to short distance. For instance in India about a million tourists arrive every year but it looks rather un-impressive being compared to its size and tourism value. It costs a visitor from Western countries quite a substantial amount to visit India for holiday. The intraregional tourism has an appreciable influence on the distribution of world arrivals. Of the total international tourist movement within Europe and North America, at least 80 per cent are intraregional. So the nearness, easy accessibility, good roads and motorable high-way facilities encourage holiday makers. Thus it is a key factor for the growth and development of tourism.

(v) Amenities

Some facilities are necessary aids to the tourist centres. A seaside resort needs the facilities of bathing, swimming, boating, yachting. Amenities can be of two types :

(a) natural, e. g. beaches, sea bathing, possibilities of fishing, opportunities for climbing, trekking etc.,

(b) man-made e.g. various types of entertainment like dancing, recreation and amusement. Beautiful sandy beaches, sheltered with bright sunshine, having palm and coconut trees and offering good bathing conditions draws large number of visitors.

Holiday-makers generally demand entertainment and recreational facilities in larger and larger measure but today tastes are changing fast and wants become more sophisticated, and if a resort wishes to attract and keep its clients, it must move with time and provide those amenities currently in fashion and in demand.

(vi) Accommodation

Accommodation is a basic necessity to any tourist destination. The term is loosely used to cover food and lodging but demand for accommodation away from one's home needs a variety of facilities. However, concept and types of accommodation have changed considerably during the last two decades. Thre has been a decline in the use of boarding houses and small private hotels while larger hotels are sharing much of holiday trade specially in metropolitan areas and popular tourist centres. In recent years some of the big suites have closed down as there has been a growing demand for more informal types of accommodation e.g. holiday villages, apartment houses, camping and carvan sites and tourist cottage etc. have become very popular.

Accommodation may in itself be an important tourist attraction. In fact a large number of tourists visit a particular place simply because a first class hotel is there which provides excellent food, rooms and other comforts. Some countries notably Switzerland, Holland and Austria have gained a reputation for good food, comfort and cleanliness.

Apart from these, amongst the factors which may influence the choice of tourist destinations, hospitality is of utmost importance. A friendly and warm attitude of local people certainly will make the visitor feel at home and help him enjoying his holiday better. A satisfied tourist can help to promote a destination in a much effective way than any other tourist promotional compaign. A compaign was launched by the Government of India recently to help people understand the importance of welcoming a tourist. A series of short films on various themes like 'Being courteous' 'Cleanliness' and 'Welcoming a Visitor' were prepared and exhibited through a wide net-work of television and cinema theatre all over the country. Slogans like 'Welcome a visitor-send back a friend', 'Be nice,' 'Tourists are our respected guests' were displayed at various exits and entry points like railway stations, airports and seaports.

Establishment of information bureaux is another step in the direction of welcoming a visitor, who is unfamiliar with the country and cannot speak or understand the language of the country. So he can get informations about places of interest and the various facilities available there immediately. Trained and competent guides who can speak local language as well as tourists' language, are also essential and are a great help to the tourists.

Apart from certain essential formalities such as health, custom and currency restrictions, the various formalities to be completed by the tourist should be reduced to the minimum. The United Nations Conference on Tourism held in Rome in the year 1963 had recommended the gradual elimination of barriers, restrictions and formalities to promote and facilitate the international tourism.

TOURISM AS A FIELD OF GEOGRAPHY

Modern geography has had its roots in mediaval cosmography, a random collection of knowledge which included astronomy, astrology, geometry and political history etc. As a result of the various scientific discoveries and development of the 17th and 18th centuries, several components of old cosmography developed into separate distinctive disciplines such as physiography, geology, geodesy and anthropology. In fact, all these aspects have made geography a fascinating study. In the 18th century, Darwinian ideas stimulated a more scientific approach to learning and geography was very much influenced by the new modes of thought. Naturally the modern geographers, with increasing knowledge and a more mature outlook, have had to specialize in a number of areas and this process has turned those specialities into many distinctive sub-disciplines within geography. Tourism is one such sub-discipline. In fact, previously it was merely an aspect of recreation but as interest in recreation seems suddenly to have exploded upon the geographical scene, both tourism and recreation have assumed new dimensions.

The discussion about tourism, its basic components and elements in detail held so far reveals that geography plays a very important role in tourism activity. But in recent tourism studies much attention has been given to its social and economic aspects while the role of geography has been more or less ignored. On all logic and rationale the study of tourism is to be placed within the broad spectrum of geography. The following arguments may be put forth :

(i) Modern geography is very much concerned with the nature of environments, the location of phenomena such as settlement patterns, spatial distribution and relationship. As tourism is particularly concerned with these spatial conditions-the location of tourist areas and the movements of people between place and place, it is clear that geography has to play a fundamental role in examining the spatial interplay of tourist demand and satisfaction.

(ii) The phenomenon of tourism is closely related to the structure, form, use and convervation of the landscape,

In its process of development tourism does bring enough change upon the landscape. However, the impact of tourism upon the landscape is basically two fold : the change which tourism brings to the physiognomy of the landscape in the form of hotels and other kinds of accommodation and the change which it brings by preserving the beauty of natural landscape through setting up of national parks, nature reserves etc. Tourism thus begets two different, almost conflicting, landscape effects. Geography has an important role to play in the reconciling of tourist activity with other demands upon particular environments.

(iii) Recent development of tourism attracted large number of people to rather barren mountain areas, which provided a new source of livelihood for the local population. This development came at a time when these regions were beginning to lose their population because they were unable to provide an ideal condition for agricultural and industrial development as compared to plains. Thus development of tourism has rescued many areas from economic disaster and depopulation. Such economic and demographic changes certainly have their relation with geography.

(iv) Tourism is a commercial activity and therefore, is an aspect of economic geography. In many Western countries, tourist activity is now a major trade employing a large number of people in the provision of accommodation, catering, transport, entertainment, other service industries and the souvenir trade. In many developing countries tourism has appeared as a solution to their regional problems. The dispersion of development to underdeveloped regions is perhaps the greatest benefit brought by tourism. This is a key factor in promotion of economic growth. Thus activity of tourism is definitely related with the geographical study. It is fully observed that "recreational studies are multifarious and complex, constituting a fruitful field for research in economic geography' (Boesch, H., 1964, p. 229).

(v) Another feature of geographical interest concerned with tourism is international trade. It is an import/export item in the economy of a country. It is not generally realized that tourism is the largest single item in the world's foreign trade and the total receipts from international tourism comes to about £10,000 in a year. Therefore tourism may play a vital role in country's balance of payments.

(vi) The far reaching social and cultural effects of tourism are of great concern to the geographers. Tourism brings a lot of money in the under-developed areas an this is perhaps the greatest social benefit of tourism. In order to develop a tourism centre, the construction of roads and system of electricity supply, water supply and sewage disposal, hospitals, churches, schools and shops becomes necessary.

Tourists bring with them their own cultural ideas, traditional practices and demands and these may have a profound effect upon the indigenous cultures. Thus tourism has proved to be the best source of international social interaction.

Now from the arguments discussed above, it is fully clear that the study of tourism very much comes within the purview of geography and it needs better and serious treatment in geographical studies. Perhaps the geography of tourism may most appropriately be studied as an applied field of geography.

Before we discuss tourism as applied geography we must at least clear the difference between applied geography and geography in general. Applied geography may be defined as the 'application of geographical methods like survey, investigation,

Growth of Tourism

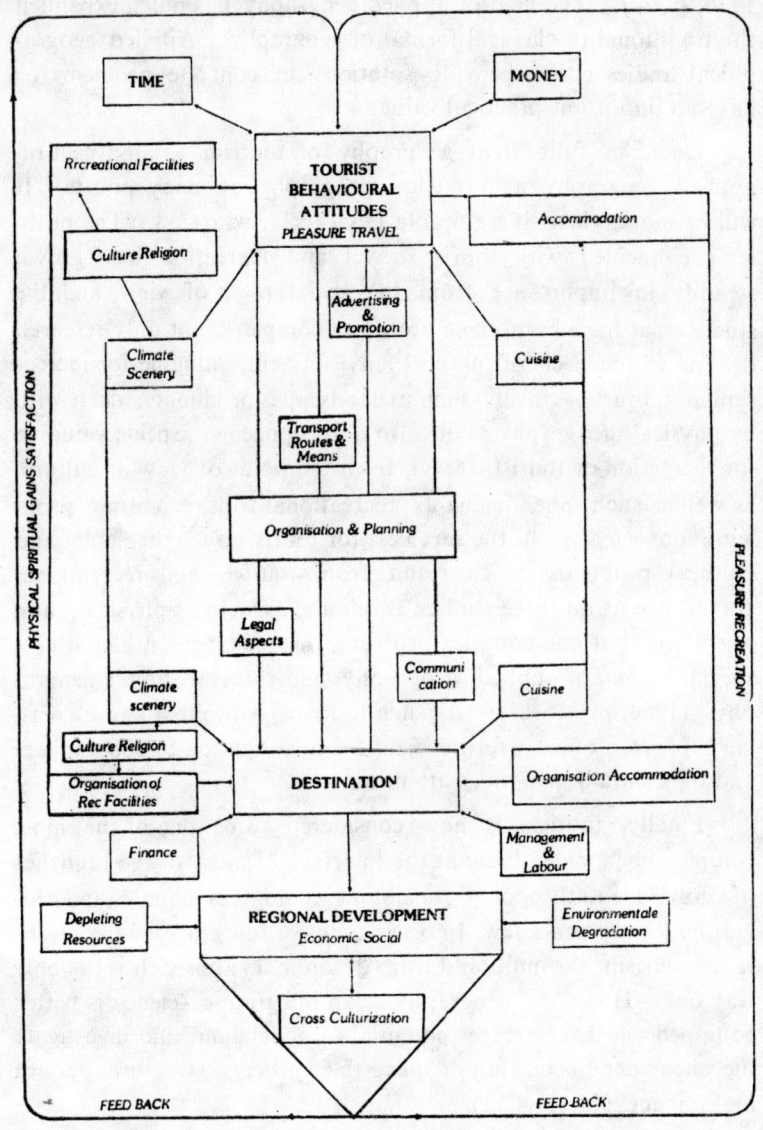

Fig. 1.1 An Intergated Model of Geography of Tourism

analysis and representation in a practical direction, e. g. physical and regional planning, urban development' etc. (Robinson, H.,

1976, p. 24). The field of applied geography has much expanded the traditional or classical format of geography. Applied geographical studies either provide solutions to concrete problems or have an important practical value.

One can fully treat geography of tourism as an aspect of applied geography as it touches geography at many points. It will be more clear if we quote Leszczycki who said, "The problems connected with tourist travel and recreation have grown steadily in importance from the social point of view and the studies that have been made are very complex...not only research dealing with aspects of natural environment valuable for recreation and tourist travel, such as landscape or climate, dealt with by physical geography ; but also anthropogenic aspects valuable for recreation or tourist travel, from the point of view of culture, as well as such phenomena as recreational trips, economic problems connected with the services for tourists and the social and cultural problems which result from tourist and recreational travel. But as all these studies, economic as well as physical, aim at solving but one complex problem, they can be considered as a special branch of applied geography, namely recreational geography...(1964, pp. 15-17). As such tourism with great and increasing expansion offers a fertile field for investigation to geographers and they should give more attention to it.

Finally, tourism is now considered to be one of the most complex phenomena lying at the interface of most of the branches of knowledge-anthropology, sociology, ecology, economics and geography to mention a few. In order to have full grasp of the multifaced tourism, the multi and trans disciplinary approach is the only way out. However, geography as an integrating science is better equipped and have greater potential to understand and investigate the phenomena occurring in space-their process, structure, pattern and impact (vide Fig. 11).

EVOLUTION OF TOURISM

As we have mentioned earlier, tourism in its present form is of rather recent origin, but man has been engaged in travel one way or the other from the very beginning of history. In the beginning when man used to lead a nomadic life, he travelled from one place to another in search of food and water. Gradually with the development of civilization, he became more and more curious about this unique world. At this point, concious travel began in order to explore and see the world. Passing through different phases of time it has now changed in its form as well as purpose.

Tourism has a multi-pronged history throughout its entire course of development. The shape, form, mode objectives and contents of travel and tourism have always been changing. An attempt is made to discuss in brief some of the salient features of tourism development.

(i) Early Travels and Travellers

The history of man and civilization itself is the history of travel and tourism. History fully demonstrates that man has always been a wanderer and explorer. Early man always on the move in search for his food and shelter. Gradually and gradually he recognised the resourcefulness of land and water and began to spend sedentary life especially in river valleys. Almost all the great world civilizations flourished in river valleys. There is a proverbial saying-civilizations flow with the flow of water.

Travel in the distant past was not a thing of pleasure as it is today. The traveller in the past was a merchant, a pilgrim, a scholar and even a curious wayfarer looking forward to new and exciting experiences. Trade and commerce were however the strongest motivator in the ancient time. The invention of money by the Sumerians (Babylonia) and development of trade around 4000 BC perhaps marks the beginning of the era of travel. 'Shulgi'-the ruler of ancient Babylonia had protected many roads and constructed rest houses for respectable way-farers.

Homer's 'Odyssey' records the wanderlust of the ancient Greeks. However, the oriental world particularly India and China attracted many ancient travellers as both the countries enjoyed the reputation of possessing fabulous wealth. India had attracted a series of invaders starting with Alexander of Macedonia, who travelled from Greece to India in 326 B.C. discovering new route between Europe and India. Chinese travellers Fahiyan (405 A.D.) and Hiuen Tsang (629 A.D.) came to India to seek knowledge. The great traveller Vasco-da-Gama reached India via Cape of Good Hope in 1498. Columbus set out to invent a new route to India and in the process discovered the New World (1492). India throughout the history had a great fascination for foreign traders. Mark Twain described India as a country of "splendour and rags, the one country under the sun with an imperishable interest, the one land that all men desire to see."

Trade and commerce remained a strong force for many travellers to set out for a long journey. This was followed by an urge to explore new lands and to seek adventurous experiences. There were many great explorers in the distant past who spent their whole life in this quest. In fact these great explorers can be credited with the distinction of being the pioneers who subsequently paved way for modern tourism.

After Alexander the great, young Marco Polo was the most famous traveller who invented many countries. He left Venice in 1217 and travelled through Persia, Afghanistan and unknown Pamir Plateau. After crossing the Gobi desert he reached China and remained there over twenty years. On his way back home he stopped in Sumatra, Java, India and Cylone. Benjamin of Tudela (1160 A. D.) was the first medieval traveller who reached the oriental world. He wrote a detailed account of his thirteen years journey through Europe, Persia and India. Ibn Batuta (1304-1324 A. D.) was another famous traveller who visited various countries in Africa and West Asia, he wrote a detailed diary of his travel experiences. There were some more European travellers who visited Asia during this period.

(ii) **Pleasure Travel**

The concept of pleasure travel as it exists in the west can be associated with the Roman Empire. Probably Romans were the

Growth of Tourism

first pleasure travellers. Wherever the Romans went they constructed a fine network of roads and developed good communication system. Travel literature was published extensively during this period. Romans travelled basically to see famous places in Mediterranean areas particularly the monuments and the famous Egyptian Pyramids. They also travelled during, holiday occasions specially the famous Olympic games.

Medicinal baths and sea-side resorts later named as 'spas' were very popular among the Romans. The patients using the spas required certain diversions and gradually they were provided various types of entertainment and amusement facilities like theatrical productions, athletic competitions, festivals etc. at the spas sites. Subsequent development of spas and sea-side resorts by Romans played a great role in development of pleasure travel all over the world.

The fall of Roman empire in the fifth century was a great set-back for pleasure travel as well as for trade and commerce. In the absence of a prosperous community with incentive to travel for pleasure, travelling ceased to exist for its own sake.

(iii) Religious Travel

Travel for religious purpose assumed a significance during the Middle Ages. By the end of the Middle Ages large number of pilgrims were travelling to the main shrines in Europe and travel again gained popularity. However, it was dominated by religious motivations. Pilgrimages strengthened religious bonds. It served as a powerful means of forging unity and understanding among people from widely different regions. The adoption and expansion of Christianity in Europe and later in America and Hinduism, Buddhism and Islam in Asia had played and continue to play a crucial role in tourism.

(iv) The Grand Tour

Evolution of Grand Tour in England in the seventeenth century marked the next important stage in the history of travel. During this period three types of people travelled Europe due to different circumstances. According to Fairburn, it was initially an Elizabethan concept. He pointed out : 'First the end of the Wars of the Roses and the gradual achievement of law and order under the strong Tuder monarch sent a mass of out-of-pocket gallants into Europe as travellers and mercenaries. Next the development of the printing press and the arrival of Renaissance learning from Italy encouraged more students to travel. Thirdly the evolution of a rich and stable monarchy helped to create a class of professional statesmen and diplomats...increasing numbers of potential diplomats, men becoming rich through England's growing foreign trade, and scholars in search of European learning, began to legitimise the gallants' jaunts which thus imperceptibly merged into the educative and political institution known as the Grand Tour (1951, pp. 118-27). By the middle of the eighteenth century it had become fashionable to take up continental tour. One of the interesting aspects of the Grand Tour was its conventional and regular form. A generally accepted itinerary was also laid down which involved a long stay in France, especially in Paris, almonst a year in Italy visiting Genoa, Milan, Florence, Rome and Venice, and then a return by way of Germany and the low countries via Switzerland. Of course, there were variations to this itinerary but this was the most popular route : it was generally believed that there was little more to be seen in the rest of the civil world after Italy, France and the low countries.

The eighteenth century is conventionally considered the golden age of the Grand Tour. It seems to have reached its peak in years immediately following the Seven Years War (1756-63). But after few years, French Revolution and the wars of Napolean which plunged the whole Europe into turmoil, brought a sudden end to the Grand Tour.

(v) Industrial Revolution and Development of Travel

The concept of modern tourism came into existence in the second half of the nineteenth century with the development of the industrialized societies of Western Europe and North America. Industrial revolution has brought tremendous changes in society.

As it has already been mentioned, travel before the industrial revolution was mainly a matter of seeking knowledge, dealing in trade and commerce and undertaking pilgrimage. During the Roman empire only the rich and leisured class indulged in pleasure travel. But the industrial revolution brought a remarkable change in this trend. The gradual introduction of regular holidays and better wages made it possible for large numbers to indulge in a holiday away from home. As the industrial momentum gathered and the concentration of population in towns and cities increased, the need for escape became even more acute. Industrialisation also brought in an increase of material wealth and certain improvements in transport and communications. Until the first World-war, the pre eminent mode of transport was the railway, the motor car was still in its infancy. This has the enough effect on concentrating development at particular points along the coast. Moreover, easy accessibility was important and this tended to stimulate regional development.

While in the beginning the sea-side resorts developed because of their natural resources, i. e. the sea and the beach, but soon the more popular thriving resorts turned their attention towards additional amenities and recreational facilities, or what may be termed 'created-resources.' There was substantial investment by both municipalities and individuals in the provision of these 'created-resources.'

(vi) The Post-War Era and Modern Tourism

The second World-war marked a watershed in tourist movement. There was considerable decline in tourist travel not only within Europe but also all over the world. But after the hostilities of war a new philosophy of holiday-making had begun to emerge and many of the old traditions had began to diminish.

Most striking feature of post-war era was the spectacular development in transport and communication facilities. Introduction of air transport for commercial travel has certainly been a key factor in the growth of modern international tourism especially in respect of long distance and intercontinental travel.

The removal of war time restrictions on international travel and the tremendous increase in speed, safety and comfort provided by the new air-crafts, expanded the tourism in those region where it had been practically unknown earlier.

Post-war era also saw a rise in the standard of living of the working and the middle classes in America and in some European countries. This period also saw the first attempt to build a 'package holiday' around air transport, the model for most of today's global tourism.

Perhaps the greatest and most significant development in modern tourism has been the quite spectacular growth of holidays abroad. In Britain also near about 8 million people annually are holidaying abroad. It is chiefly due to the extraordinary development of the inclusive (package) tour which has transformed the holiday habits of millions. The motor car too has had a big impact on holiday-making and been responsible for the rapid growth in the touring, camping and caravanning type of holiday which largely, if not entirely, ignores the traditional resort tours.

ROLE OF ORGANIZATION IN THE DEVELOPMENT OF TOURISM

For the growth and development of tourism organization plays an important role. It is a frame-work within which tourism as an industry operates. The main purpose of organization is to achieve through group-actions the objectives for which tourism has been set up. The basic determinants of success in the field of tourism can be divided into three parts :

1. Attractions — climate, scenery, historical, religious and cultural features ;
2. Accessibility — distance of destination and transport facilities ;
3. Amenities — accommodation, catering, entertainment.

These three are the necessary components for the development of tourism. The organization of tourism falls into two parts :

1. There are sectors of tourism-the various providers of tourist services, transport, hotel and catering, entertainments etc.
2. There are the levels of tourist organization, the activities concerned with tourism can be organised at international, national, regional and local levels.

The first part shows the horizontal organization and the second vertical organization of tourism.

Today many countries have tourist organizations and are getting economic, financial and social advantages from them. Mostly after the second World-War many countries have managed tourism on scientific lines and set-up organizations to deal specifically with the subject of tourism. The development of tourist organization of any country depends on a number of factors.

The political, economic and social system in a particular country has the important bearing on the development of tourist organization. In a country where government is centralised it is likely to be reflected in its Tourist Organization such as Spain, U.S.S.R. etc. In these countries tourist industry is centralised and dominated by Central Government and here tourism industry is well developed, but in Great Britain, West Germany, Switzerland and Austria with a minimum of government interference tourist industry consists of one or more co-operative bodies at the national and regional level.

The importance of tourism in national economy is another factor for the Development of Tourist Organization. In a country where tourism industry is much developed than other industries there tourism organization will be developed on a much more sound footing and government will be actively concerned for tourism industry.

The stage of tourism development in any country is another important factor for the development of tourism organization. In the country where tourism industry is less developed or is in its beginning, organizational base would be somewhat weak.

So for the quick result from tourism, it should be centralised or brought under the direct government control as in the case of India. Here tourism industry is in its primary stage and government is spending big money for the development of infrastructure and for the attraction of domestic and foreign tourists.

The organization of tourism also depends upon traditional influences and historical considerations. Wherever these components are strong tourist organization is somewhat better developed. Organizations are broadly categorised into two major groups :

(i) **World Tourism Organization**

For the first time in 1908 France, Spain and Portugal realised the need for the development of their recreational and historic resources from tourism point of view and founded 'FRANCO, HISPANO, PORTUGUESE' federation of tourist association. After the first World-War many other countries felt the need of international collaboration in the field of tourism and in 1924 'International Union of Official Organization of Tourism Propaganda' was established. The first congress of this organization was held at the Hague, Holland in 1925. Fourteen national tourist organizations' delegates from European countries attended this congress. The aim of this congress was to exchange informations on tourist publicity, export and import of tourist publicity materials from different countries. In the year of 1947 the organization was transformed into the 'International Union of Official Travel Organization.' In 1963 the organization was recognised by the United Nations Conference on 'International Travel and Tourism' in Rome. This conference recommended that the United Nations should consider the International Union of Official Travel Organization as its main instrument for the promotion of tourism.

This is the only organization on the tourism which aims to stimulate and increase the free flow of persons in the interest of economic development and to strengthen social and cultural relations. This organization has closer co-operations with the United Nations Economic and Social Council, the World Health Organization, the International Labour Organization, the International Civil Aviation Organization and also direct link with the regional commissions of the United Nations. Some of the main objectives of the organization are :

1. To promote economic development through tourism,

2. To increase social and cultural role of tourism in the life of nations,

3. To improve international trade,

4. To gain recognition of the value of tourism as a means of promoting international understanding and world peace.

The apex body of the organization is the General Assembly which holds its meeting once a year. This organization also has various committees and commissions which are engaged in different persuits.

In January, 1975 I. U. O. T. O. was changed into the World Tourism Organization (W. T. O.) to deal with tourism problem at the world level. The head office of this organization is Madrid (Spain). The aim of the organization is the promotion and development of tourism for economic development, international understanding, world peace, observation of human rights, fundamental freedom for all without distinction to race, sex, language, religion etc. This is an inter-government organization in a United Nations General Assembly resolution and plays a central and decisive role in the field of tourism. The organization has these categories of members :

1. Full members ; sovereign states .

2. Associate members ; territories or a group of territories.

3. Affiliated members ; international bodies both governmental and non-governmental concerned with specialised interest in tourism.

On October 1st, 1984 this Organization had 107 full members, 2 associated members and one affiliated member.

Besides this organization, Pacific Area Travel Association (P.A.T.A.), International Air Transport Association (I.A.T.A.), International Civil Aviation Organization (I.C.A.O.) are some other important associations for the development of tourism at international level. Among them P. A. T. A. is the important association founded in the year of 1951 with 44 founding members. This is a non-profit organization and the aim of this organization is developing and promoting facilities of travel within the Pacific area and the South East Asian region.

(ii) National Tourist Organization

All the countries of the world which are engaged in tourism have their own tourism organizations at national level. They are called by different names in different countries. The arrangement and the constitution of national tourism organization also vary from country to country based on the political structure of the country, the level of economic development and potential value of tourism to the national economy etc. The role of the national tourist organization is more appropriate to countries where tourism is already fairly advanced and where the private sector is active in it. National tourism organization would normally undertake the following functions : (1) Research ; (2) Information and promotion within the country ; (3) Regularizations of standards of lodging and restaurants ; (4) Control of activities of private travel agencies ; (5) Publicity overseas ; (6) Technical and Juridical problems ; (7) International relation ; (8) Development of selected tourist areas ; (9) Overall tourism policy and promotion. (Tourism Development and Economic Growth Estoril Seminar, O.E.C.D., 1967, p. 20).

TOURISM DEVELOPMENT IN INDIA

India being a vast and diverse country has always something to offer to everyone. Its glorious traditions and rich cultural heritage are linked with the development of tourism. Its magnificent monuments attract large numbers of visitors from all over the world. Besides its cultural heritage, India also occupies a unique geographical position. It has an exceptionally varied climate ranging from the extreme cold in high altitudes in Himalayan region to the hot summers in plains. The wealth of cultural traditions extending over thousands of years, the natural surrounding, the architectural masterpieces, the music, dance, paintings, customs, languages etc.-all these make India a tourist paradise. Only few countries in the world possibly provide such aforesaid interests to a visitor.

However, due to some historical reasons India started taking interest in the modern concept of tourism rather quite late. The economic and social advantages of tourism which were being fully exploited by many countries, especially in the West, came to be recognised in India only in the sixties. Although considerable time and attention were devoted to the development of tourist traffic immediately after independence, it was, however, only two decades later that tourism received the priority it actually deserved.

The first conscious and organised effort to promote tourism in India was made as early as in the year 1945, when a committee was set up by the Government of India under the supervision of Sir John Sargent. The main objective of this committee was to make a detailed survey of the tourist traffic in India and suggest new potential areas in the country. One of the major recommendations of this committee was to set-up a separate representative organization for the promotion of tourism. The committee recommended that the question of promoting and developing tourist traffic was a matter of great national importance and therefore, it deserved the whole time attention of a separate organization. The recommendations of the committee mostly formed the guidelines for the establishment of tourist organization in the country after independence.

A separate tourist traffic branch was set-up in the Ministry of Transport in the year 1949. With the increase in its activities the Tourist Traffic Division expanded considerably and during the year 1955-56 the headquarters establishment was increased from one branch to four branches, each having wide ranging duties. The four sections looking after various subjects were : (i) Tourist Traffic Section, (ii) Tourist Administration Section, (iii) Tourist Publicity Section, and (iv) Distribution Section.

Another important step during this period was the opening of a chain of tourist offices both in India and overseas for the dissemination of tourist informations. Regional offices were set-up at important ports of entry. Tourist offices were opened in Delhi, Bombay, Calcutta and Madras. Tourist information offices were also set up in some of the foreign countries : New York-U.S.A. (Dec., 1952), London-UK (July, 1955), Paris-France (Feb., 1956), Melbourn-Australia (Sep., 1956) etc.

It was on March 1, 1958 that a separate department was created in the Ministry of Transport to deal with all matters concerning tourism. However, the Ministry was reorganized again on March 14, 1967 as the Ministry of Tourism and Civil Aviation with two dəpartments—(i) Department of Tourism, and (ii) Department of Civil Aviation.

The functions of the Depprtment of Tourism are both promotional and organizational which are conducted by the following seven divisions : (i) Planning and Programming, (ii) Publicity and Conference, (iii) Travel, Trade and Hospitality, (iv) Accommodation, (v) Supplementary Accommodation and Wild Life, (vi) Market Research, and (vii) Administration.

The work of this department has increased enormously. They can be summarised as in table 1.3.

TABLE 1.3

Organization of Tourism Administration in India

Department of Tourism
Ministry of Tourism and Civil Aviation
Government of India, New Delhi

Minister
Deputy Minister
Secretary
Director General
Additional Director

Joint Director General	Deputy Director General	Deputy Director General	Deputy Director General	Deputy Director General	Director Tourism	Director Market Research
Hotels	Publicity Promotion Training Programmes Conferences	Travel Trade Hospitality Programmes	Planning Programming	Supplementary Accommodation Wild Life	Administration Finance Coordination	Travel Statistics

India Tourism Development Corporation Ltd. (I. T. D. C.)

The India Tourism Department Ltd. was incorporated on March 31, 1965, by amalgamating three separate undertakings then in existence, namely, the Hotel Corporation of India Ltd., Indian Tourism Corporation Ltd., Tourism Transport Undertaking Ltd., under the provision of the Companies Act, 1956. On the 1st October, 1966 the I.T.D.C. started its formal functioning. In pursuance of the recommendation of the Administrative Reforms Commission (A.R.C.), the control of Ashoka Hotel Ltd. and the Janpath Hotel Ltd. was transferred from the then Ministry of Works, Housing and Supply to the Ministry of Tourism and Civil Aviation from July 2, 1968. Ranjit and Lodi Hotels were also amalgamated with I.T.D.C. from March, 1970. The main objectives of this corporation are :

(i) Construction and management of hotels, motels, tourist bungalows, guest houses, restaurants and beach resorts at various places for accommodating tourists.

(ii) To provide comfortable transport facilities for tourists.

(iii) To provide entertainment facilities for tourist by way of organising cultural shows, music concerts, sound and light shows etc.

(iv)) To provide shopping facilities for tourists.

(v) To provide publicity service in India and overseas.

In the year of 1969 I.T.D.C. had 125 rooms and a transport fleet of 50 cars and coaches. The I.T.D.C. today is the largest accommodation chain with 3000 hotel rooms and a tourist transport fleet of over 300. I.T.D.C. services include accommodation and restaurant, duty free shops at International Airports, sound and light shows and the production of quality publicity material. This corporation has established a marketing division at its headquarter in New Delhi.

According to its seventeenth annual report 1981-82, I.T.D.C. had seven 5 star hotels, three 4 star hotels, eleven 3 star hotels, and twelve 1 star hotels with 3800 bed capacity and a tourist transport fleet of 113 luxury cars, 99 ambassadors, 49 big coaches, 2 mini coaches. Today it is the apex organization fully involved with all the developmental and promotional activities pertaining to tourism in India.

MAJOR CONTRIBUTIONS

It has been clear that geography of tourism is an aspect of applied geography. The expansion of tourism has many ramifications which are of concern to the geographers ; migration of people, changes in transport, increased accessibility, changes in land use, urban development, cultural diffusion etc. But surprisingly geographers have directed their attention to tourism rather late.

First time in 1930, an economic geographer K.C. McMurry published a paper discussing the significance of recreational land use of Northern Michigan. In this paper he had discussed types of land, useful to hunters and fishermen in detail. In 1935 another paper was published by Robert M. Brown, in which he explained the phenomenon of tourism and analysed the techniques for measuring its magnitude, patterns and economic values. In 1938 Durant in his paper on leisure elaborately discussed the importance of holiday. He also sketched out a brief history of tourism development. Gilbert throwing some light on the environmental attributes of tourism critically examined the sea coast as an effective health resort. After this few more papers were published on recreation in specific regions such as 'Part-Time Farming and Recreational Land-Use in New England' by R. B. Greeley, 'Tourism as Recreation in West' by C. M. Zierer etc.

The out-break of the World-War second almost slackened the speed of writing on the subject like tourism and recreation. Possibly no literature was published during the period (1939-45). However, after the war, the reconstruction of the world economy and social order paved the way for many new things. Tourism is, literally speaking, a post-war phenomenon. Together with increase in international travel a number of papers and other literatures began to pour in on different aspects of tourism, albeit most of the literatures were related with practical sides of tourism and recreation. More or less they were informative and descriptive.

Between 1947 to 1951 quite a number of surveys were made by state agencies for recreational patterns and expenditure in the United States. Several research papers were published on the basis of these surveys, such as—'Business Aspects of Vocation Travel' by G. H. Stedman and 'The Wisconsin Tourist' by V. H. Lanning-all these papers were based upon questionnaires filled by the tourists.

During the sixties some research work were also initiated on tourism by geographers when they realized that it offered a varied field for investigation. But the first systematic work on tourism was done by G. Sigaux in the year 1966. This brought a marked change in the development of tourism. Another book written by Clawson and Knetsh on out-door recreation may also be mentioned. In 1967 J. White wrote a book on history of tourism. But the book which may be considered as a landmark in the study of tourism is Michel Peters' International Tourism (1969). Patmore had also made a notable contribution in his study of land-use and recreational activities (Patmore, J. A., 1970). In 1970, T. L. Burton edited a book 'Recreational Research and Planning'. Another important book written in 1972 by Cosgrove and Jackson deals with geography of recreation aud leisure in quite detail.

During the eighties tourism assumed quite a new dimension and it has become more or less a subject of studies (both at degree and diploma level) specially in the West. Quantum of literature on the various aspects of travel, tourism and recreation began to pour in on a considerable scale. But one thing that is specially to be noted in this regard is that most of the publications on the theme are of applied nature and they have come mainly from a number of organizations, institutions and agencies that are practically involved in organising and promoting tourism in different parts of the world. Text books or research monographs on tourism dealing with its academic or conceptual aspects are very few and far between. However, in the developing countries too, now it is gaining momentum and a number of books containing informations on national, regional and local tourism and tourist spots are comming to light. Tourism as a field of geographical enquiry and analysis has a bright prospect and the subject can very well be studied on scientific lines.

Tourism and recreation as a field of geographic study and research were introduced in India quite late. Though with the setting up of the Department of Tourism in 1956 a number of steps were being taken for the promotion and development of tourism in India, it went almost unnoticed by the academicians. Tourism has no doubt been introduced now in some of the Indian Universities and Institutions, but it is often at diploma stage everywhere. It has hardly been able to make any grounding in academic curricula either at the college or university level. Therefore literature on the various aspects of tourism are quite meagre. Most of the books or pamphlets that are written, they are mainly by the persons, in-charge of travelling, hotel management, recreation or marketing etc. at the government level. Books written on regional geography, development, planning, trade and commerce etc. also touch tourism though partially and that too only on their fringe. Some regional monographs dealing with history, culture, geography and environment in some parts of India also throw light on certain aspects of tourism. Monographs published on mountanious, coastal or desert areas etc. also touch upon this aspect in some way or the other. But the works directly dealing with tourism as a scientific field of investigation are quite few in India. The beginning has, however, been made with the scattered research work being conducted at the university level though in piecemeal way. In this respect the name of T. V. Singh may specially be mentioned who has contributed significantly towards the development to tourism geography is India in his own way. Some of the Indian Universities such as Garhwal (Srinagar), Kumaun (Nainital), Rajasthan (Jaipur) and Marathwara (Aurangabad) have started certificate, diploma and degree courses on tourism. Courses on tourism and hotel management etc. are also conducted at Delhi, Calcutta, Bombay, Madras and Nagpur.

2

Hill Region of Uttar Pradesh : Physical and Cultural Setting

LOCATION, EXTENT AND ADMINISTRATIVE DIVISIONS

The Himalaya has always been a nursery of peace and religion. It has been the cradle of everything precious and beautiful in India's heritage. Poets, painters, sages and saints have always been spell-bound by the natural grace and charm of the Himalaya. The poet Kalidas conceived the Himalaya to be a much larger mountain than its present form and described it as a celestial entity in his famous epic 'Kumarsambhavam' in the following lines :

अस्त्युत्तरस्यां दिशि देवतात्मा
हिमालयो नाम नगाधिराजः ।
पूर्वापरौ तोयनिधी वगाह्य
स्थितः पृथित्या इव मानदंडः ॥ 1:1

"There is a mountain in the north ensouled by Divinity named Himalaya, the King of all mountains. Stretching from

East to West coast, it is located on the earth as a measuring rod".

External boundaries of some nine states touch or pass through this highest mountain wall. They are Pakistan, Afghanistan, the U.S.S.R., China, India, Nepal, Bhutan, Bangladesh and Burma.

In the West the Himalays start from Baluchistan and stretch up to Burma in the East. In case of India the Himalayan ranges spread from Kashmir in the north-west to Naga hills in the north-east through Himachal Pradesh, Uttar Pradesh (Uttara Khand), Sikkim, Assam and Arunachal Pradesh (vide Fig. 2.1).

Uttarakhand comprises the main part of U. P. Himalaya* including Garhwal Himalaya and Kumaun Himalaya, lying between 29°5′N to 31°25′N lat. and 77°45′E. to 81°E. long and covering about 46485 Km^2 of area. The maximum length of U. P. Himalaya from east to west is 357 Km. and width from north to south comes to about 294 Km. In the west the Tons river separates this region from Himachal Pradesh while in the east it is bifurcated from Nepal by the river Kali. From the foot-hill zone of Uttar Pradesh in the south this region extends up to the snowclad peaks in the north making the Indo-Tibetan Border.

U. P. Himalaya incorporates the entire administrative divisions of Garhwal and Kumaun. Thus eight northern districts of Uttar Pradesh i. e., Dehra Dun, Uttarkashi, Chamoli, Tehri Garhwal, Pauri-Garhwal (Garhwal division) ; Nainital, Almora, Pithoragarh (Kumaun Division) are the constituents of the study area (Fig. 2.2). Districts are divided into 'tahsils' which are further sub-divided into 'parganas' and Community Development Blocks. In all, there are 30 tahsils and 89 Community Development Blocks in this region. There are also a number of local

---

*Previously known as Kumaun Himalaya. Some of the authors now term this part of Himalaya as Garhkum (Garhwal-Kumaun) Himalaya.

Hill Region of Uttar Pradesh

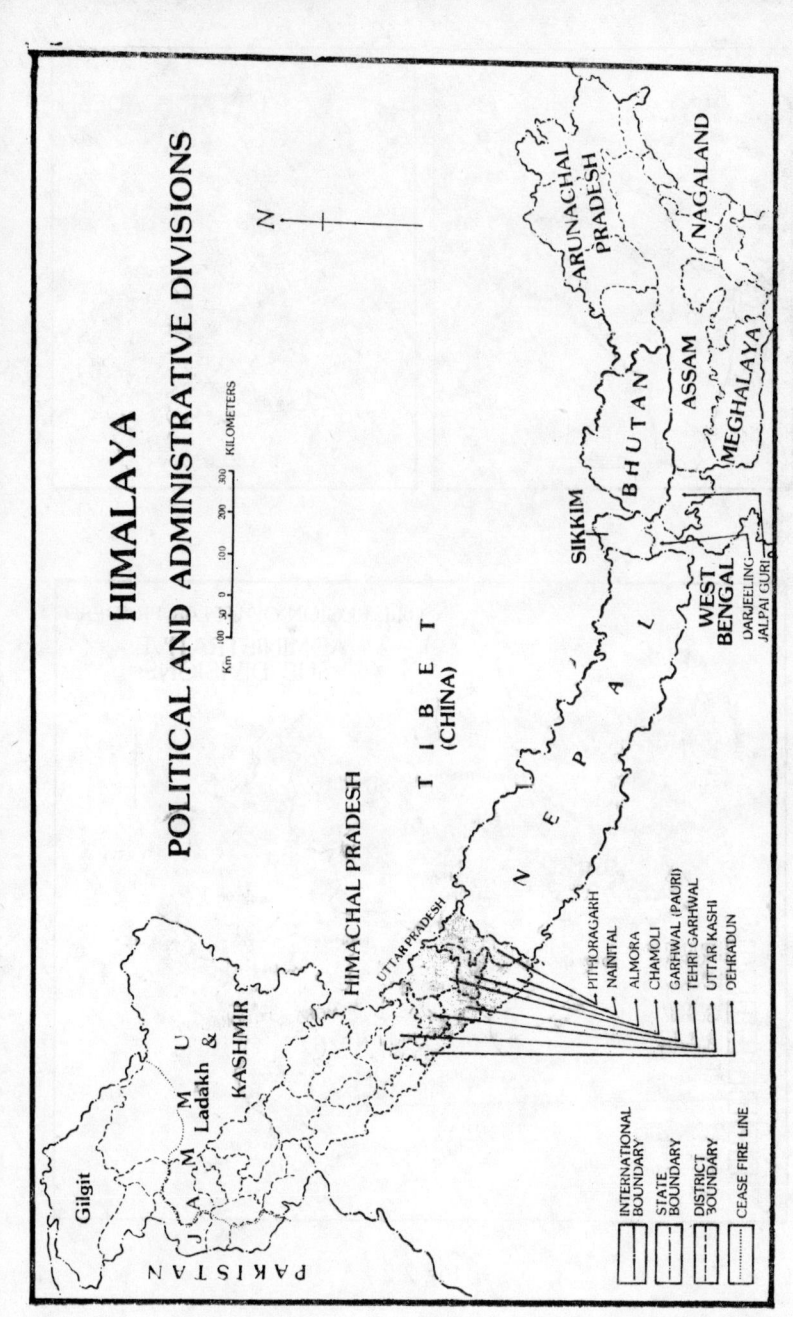

Fig. 2.1

Himalayan Environment and Tourism

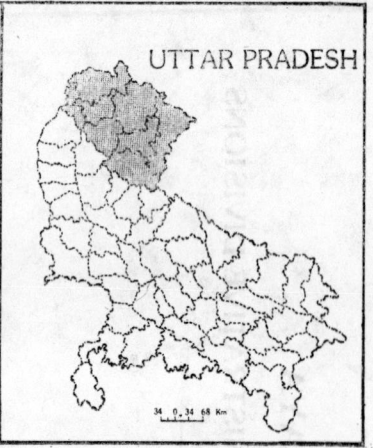

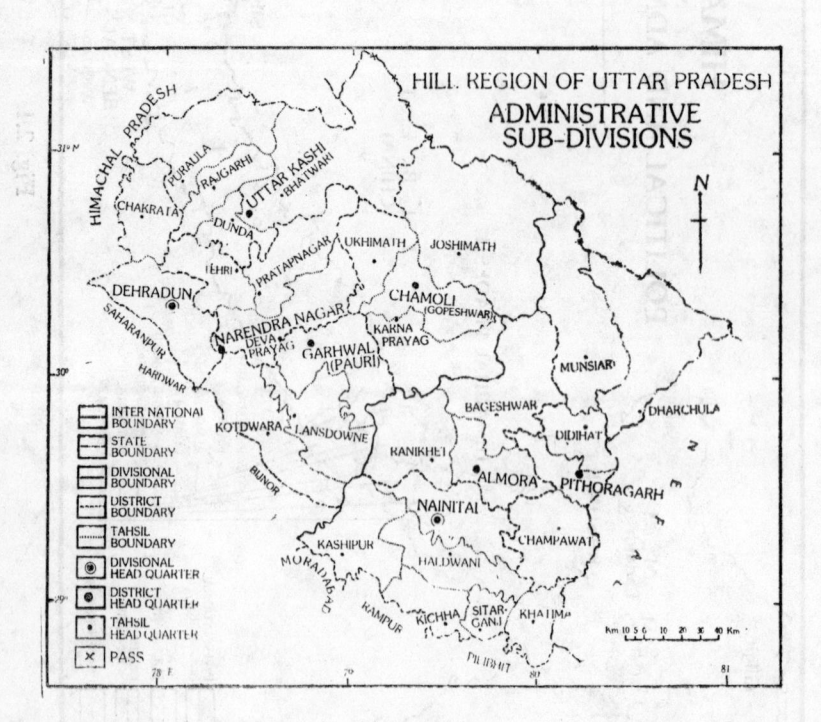

Fig 2.2

bodies for the administration of rural and urban areas of the districts. In all, there are 8 District Boards (one in each district), 21 Municipal Boards, 16 Town Area Committees, 14 Notified Areas, 8 Cantonment Boards and 3 Census Towns (vide Table 2.1).

PHYSIOGRAPHY

The northern part of Uttar Pradesh is completely covered with Himalayan ranges normally called the U. P. Himalaya. This region has a rugged topography with a number of valleys, glaciers, lakes and 'tals' strewn all over the area.

(i) Structure

The geological structure of this area is quite complex and complicated. However, the whole region can be broadly divided into three stratigraphical zones :

(a) Outer or Sub-Himalayan or Siwalik Zone;

(b) Central or Lesser Himalayan Zone;

(c) Greater Himalayan Zone.

The starting point of the Sub-Himalayan Zone is the upper Ganga plain. According to geologists this belt is formed by tertiary and upper tertiary sedimentary river deposits. The rocks of this region are mostly of great thickness of detrital material, clay and conglomerates, their thickness ranging between 5000 to 5500 m. The beds of this region are mostly filled with sand-stone and shale.

The Central or Lesser Himalayan Zone is separated from the Siwalik Zone by a greater thrust known as the 'Main Boundary Fault' (Fig. 2.3). This zone is composed of granite and other crystalline rocks of unfossiliferous (or poorly fossiliferous) sediments with complex tectonics. Rocks have been metamorphosed to a larger extent and they vary in age from Algonkian to the Eocene. "Lithological variations present a mosaic of colours-buff, cream, white, purple, pink, gray, green, yellow and slaty

TABLE 2.1
Area and Administrative Divisions of U. P. Himalaya

Details	Kumaun Division Almora	Nainital	Pithoragarh	Chamoli	Garhwal Division Dehra Dun	Pauri-Garhwal	Tehri Garhwal	Uttar-kashi	U. P. Himalaya Total
1. Total Geographical Area (Km²)	5385	6794	8856	9125	3088	5440	4421	8016	51125
2. Number of Tahsils	3	6	5	4	2	3	3	4	30
3. Number of Community Development Blocks	14	15	12	11	6	15	10	6	89
4. Number of Towns :									
(i) Municipal Boards	5	18	5	7	11	8	5	3	62
(ii) Town Areas	2	8	1	—	3	4	2	1	21
(iii) Cantonments	—	1	3	1	4	1	—	2	16
(iv) Notified Areas	2	1	1	—	1	1	3	—	8
(v) Census Towns	1	—	—	6	2	1	—	—	14
									3
5. Total Population :	757373	1136523	489267	36446	761668	637877	497710	190948	4835712
(i) Rural	709777 (93.72%)	824080 (72.51%)	462248 (94.48%)	335172 (91.99%)	389527 (51.14%)	575208 (90.18%)	477164 (95.87%)	177676 (93.05%)	3950852 (81.7%)
(ii) Urban	47596 (6.28%)	312443 (27.49%)	27019 (5.52%)	29174 (8.01%)	372141 (48.86%)	62669 (9.82%)	20546 (4.13%)	13272 (6.05%)	884860 (18.3%)
6. Population Density (per km²)	141	167	55	41	247	117	113	24	95

Source : Census of India 1981, Part 2B.

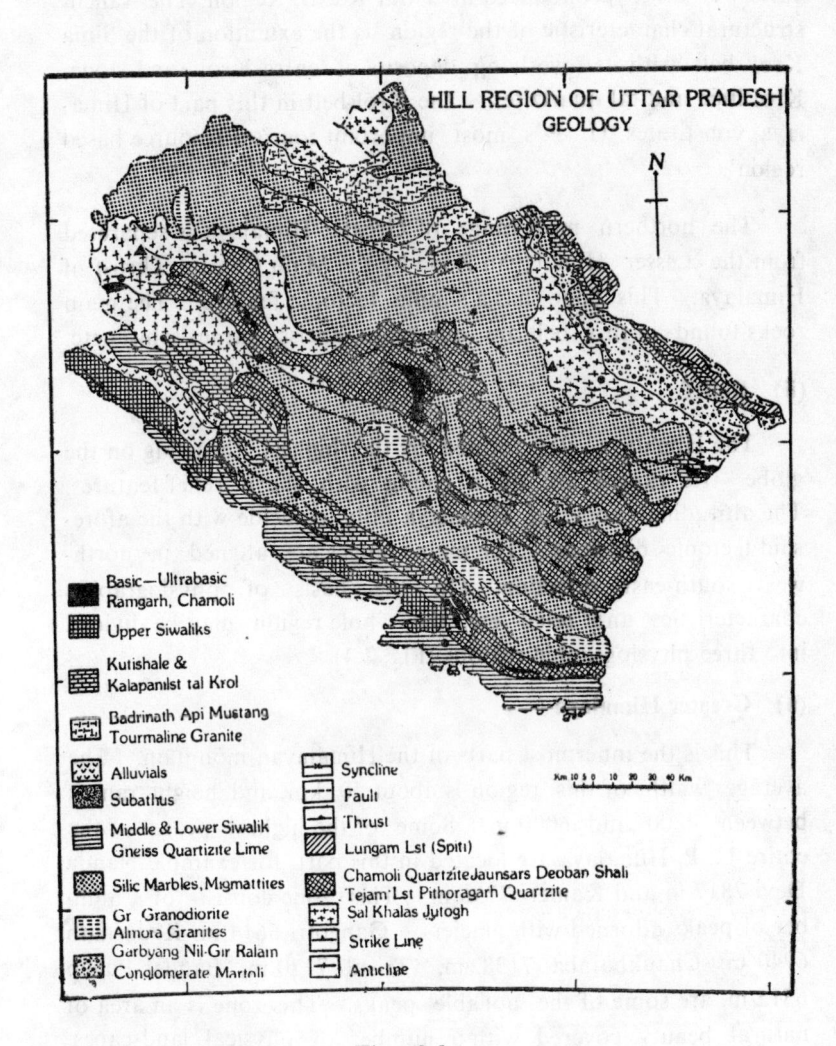

Fig. 2.3

presenting a feast to the eye" (Singh, T. V. 1974, p. 8). The variety is most pronounced in Uttar Kashi Region. The salient structural characteristic of the region is the extention of the Sima Krol belt with its overlying deposits of enfra Krol sand-stone, Krol lime and tal quartzites. The Krol-belt in this part of Himalaya constitutes 'U. P.'s most important tourism resource based region'.

The northern most range of Greater Himalaya is separated from the Lesser Himalayan Zone by the Main Central Thrust of Himalaya. This Zone has a simple tectonic feature. The main rocks found in this belt are quartzites, gneiss, garnet-schists etc.

(ii) **Relief**

The Himalaya was formed by the highest thrusting on the globe. Its ranges are quite young with sharp relief features. The altitudinal zones of Himalaya fully coincide with the aforesaid tectonic divisions. The main ranges are aligned in northwest south-east direction. On the basis of physiographic characteristics and relief etc. the whole region may be divided into three physiographic regions (Fig. 2.4) :

(a) **Greater Himalaya**

This is the innermost part of the Himalayan mountain. The average width of this region is about 50 km. and height ranges between 4800 and 6000 m. Some of the highest peaks of the entire U. P. Himalaya are located in this part, for example Nanda Devi 7817 m and Kamet 7756 m. This zone consists of a number of peaks adorned with glaciers. Gangotri 6614 m, Kedarnath 6940 m, Chaukhamba 7138 m, Trisul 7120 m, Bander-Punch 6315 m, are some of the notable peaks. This zone is an area of natural beauty covered with a number of physical landscapes. There are also many prominent river valleys such as Bhagirathi, Alaknanda, Dhauli Ganga etc. The region also abounds in glacier lakes. Hemkund, Roop Kund, Chaukhamba are notable among them. The landforms obtaining in this part of Himalaya

Hill Region of Uttar Pradesh

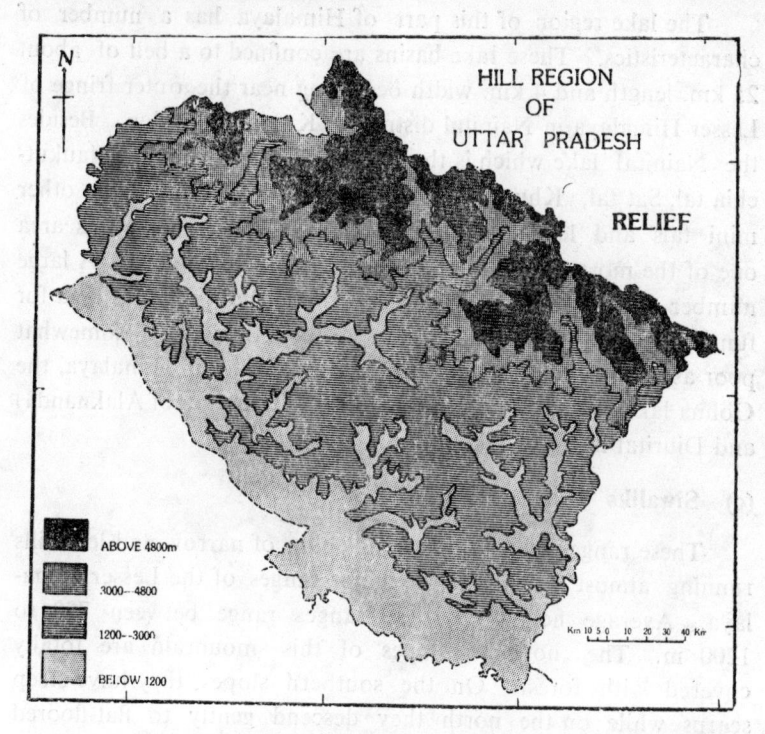

HILL REGION OF UTTAR PRADESH

RELIEF

ABOVE 4800m
3000—4800
1200—3000
BELOW 1200

Fig. 2.4

show ample proofs of ice-sculpture. 'Presence of the fluvio-glacial drifts and matter, glacial lakes formed of plugging of valleys (e. g., Hemkund, Rupkund, Satopanth, Chobarital and Chaukhamba) and broad glacial terraces are the evidences that the region was affected by at least one glacial age (Wadia, D. N. 1968, p. 43).

(b) Lesser Himalaya

The central part of Himalaya comprises of a number of ranges, hills, valleys and lake basins. The approximate width of the region is 75 km. and the average height is 1500 to 2700 m. The whole region is full of ridges divided from each other by deep valleys.

The lake region of this part of Himalaya has a number of characteristics. These lake basins are confined to a belt of about 25 km. length and 4 km. width occurring near the outer fringe of Lesser Himalaya in Nainital district of Kumaun division. Besides the Nainital lake which is the queen of lakes, Bhimtal, Naukutchia tal, Sat tal, Khurpatal, Sukha tal, Saria tal and many other mini tals and lakes abound in the region which make this area one of the most important recreation resource regions. A large number of visitors both inland and foreign come to this area for fun and frolic. Garhwal part of Lessor Himalaya is somewhat poor as regards lake endowment. In the Garhwal Himalaya, the Gohna lake in the valley of Birhi-Ganga (Tributary of Alaknanda) and Diurital north of Ukimath are noteworthy.

(c) Siwaliks

These ranges constitute a long chain of narrow and low hills running almost parallel to the major ranges of the Lesser Himalaya. Average height of these ranges range between 750 to 1200 m. The northern slopes of this mountain are totally covered with forest. On the southern slopes they have steep scarps while on the north they descend gently to flat-floored structural valleys called 'duns' (Singh, R. L. 1971, p. 449). These duns are covered with recent gravels of Lesser Himalaya to a height of 350 m. above the plains. DehraDun about 35 km. long and 25 km. wide is the biggest and most developed in the whole Garhwal region. With its natural splendour and human articulation this valley provides one of the best spots for tourists. Other duns like Patti, Chaukhamba, Kohtri and Kota are quite small.

(iii) Drainage System

Rivers have been the Key factors in the human civilization from its very advent. *Civilizations almost flows with the flows of water*. Most of the civilizations have been named after the important river systems. India has a unique position in this regard. A lot of worldly and spiritual significance were attached to these rivers and they were called as *'sacred mother and goddess'*. Their water cleaned their body and soul and brought them into communion with the benign water spirit and the honoured dead whose ashes they consigned in them (Singh, T. V., 1974, p. 14).

U. P. Himalaya has a wonderful river system in the whole country. It is well-drained by a number of rivers and rivulets of various magnitude (Fig. 2.5). Besides its rivers, the region

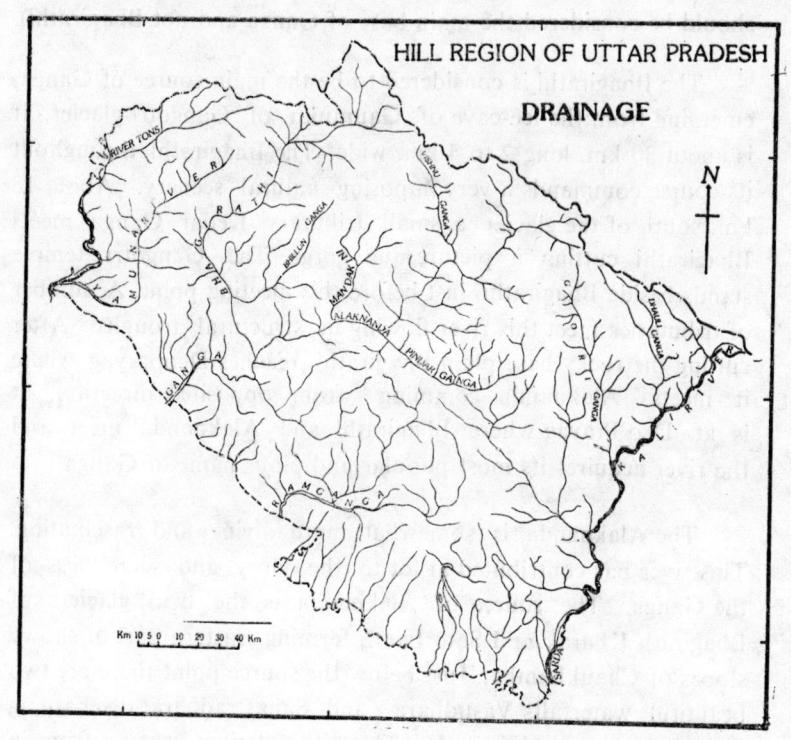

Fig. 2.5

abounds in numerous lakes and tals of varying shapes and sizes. The drainage of the region can be categorized into three major systems :

(a) Ganga System

The historical hydrography of the Ganga is a topic of multi-disciplinary interest. The source materials for such studies are found in the ancient texts like the *Ramayan*, the *Mahabharat* and the *Puranas*. A lot of descriptions of this river have also been made by foreign travellers who visited India in ancient time. These source materials generally regard Bhagirathi as the main source of Ganga. But according to the volume of water Alaknanda seems to be bigger than Bhagirathi. (As such Alaknanda should be considered the main base of Ganga and not Bhagirathi).

The Bhagirathi is considered to be the main source of Ganga, emerging from the ice-cave of Gaumukh of Gangotri glacier. It is about 30 km. long 2 to 4 km. wide. The Bhagirathi throughout its course commands a very imposing natural scenery. About 18 km. south of the glacier a small tributary Kedar Ganga meets Bhagirathi cutting a picturesque gorge. The Gangotri temple stands beside Bhagirathi, just before this meeting point. A number of tributaries meet this river flowing in structural troughs. After cutting the rocky base plain Bhagirathi reaches Deoprayag where it meets Alaknanda comming from opposite direction. It is at Deo Prayag where Bhagirathi and Alaknanda meet and the river acquires its most popular and pious name of Ganga.

The Alaknanda is somewhat more divine and fascinating. This river has contributed at lot to the glory and sacredness of the Ganga. The source of Alaknanda is the twin glaciers of Bhagirath Kharak and Sato Panth farming eastern part of snowy slopes of Chaukhamba. Just below the source point there are two beautiful waterfalls Vasudhara and Sahastradhara discharging their water into Alaknanda. The river derives waters from a number of tributaries. At Badrinath, Rishi Ganga meets the main stream giving a hanging valley perception. The Khiraon Ganga merges into Alaknanda just below Hanuman Chatti. The Bhyunder Ganga flowing along the valley of flowers meets Alaknanda near Govind-ghat. Other important tributaries meet

Alaknanda at certain intervals. Below Joshimath the Dhauli Ganga comes down from the Niti Pass to join it at Vishnu Prayag, the Nandakini meets it at Nand Prayag. At Karn Prayag, the Alaknanda is joined by the Pindar Ganga which arises from the Pindari glacier on the eastern flank of the great Nanda Devi (7816 m). The Mandakini river comming from near Kedarnath temple joins Alaknanda at Rudra Prayag. After flowing about 70 km. from here Alaknanda finally merges into Bhagirathi at famous Deva Prayag to acquire the name of the Ganga hereafter. All these Prayagas (confluences) are quite sacred for Hindus. A large number of pilgrims and inland tourists come here every year.

(b) Yamuna System

The source of Yamuna is the Yamunotri glacier on the south-west slopes of Bander-Punch peak (6387 m) in Uttar Kashi district. It has lesser number of tributaries but they are somewhat more turbulent and rapid. The Tons and Pober are the main tributaries. The Tons rising from the northern slope of Bander-Punch flows in a valley north-west of the Yamuna and meets it below Kalsi. The Tons nearly brings double the volume of water of the Yamuna. After this point the Yamuna comes out of the Lesser Himalaya and intrudes in the famous Dun Valley.

The river Yamuna though the most important tributary of the river Ganga has no place or spot of pilgrimage in its entire course in U. P. Himalaya except at its source itself. The Yamunotri temple with its geysers and hot springs is the best attraction for the pilgrims and the tourists.

(c) Kali System

The river Kali and its tributaries drain almost 25 per cent area of the entire U. P. Himalaya covering the district of Pithoragarh and the eastern parts of Almora and Nainital. A number of tributaries meet Kali at intervals. The Gori Ganga meets it at Jaulgiri, the Sarju a major feeder of the Kali meets 45 km. below this point. The Kali ultimately enters the plain at Baramdeo where after the river takes its popular name Sarda.

Some of the important rivers flowing the eastern part of U.P. Himalaya are Ramganga, Kosi, Gola, Nihal and Dabka etc. These rivers have generally formed deep valleys following the lithological structure of the area. The dendritic type of drainage pattern is the most common.

CLIMATE AND CLIMATIC ZONES

Very few studies have been made of the total climatic panorama of the Himalayan region. The climate of this region is highly varied mainly because of the variations in altitude and their slope sides. The micro climatic conditions normally differ from place to place according to the (1) direction of ridges, (2) degree of slope, (3) sunny or shady aspects of slope, (4) intensity of forest cover, and (5) nearness of glaciers (Singh, R. L., 1971, p. 435).

Altitude is the most important factor behind the intra and inter regional variation in temperature distribution. The lapse rate which is the result of the vertical distribution of height mainly works as a temperature controlling phenomenon in this region. For example in the summer season the valleys have tropical climate while only few km. away the great Himalayan Range touches the cool climate. The following verse from the 'Kumarsambhavam' is testimony to this fact :

आमेखलं सच्चरतां घनानां,
छायामघः सानुमतां निषेव्य ।

अद्वेजिता वृष्टिभिरा श्रमन्ते,
श्रृणानि यस्या तपवन्ति सिद्ध: ॥ 1:5॥

"After enjoying the cool shade under the cloud around whose girdle, the saints, being troubled by rain, take refuge in the sun-drenched high peaks above."

Hill Region of Uttar Pradesh

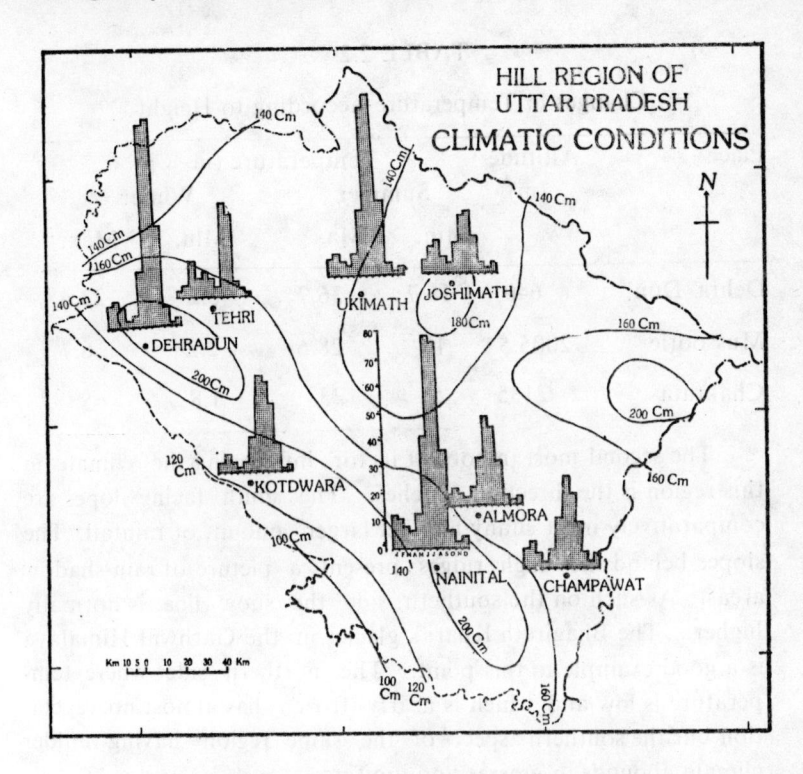

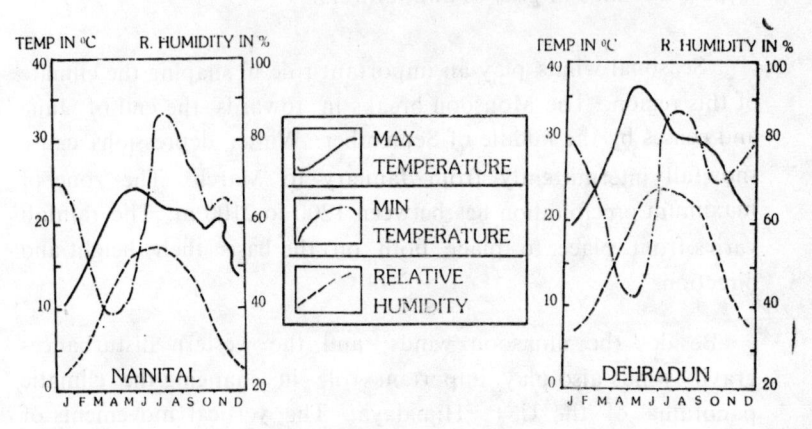

Fig. 2.6

TABLE 2.2

Changes in Temperature according to Height

Place	Altitude (m)	Summer Min.	Summer Max.	Winter Min.	Winter Max.
Dehra Dun	640	16.7	36.7	5.2	23.4
Mussoorie	2005.5	10	28.6	2.2	6.7
Chakrata	2135	5	23	1.8	5

The second most important factor influencing the climate in this region is the direction of relief. The south facing slopes are comparatively most sunny and get larger amount of rainfall. The slopes behind the high ridges present a picture of rain-shadow areas. As such on the southern side the snow line is normally higher. The Bhagirath Kharak glacier in the Garhwal Himalaya is a good example to this point. The northern side where temperature is low and which is nearly frozen has almost no vegetation but the southern aspect of the same region having milder climate abounds in grasses and junifers.

Seasonal winds play an important role in shaping the climate of this region. The Monsoon breaks in towards the end of June and ceases by the middle of September. Winter depressions cause snowfall intermittently from January to March. The zone of maximum precipitation lies between 1200 to 2100 m. The rainfall varies from place to place both on the basis their height and direction.

Besides the monsoon winds and the western disturbances gravity winds also play important role in changing the climatic panorama of the U. P. Himalaya. The vertical movements of air produced by change of temperature as the day advances, are called gravity winds. With the sun-rise mists start warming up

TABLE 2.3
Altitudinal Variation in Rainfall

Station	Altitude (m)	Rainfall (cm)
Tehri	778	80
Deoprayag	457	70
Karnprayag	884	136
Srinagar	550	93
Pithoragarh	1636	122
Almora	1676	104
Dehra Dun	682	212
Nainital	1934	270

and ascend like a white balloon and soon they cover up the snow views in the distance. After sun-set with the downward movement of the air, mists roll down the slopes into valleys. Normally by mid-night the mists reach the valley bottom as to take rest for the night and thus the sky becomes more clear and bright. Some of the tourists who come for the sake of fun, frolic and adventure often enjoy the glorious scene in the morning and brighter sky at mid-night.

Broadly speaking the seasonal changes in this mountainous region is quite marked. Normally in winter i.e. from December to March Upper Parts of Himalaya are covered with snow and get an average snow-fall of 8 to 10 days in every month. In April the weather on the whole is clear and bright. May and June are marked by thunder, lightning and occasional hail storms. The monsoon breaks in sometime in mid-June and from July to September there is heavy rain. The amount of rainfall gradually decreases from East to West. In October and November the weather normally becomes clear and the days are very sunny and bright.

Thus the cycle of seasons itself indicates two clear-cut occasions for tourists coming to this region. Mostly they visit this area either from mid-September to mid-November or from April to mid-June.

It is quite difficult to delineate zones of identical climatic conditions within such a complex and complicated framework. Only the broad generalizations can be made that stand greatly modified in view of local conditions. The suggested climatic regions are more or less altitudinal :

(i)	Sub-Tropical Zone	below 900 m
(ii)	Warm Temperate	900 to 1800 m
(iii)	Cool Temperate	1800 to 2400 m
(iv)	Cold Zone	2400 to 4000 m
(v)	Permafrost Zone (Permanently frozen)	above 4000 m

FLORA AND FAUNA

The things which attract the lovers of mountain most are their flora and fauna. Different types of trees, plants and shrubs give a touching green look to the bare rocky hills. The romance of wilderness is found in colourful fauna wandering in its lush green meadows. In addition, the soft twitter, sweet chirp and wild cries of forest birds and animals within themselves are a treat to the tourists. Perhaps they are our real national heritage. Even when 'Nature' comes to town, garden cities grow and generally punctuates the congested industrial or residential landscape--"so much of green belt can always be discovered on the town planners' blue print". Trees are essential ingredients in any landscape, vestiges of Nature's primeval glory before "man made extensive in-roads upon the grandiose world of vegetation" (Blache, 1950, p. 193).

(i) Flora

The major portion of the U. P. Himalaya is covered with forest, and with all its aspects it is the source of enormous wealth of this region. Height has its major effect on the natural vegetation in every mountainous area. That is why a vertical differentiation of vegetation is found in mountains. Some lime formation, lithological and chemical composition of rocks play the dominant role in the distribution of vegetation, while the altitude and climate have also much effects on it. In all, there are three main factors which affect the nature and types of vegetation in this region--(1) atmospheric, (2) edaphic, and (3) biotic.

On the basis of the above factors we can divide the natural vegetation of this region into following groups (vide Fig. 2.7) :

(a) Sub-tropical zone

(b) Temperate zone

(c) Sub-Alpine zone

(d) Alpine zone

The sub-tropical type of vegetation is found throughout the sub-Himalayan tract, extending from north-west to south-east. The height of this zone is about 750 m in southern part while in the north it is around 1200 m. The most significant tree of this zone is 'Sal'. The wood of this tree is of very high quality and has its own commercial value. The other trees found in this type of forest are Khair, Shisham, Haldu, Teak, Euclyptus, Sain etc.

Temperate zone is generally found between 1050 and 1990 m in south and between 900 and 1800 m in north. Chir and Fir are the two trees which are found mostly in this entire zone. The wood of Chir is used in making packing boxes for tea, fruits and for a number of other things.

In sub-Alpine zone coniferous type of forest is found on the height of 1800 to 3200 m. Several types of coniferous trees are found in this area in general, but the types of trees differ accord-

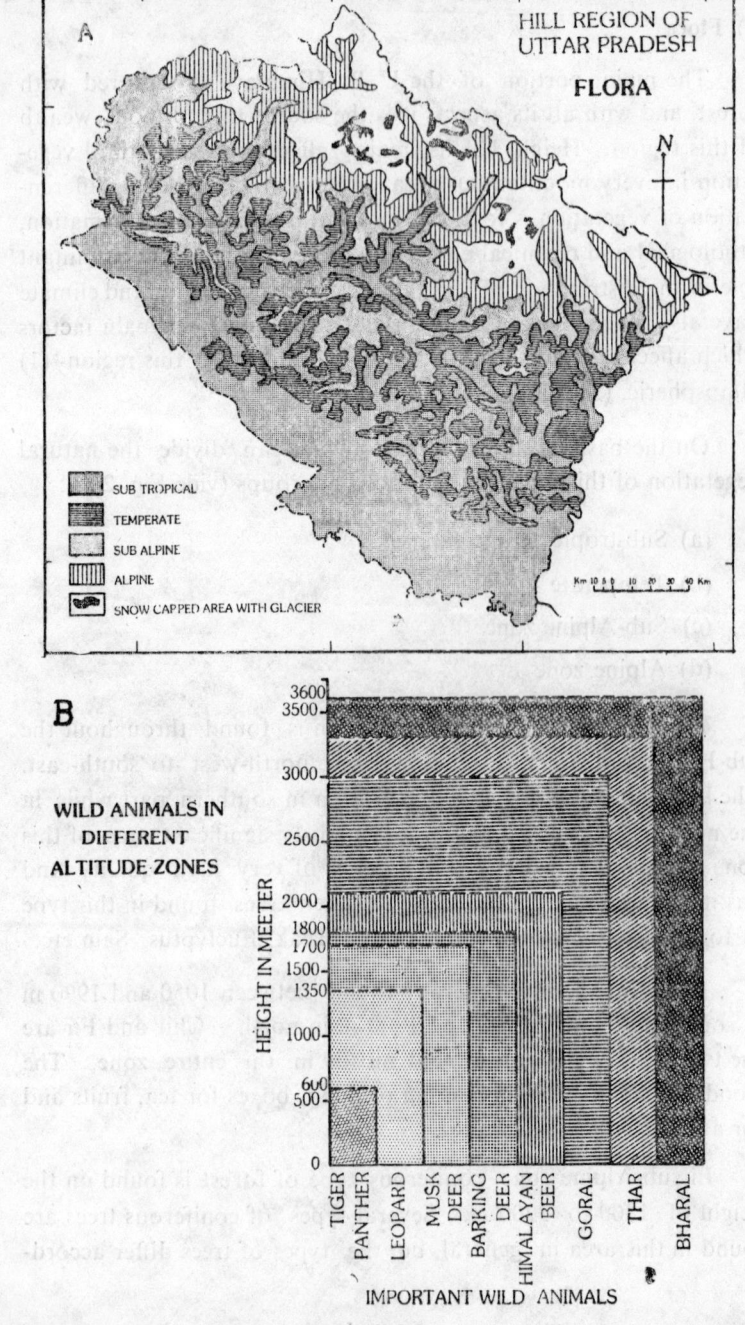

Fig. 2.7

ing to height. Cypress and Spruce are found between 2000 and 2500 m, Deodar from 2400 to 3050 m, Blue pine, Silver pine, Fir etc. are found from 1900 to 3100 m in patches.

Alpine pastures are found usually above 3200 m. They can be divided further into two sub-groups :

A. *Alpine Shrub Land* : Because of severe climatic conditions on the height of 3200 m and above, only different types of shrubs are found, of which varities of sweet edible berries and several types of herbs as pulsatillum, aconitum etc. and wild flowers are common.

B. *Alpine Grass Land* : The snowline begins above 3800 m, so this region lacks in vegetation. During the span of two or three months in summer when snow melts only some sort of grasses are found.

(ii) **Fauna**

Wildlife is always connected with forest. Actually the fauna is the manifestation of flora. Wildlife varies from place to place on the basis of forest and climate. In U. P. Himalaya different types of forest is the source of various colourful wildlife as majestic tigers and elephants in the Tarai, snow leopord, brown bear and morals in the Alpine region. These wild animals are the integral part of our national heritage and also are attractions for tourists. The fauna of U. P. Himalayas can be classified into following groups :

(a) Wild animals of Lower Himalaya, 600 to 1800 m

(b) Wild animals of Middle Himalaya, 1800 to 3200 m

(c) Wild animals of Inner Himalaya, 3200 to 3800 m

Between 600 and 1800 m important wild animals are panther, tiger, wild bear, leopard, musk deer, swamp deer etc., while on the height of 1800 to 3200 m the most common animals are barking deer, sloth bear, bluebull, black buck etc. Above 3200 m severe cold and absence of vegetation do not encourage the wildlife. So on higher altitudes few animals like thar, goral, bharal of sheep family are found.

TABLE 2.4

Distribution of Wild Animals in Different Altitude Zones

Sl. No.	Altitude Zones (m)	Important Wild Animals
1.	Below 600	Tiger, Panther
2.	600—1300	Leopard
3.	1300—1700	Musk Deer
4.	1700—1800	Barking Deer
5.	1800—2100	Himalayan Bear
6.	2100—3000	Goral*
7.	3000—3300	Thar*
8.	3300—3600	Bharal*

*Different kinds of sheep

For the preservation of wild animals in U. P. Himalaya, a number of programmes have been initiated by the government. These wild animal are not only our national heritage but an important source for developing tourism industry. There is a National Park and four famous sanctuaries in this region which attract a lot of visitors every year.

SOILS AND MINERALS

(i) Soil

Soil of this region is not a significant thing. Mostly stony and unmature type of soil is found here. It does not have any system nor it forms a compact block. It differs from valley to valley and slope to slope according to ecological conditions. On the foothills of the mountains, deposits of gravel and coarse sand are found which are very poor as far as fertility is concerned. While on the fore side of the rivers, narrow strips of alluvial soil are found, red loam soils are found in small patches. Soil of Garkhum region at some places is good for potato cultivation as it is hard and sandy. On the higher altitudes soils are of glacial type.

On the basis of altitude soils of this region can be classified into a number of groups (Table 2.5).

TABLE 2.5

Vertical Arrangement of Soils

Pedo	Ecological Zones	Altitude (m)	soil Type
1.	Alpine Zone	Above 3000	Glacial Soil.
2.	Upper Bhagirathi & Alaknanda Zone	2000—3000	Brown deciduous gray coniferous and frost soils.
3.	Lower Bhagirathi & Alaknanda Zone.	1000—2000	Brown frost soils.
4.	Siwaliks and Duns	Below 1000	Alluvial soils.

(ii) Minerals

As far as mineral deposits are concerned it depends mainly on the structure and formation of the region. Himalayan region is one of the newly formed areas of the world due to sedimentation in the water. As such in this region mostly minerals of sedimentary origin are found like lime stone, magnesite, gypsum phosphorite etc. The Deoban Tejam belt and Siwalik have rich deposits of lime stone of cement grade, magensite and gypsum. In the outer zone of Siwalik, small deposits of limestone, phosphorite, silver and some atomic minerals are found. Another useful mineral 'shilajeet' is found in the hard rocks of high altitude. In the low area copper is found in Almora, lignite coal in Barkal, soap slate in Sarju valley of Almora, iron-ore in Pithoragarh, lime slate, phosphorite in DehraDun and Mussoorie. But these deposits are not very significant as far their industrial use is concerned.

POWER AND INDUSTRY

This region has rich source to generate hydrolectric power because a number of water falls and rapid streams are flowing down throughout the region. Several types of fruits and woods are also available for timber and food canning industries but due to certain reasons U. P. Himalaya is still a less developed region as far as power and industries are concerned. In the last two Five-Year Plans Government have made many new proposals to develop this region by setting up new hydro-electric stations and provide facilities to develop industries and improve the conditions of poor hill people.

(i) Power

Before independence there were very few small hydroelectric stations in Nainital, Almora, Mussoorie and Ranikhet etc. No major power project was set-up by the British Government. But after independence utmost priority was given to generate hydro-electrical power in this area and many big power projects were setup. A new hydro-electric power plant has just been completed over Tons river (a tributary of Yamuna). The slope of this river is steep and 'S' shaped. Three power stations have to be set up at three places of this 'S' shaped slope one at the top, second at middle and the third at the bottom of the slope. An underground tunnel has been constructed on the top of the 'S' down to its bottom. The capacity of this plant is 324 MW. Another hydro-electric project of a capacity of 134.4 MW has been setup over Ram Ganga River near Ramnagar Mandi at Kalagarh. Other important power project of this region is over Sharda River near Tanakpur. Capacity of this plant is 41.4 MW, another one is over upper Ganga Canal at Pathri near Hardwar with a capacity of 21.2 MW. A small power unit has been constructed at Bageshwar (Nainital), another one at Badrinath. The biggest power plant of this region is being constructed over Bhagirathi River in Tehri-Garhwal district named as Tehri Dam. However, two new power stations are under construction at Pancheshwar over Kali River and at Jamrani over Gola River.

(ii) Industry

U. P. Himalaya is the most backward region as far as industrial development is concerned. It is not easy to set-up industries in such a region with so many drawbacks. Although there is no problem of raw materials and hydroelectric power in this region, but inadequate facilities of transport and communication, paucity of local enterpreneurs and economically poor people do not encourage an industrial development.

There are many corporations which have been working for the industrial development of this region such as Garhwal and Kumaun Development Corporations, State Minerals Development Corporation, State Industrial Development Corporation, State Forest Corporation, State Cement Corporation, State Sugar Corporation, U. P. Textiles Corporation etc. Some major industries developed by Kumaun Development Corporation are- Trans Cable Limited at Kathgodam, Rasin and Tarpentine Project Limited at Champawat, Varnish Project (Champawat). Thi Corporation has also developed the Salwant Extraction Plant (Kathgodam), Soap-stone Mining (Bageshwar), Paper Mill Plant at Almora. Garhwal Development Corporation also has developed many industries in Garhwal Division such as Rasin and Tarpentine Project, Tilwara ; Wood Project, Muni-ki-Reti ; Wood Project Garwara (Uttar Kashi). This Corporation has also planned to set-up couple of cement, paper and medicine plants in comming years. State Industrial Development Corporation has developed a small industrial complex at Mohan (Almora) and a magnesite development project also at Almora and Bhowali (Nainital). This Corporation has planned to set-up a watch and paper-pulp industry in Garhwal region. State Cement Corporation has planned to set-up Cement Plants at Pithoragarh (4 Lakh MT), at DehraDun (4.6 Lakh MT) and five other small cement plants at other places. Co-operative Sugar Mill Limited has planned to set-up sugar mills at Bajpur and Sitarganj. Apart from these, industrial training centres have been opened at Bageshwar, Kapkot. At these centres a number of wooden goods, Thulma (blanket) and Chutikan (carpet) are produced. At some other centres several items of deer skin are also manufactured.

In the current (7th) Five-Year Plan Government have many programmes to develop small-scale industries in this hill region and to improve poor economic conditions of hill people. Government are providing loan to hill people at low interest to initiate the industrial development of the region. After implementing the above said programmes, the over all conditions of this region would definitely improve and the problem of unemployment would also be minimised.

TRANSPORT AND COMMUNICATION

"Transport is life-blood of the present industrial framework, as between the producer and consumer lies a distance which has to be covered by transportational facilities" (Jones & Darkenwald 1947, p. 575).

Himalayan region does not provide ideal conditions for the Development of Transport and Communication because of folded mountain chains, steep slopes, sterile and unstable rocks. That's why roads are the major means of transportation here. Development of this region is directly connected with the development of transport. Since 1960 both the Central as well as the State Governments have started a lot of programmes for the Development of Transport and Communication System in the region. Many new roads are constructed and some are under construction in order to encourage trade, commerce and tourism in the region. As far as the rail transport is concerned it is less developed due to the rugged topography of this hill region. The present rail heads-North-Eastern Railway (meter gauge Tanakpur, Kathgodam, Ram Nagar), Northern Railway (broad gauge Kotdwara, Rishikesh, DehraDun) handle the total rail service of this region :

As the major means of transport, there are three types of roads in this region :

(i) State Highways

(ii) District roads

(iii) Village roads

State Highways Nos. 6, 29, 37, 45, 47, 53, 55 and 57 pass through this region. All major roads start from the last railway terminus. From Tanakpur rail-head one road goes towards Lipulekh while from Kathgodam railway station two roads stretch towards the inner parts of Himalaya. One road goes straight to Nainital and other to Bhimtal. From Nainital roads proceed towards Almora, Ranikhet and Mukteshwar. In the lower part Rishikesh is the most important rail-head, from where many roads start for Dehra Dun, Mussoorie, Yamunotri, Gangotri, Badrinath and Kedarnath. Some major routes of this region are as follows :

1. Rishikesh-Yamunotri Route

This route starts from Rishikesh and extends upto Hanuman Chatti, its length being about 220 km. Distance of Yamunotri temple from this place is only 12 km. This is a trek route and vehicles could not move on it due to unstable mountainous rocks, so pilgrims have to go there on foot. This route is only seasonal and is opened only during summer.

2. Rishikesh-Gangotri Route

From Rishikesh this route goes upto Gangotri (245 km). Tourists and pilgrims can go there easily by bus or taxi. The

66   *Himalayan Environment and Tourism*

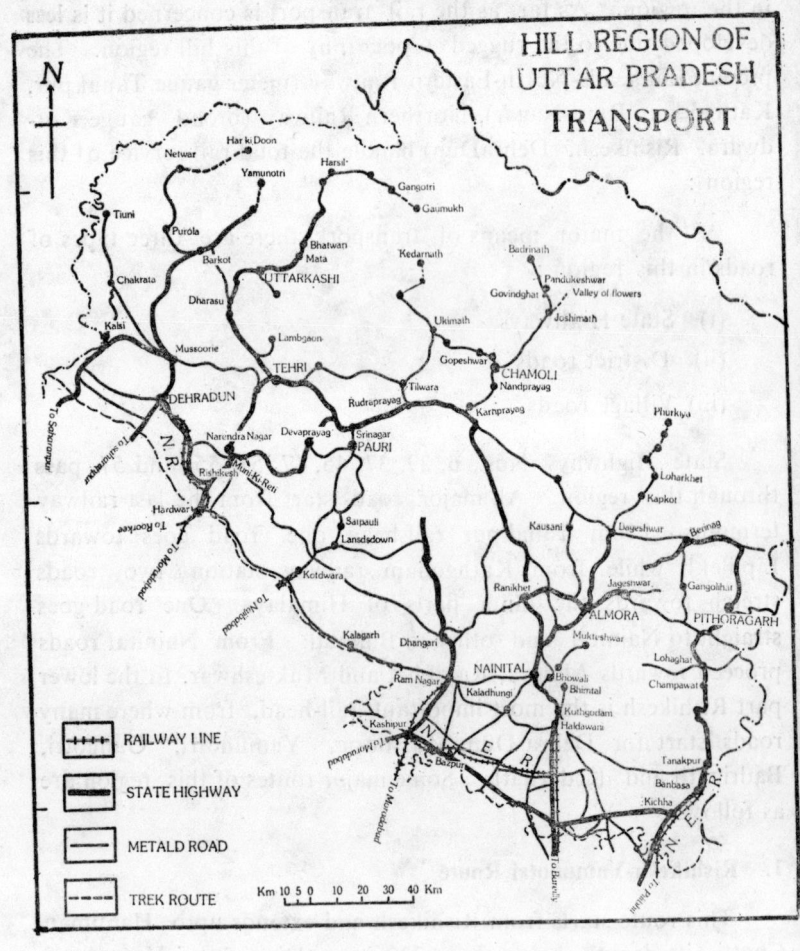

![Map: HILL REGION OF UTTAR PRADESH TRANSPORT]

Fig. 2.8

distance of Gaumukh from Gangotri is 18 km. and pilgrims have to go there on foot through trek route.

3. Rishikesh-Kedarnath Route

This route starts from Rishikesh and goes up to Gaurikund (214 km.) from where the distance of Kedarnath is 14 km. which is seasonal trek route.

4. Rishikesh-Badrinath Route

This route starting from Rishikesh goes straight up to Badrinath. There is also a trek route which goes from Govind-Ghat to the Valley of Flowers and Hemkund.

In the entire U. P. Himalayan Region K.M.O.U. (Kumaun Motors Operators Union) and G.M.O.U. (Garhwal Motors Operators Union) buses provide regular services to tourists and pilgrims as well as to local people. Department of Tourism and many travel agencies are also involved in providing transport facilities to tourists. But in all, the transport facilities are not enough to meet the demands. Much more attention should be needed not only to construct new roads but also to the maintenance of these roads. In 1984 tourism was declared as an industry so many new roads and other facilities are proposed to be provided to give a push to this industry.

As far as air service in the region is concerned it is not available for civilians. It is used only for military purposes. In the entire U. P. Himalayan region minor air service is available only in Pantnagar (Nainital) and Dehra Dun. However, air services through Vayudoot has recently been introduced in the region.

POPULATION

(i) Size, Distribution and Density Pattern

U. P. Himalaya is the most sparsely populated region of the State. The total population of this region is only 48,35,712 (4.4% of the total population of U. P.), while it comprises about 17.30% of the total area of the State. The population growth of this region was 47.34 during the last eighty years (1901-1981), while this figure for U. P. was 56.14%. The decennial growth of population was 43.42% (highest) in Nainital and it was 12.88% (lowest) in Pauri-Garhwal. The maximum increase in population was in Chamoli district (135.79%) and the minimum in Almora district (18.42) during 1971-81.

68 *Himalayan Environment and Tourism*

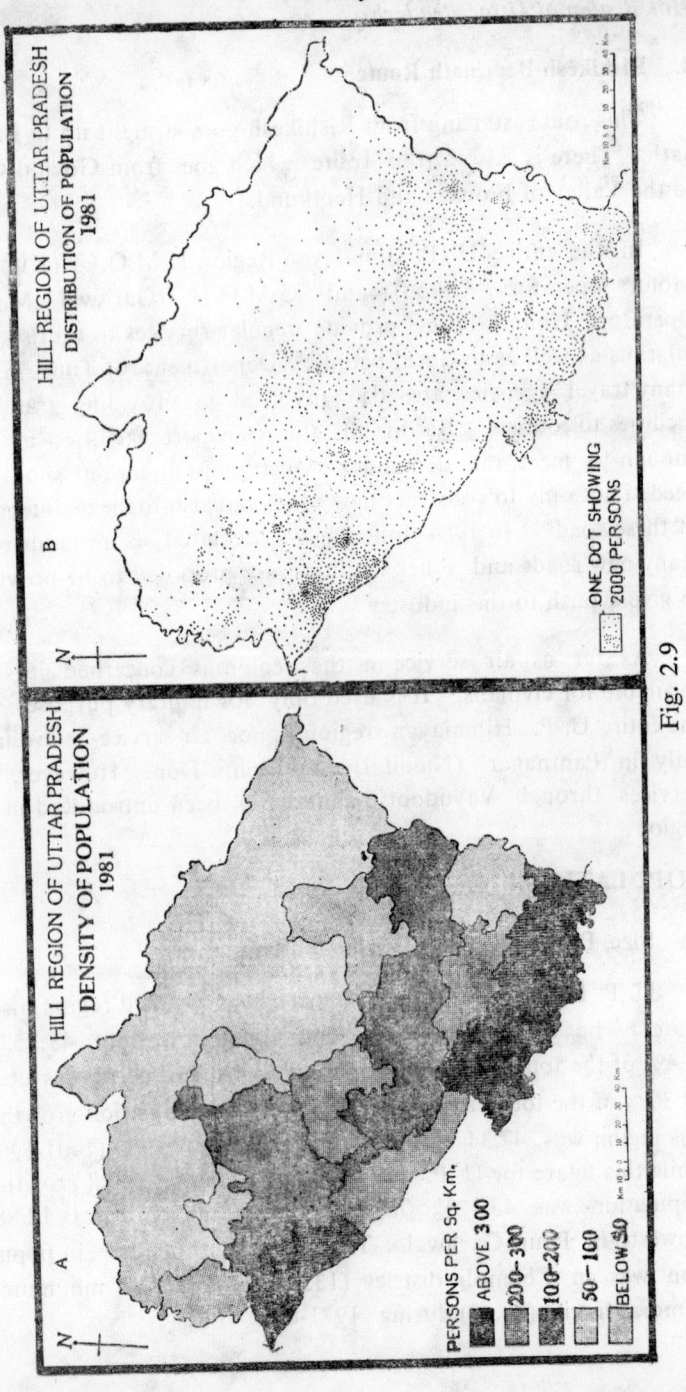

Fig. 2.9

The average density of population of this region is 95 persons per Km² (1981), while this figure for U. P. is 377 persons per Km². Density of population in U. P. Himalaya differs from place to place on district level. A maximum density of 247 persons per Km² is found in Dehra Dun District while the minimum (24 persons per Km²) is in Uttarkashi District. On tahsil level this variation is somewhat more pronounced. The maximum population density of 349 persons per Km² has been recorded in Dehra Dun tahsil while Munsari in Pithoragarh District has the minimum density of 14 persons per Km².

Mountains do not provide an ideal condition for human habitation always. Steep slopes, exposures, narrow valleys and ruggedness play their part in restricting human access, habitation and cultivation. Though all these disadvantages can be overcome by developing new technology, yet one could not overcome the drastic reduction in the atmospheric and oxygen pressure and severe cold climatic conditions in high altitudes.

(ii) Population Structure

(a) Sex-Ratio

In the total population of 48,35,712 there were 24,68,000 males and 23,67,712 females, thus the percentage of males is 51.04% as compared to 48.96% of females in the total population of U. P. Himalaya. So the sex-ratio of this region is 959 females per 1000 males, which is higher in comparison to U. P. that is 885 females per 1000 males. But this ratio varies from one district to another. It is the highest (1088) in Tehri-Garhwal and the lowest (811) in Dehra Dun.

(b) Literacy

Urbanization and literacy are always inter-related with one another. As U. P. Himalayan region is high urbanized, than total U. P. the average literacy rate is 39.2% while the literacy rate of U. P. is 27.38%. In rural areas this rate is very low, while in urban areas this figure is rather impressive, where 61.2% of total population is literate. Males (53.8%) outnumber females (24.2%) as far as literacy is concerned. But in comparison to the state where 54.44% males and 35.82% females are educated, the above figure is somewhat low. The highest literacy rate (52.6%) was observed in Dehra Dun District. The literacy rate in other seven districts are Pauri-Garhwal (41.1), Pithoragarh (39.1), Nainital (37.8), Almora (37.8), Chamoli (37.5), Uttarkashi (28.9), and Tehri-Garhwal (27.9) percent.

(c) *Scheduled Castes and Scheduled Tribes*

In U. P. Himalaya Scheduled Castes and Scheduled Tribes together constitute 19.73% of the total population, of which about 15.96% are scheduled castes and 3.76% scheduled tribes. Some notable tribes living in this hill region are Tharu, Bhotia, Raji etc.

URBANIZATION AND URBAN CENTRES

Urbanization plays an important role in the development of a region. Urban centres being nodes of settlements are the real foci of social contacts and economic growth performing a number of important activities. They do not exist for themselves alone, rather they are a part of a whole complex and serve the surrounding countryside with which they are spatially and functionally knit-together.

The term 'urbanization' suffers from confusing variety of definitions as given by sociologists, economists, geographers, urban planners from their different points of view. In general, most of the studies of urbanization have been made in social, economic and demographic contexts.

From social and cultural viewpoints urbanization means the way of life and living different from rural life. It shows the changing behaviour pattern from rural to urban, which includes qualitative and quantitative improvements in the systems of housing, water supply, means of Transport and Communication,

Administrative and Educational Institutions and many other micro aspects of life as culture and tradition. According to Kingsley Davis (1962, p. 1), who has made an intensive study of urbanization in India "Urbanization usually is said to be taking place when the proportion of total population that is residing in places defined as urban is rising or when urban population is growing at faster rate than the average rate of growth for a nation". According to Bose (1973, p. 3) "Urbanization in demographic sense is an increase in the proportion of urban population (U) to total population (T) over a period of time. As long as U/T increases there is urbanization".

So it is clear that the measuring of the processes of urbanization involves a combined set of socio-economic and demographic factors. Mitchell (1969, p.3) refers to "urbanization as being the process of becoming urban, moving to cities, changing from agricultural to other pursuits common to cities and corresponding changing of behaviour patterns".

Everywhere in the world and in India, the increase in urban population is an important index of measuring urbanization of a region. Urbanization of any region is the result of (1) natural growth (birth rate high and death rate low), (2) increase in the number of towns (either by origin or by rural urbanization), and (3) migration of people from rural to urban areas (because of industrialization or urbanization).

U. P. Himalaya is a region being exposed to urbanization only just recently. Development of new urban centres, conversion of villages into towns and natural growth of population are the basic trends of urbanization in this area. In rural areas of this region people have their employment mostly through different agricultural activities. So their income is low. As youths of today, whether they are literate or illiterate are not interested in agriculture, they move towards urban centres in search of better employment and higher income. Other facilities such as higher educational institutions, better medical facilities, sanitation, drinking water, electricity etc. also attract them to adopt urban life. In short, in U. P. Himalayan region migration of rural people towards urban areas is the main feature of urbanization.

(i) Growth and Trends of Urbanization

U. P. Himalaya is one of the backward regions of the State. Most of the region is dominated by agriculture. So economic condition of the people is very poor. Industrialization of the region is only in its initial stage and has not been able to take a concrete shape so far on account of weak infrastructure. As such in this Economically Backward Region of U. P. Himalaya, the process of urbanization has been very slow since the beginning of this century. During 1901 to 1981 the total growth of urban population was 807.7% when the growth of total population during the same years was 230.8%.

However, the decadal growth of urban population was recorded 51.9, 30.9, 49.9 and 57.6 percent in the successive years of 1951, 1961, 1971 and 1981 respectively. For the same years, these figures were 22.9, 9.9, 30.9 and 60.7 percent respectively for Uttar Pradesh and 41.4, 26.4, 38.2 and 46.4 percent respectively for the country as a whole.

Table 2.6 denotes that the total urban population in U. P. Himalaya was 97486 in 1901 which increased by 24.95 percent during the first decade of this century and thus it remained to be 121812 in 1911. The rate of urbanization was very low during the first three decades 1901-31. The growth rate was only 35.5 percent. But thereafter, urbanization proceeded with faster rates and as a result, during the last five decades (1931-1981), urban centres experienced 250 percent increase in their population. Thus in 1941, 1951, 1961, 1971, and 1981, urban population of the region had reached at 1.89, 2.87, 3.74, 5.61 and 8.85 lakhs. In this way during the last 80 years, U. P. Himalaya had experienced 807.7 percent growth in its urban population, while this growth for whole U. P. was 269.14 percent during the same years.

TABLE 2.6
Growth of Urban Population in U. P. Himalaya (1901-81)

Year	Urban Population in U. P. Himalaya — Population	Decadal variation in percent	Urban Population in Uttar Pradesh — Population	Decadal variation in percent	Decadal variation of urban population in India in percent
1901	97486	—	5300611	—	—
1911	121812	24.95	4906673	− 8.98	− 0.35
1921	131721	8.13	4936416	+ 0.61	− 8.27
1931	132135	0.31	5568789	+12.81	+19.12
1941	188882	42.92	7016490	+26.00	+31.97
1951	286834	51.85	8625699	+22.93	+41.42
1961	374408	30.83	9479895	+ 9.90	+26.41
1971	561306	49.91	12388596	+30.68	+38.23
1981	884860	57.64	19899115	+60.72	+46.39

Source : Census of India 1981, Series 22, Uttar Pradesh, Part X-A.

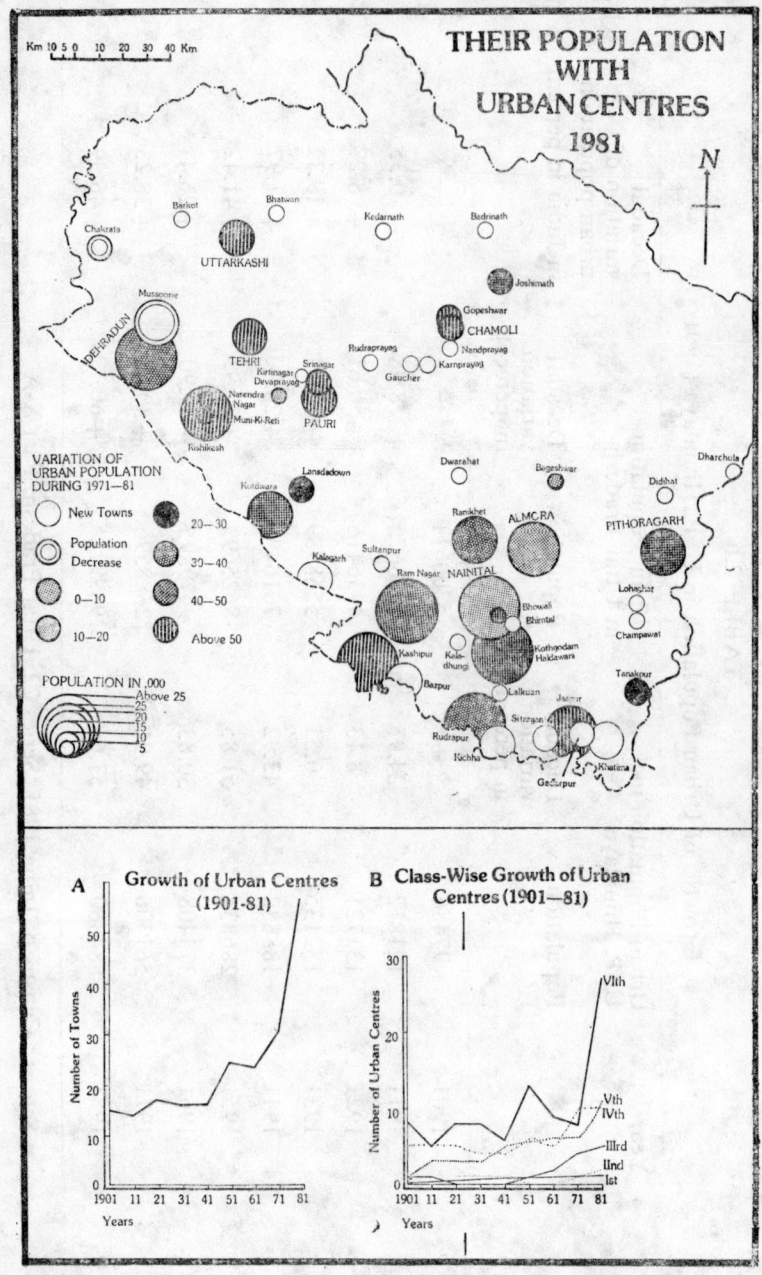

Fig. 2.10

(ii) Urban Centres and Their Class-wise Distribution

There were 15 urban centres in the entire U. P. Himalaya in the census year of 1901, but in 1911 census one urban centre was declassified and as such only 14 urban centres were left. In the next 30 years there had been mild increase as in the census years of 1921, 1931 and 1941, there were 17, 16 and 16 urban centres respectively. During these years growth rate was 21.4% (1921), —5.9 (1931) and in the census year of 1941 the growth rate was zero. In the census year of 1951 eight new urban centres developed—five in Tehri, two in Pauri-Garhwal and one in Uttarkasi. The growth rate of urban centres between 1941 and 1951 was 50%. In the census year of 1961 although two towns increased one each in Nainital and Uttarkashi, three towns were declassified, two in Tehri-Garhwal and one in Pithoragarh. In the next ten years in the census year of 1971 eight urban centres developed two each in Tehri-Garhwal and Chamoli, one each in Almora, Dehra Dun, Nainital and Pithoragarh, but one town in Uttarkashi was declassified. During this year growth rate was quite high (30.1%). But in between 1971-1981, the number of urban centres almost doubled and in 1981 census there were 26 urban centres having increased due to the definitional change of urban centres nine in Nainital, five in Chamoli four in Pithoragarh, three in Pauri-Garhwal, two each in Dehra Dun and Uttarkashi and one in Almora. During 1971-81 the growth rate of urban centres was 86.7%. As such the total number of urban centres came to be 56 (excluding six urban centres which are included in four Urban-Aglomerations) including 26 new urban centres. Distribution of these urban centres is quite interesting, seventeen of them are situated in Nainital alone while there are eight in Pauri-Garhwal, seven each in Chamoli and Dehra Dun, five each in Tehri-Garhwal and Pithoragarh, four in Almora and three in Uttarkashi district.

From the Table 2.7 it is noticed that in between 1901 and 1981 the total growth of urban centres in the entire U. P. Himalaya is 273.33%. But this growth rate varied from time to

TABLE 2.7
Variation in the Number of Towns in U.P. Himalaya during 1901—81

Sl. No.	Districts	1901	'11	'21	'31	'41	'51	'61	'71	'81
1.	Almora	2	2	2	2	2	2	2	3	4
2.	Chamoli	—	—	—	—	—	—	—	2	7
3.	Dehra Dun	4	4	4	4	4	6	4	5	7
4.	Nainital	6	5	7	7	6	6	7	8	17
5.	Pauri-Garhwal	3	3	4	3	3	5	5	5	8
6.	Pithoragarh	—	—	—	—	1	1	—	1	5
7.	Tehri-Garhwal	—	—	—	—	—	5	3	5	5
8.	Uttarkashi	—	—	—	—	—	1	2	1	3
	Total	15	14	17	16	16	24	23	30	56
	Decadal variation (in percentage)		−6.7	+21.4	−5.9	±0	+50%	−41%	+30.1	86.7

time. It was very slow in the first four decades between 1901 and 1941. It was only 6.67% but increased rapidly in the next four decades as during 1941—1981 the growth rate was 250%.

As regards the class-wise* distribution of towns in this Himalayan region, towns of lower classes predominated from the very beginning. The variation in the number of different categories of towns are fully marked as is clear from the Table 2.8 and figure 2.10-C.

(iii) Level of Urbanization

The level of urbanization means ratio between urban and total population. The level of urbanization in U. P. Himalaya is 18.93% while it is 17.95% in U. P. and 23.31% in India. Even this ratio is not evenly distributed throughout the U. P. Himalayan region and it differs from district to district. Dehra Dun district has the heighest level of urbanization which is around 48.8% white it is the lowest in Tehri Garhwal district (4.12%). On the tahsil level, the level of urbanization is the highest in Dehra Dun tahsil (54.4%) and the lowest in Ukimath tahsil of Chamoli district (0.14%). All the 30 tahsils of U. P. Himalayan districts may be grouped into five categories on the basis of their level of urbanization (vide Fig. 211A) :

(a) Non-urbanized area,

(b) Very low urbanized area (below 5 percent),

(c) Low urbanized area (5 to 15 percent),

(d) Medium urbanized area (15 to 25 percent), and

(e) High urbanized area (above 25 percent).

Among the eight districts of U. P. Himalaya, Tehri Garhwal belongs to the second category of very low urbanized area

---

* In the Indian Census, the urban centres are categorised into six urban classes on the basis of population size. Class I-1,00,000 or more, II-50,000-99,999, III-20,000—49,999, IV-10,000-19,999, V-5,000-9,999 and VI-less than 5,000 persons.

TABLE 2.8
Class-wise Growth of Urban Centres (1901-81)

Sl. No.	Class	1901	'11	'21	'31	'41	'51	'61	'71	'81
1.	I	—	—	—	—	—	—	1	1	1
2.	II	—	—	1	—	1	1	—	1	2
3.	III	1	1	1	—	1	—	2	4	5
4.	IV	1	3	3	5	5	3	6	6	11
5.	V	5	5	5	4	4	6	5	10	10
6.	VI	8	5	8	8	6	13	9	8	27
	Total	15	14	17	16	16	24	23	30	56

Fig. 2.11

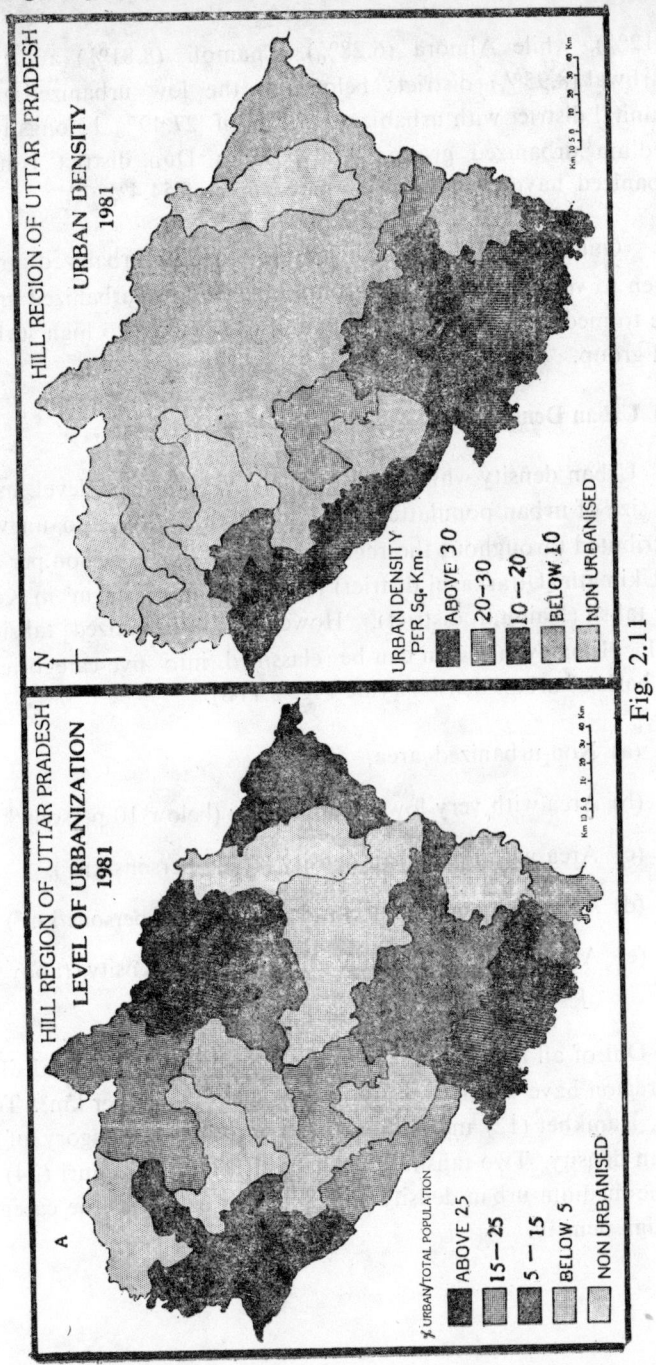

(4.12%), while Almora (6.28%), Chamoli (8.81%) and Pauri Garhwal (8.95%) districts belong to the low urbanized group. Nainital district with urbanization level of 27.49% belongs to the medium urbanized group. Only Dehra Dun district is highly urbanized having urbanization percentage of 54.4%.

Out of 30 tahsils, four belong to the non-urbanized group, seven to very low urbanized group, nine to low urbanized group, five to medium unbanized group, and five belong to high urbanized group.

(iv) Urban Density

Urban density which is also analysed on tahsil level, means the size of urban population per Km^2 area. It is also unevenly distributed throughout the region ranging from 1 person per Km^2 in Ukimath (Uttarkashi district) to 140 peasons per Km^2 in Kashipur tahsil (Nainital district). However, all urbanized tahsils of U. P. Himalayan region can be classified into five categories on the basis of urban density (vide Fig. 2.11B).

(a) Non-urbanized area,

(b) Area with very low urban density (below 10 persons/km^2),

(c) Area with low urban density (10-20 persons/km^2),

(d) Area with medium urban density (20-30 persons/km^2) and

(e) Area with moderately high urban density (above 30 person/km^2).

Out of all the 30 tahsils 4 are non-urbanized, 13 tahsils of the region have urban density below 10 persons per km^2. Tehri (13), Ranikhet (12) and Almora (16) are in the category of low urban density. Two tahsils of Pithoragarh (20) and Pauri (24) are of the medium urban density and 8 tahsils belong to the category of high density.

In the entire U. P. Himalaya high urban density of 121 persons per km^2 is observed in Dehra Dun district and low urban density in Uttarkashi district (only 2 persons per km^2).

(v) Regional Pattern of Urbanization

Areal differentiation and spatial organization are the two major aspects of geographical studies. Spatial analysis of the number and size of urban centres and the growth rate of urban population can better be explained on sub-regional basis.

A. *Kumaun Region*

This region consisting of the districts of Almora, Nainital and Pithoragarh contains a population of 22.8 lakhs according to 1981 census. The urban population of this region is 3.87 lakh which is about 16.24% of its total population. The level of urbanization in all the three districts is not the same. In Nainital district the percentage of urban population is 27.70% while in Almora and Pithoragarh it is 5.99% and 5.64% respectively. There are 28 urban centres in the enitre Kumaun region—10 M. B., 3 Cantt. 3 N. A., 12 T. A. As far as the towns and their categories are concerned there is no Ist class town in the entire Kumaun region while there is one IInd class town in Nainital district. As many as 6 class III towns (2 in Almora, 4 in Nainital district), 4 class IV towns (1 in Pithoragarh, 1 in Almora and 2 in Nainital district), 4 class V towns (all in Nainital district), 11 class VI towns (4 in Pithoragarh, 2 in Almora and 5 in Nainital district) are the main towns in the entire Kumaun region. There are also two urban agglomarations (U. As.) in Kumaun region which includes Nainital M. B. and Nainital Cantt. in Nainital, and Almora M. B. and Almora Cantt. in Almora.

The decennial growth rate of urbanization of this region is interesting one. It is 79.50% in Nainital, 18.4% in Almora and 120.54% in Pithoragarh during 1971—1981.

B. *Garhwal Region*

It comprises five hill districts of U. P.—Dehra Dun Pauri-Garhwal, Tehri-Garhwal, Uttarkashi and Chamoli. About 20.7%

TABLE 2.9
Hill Towns—Their Population and Decadal Variation

Sl. No.	Name of Towns	Population 1971	Population 1981	Population variation during 1971-81 (in percent)
1.	Dehra Dun—U. A.	220571	293010	+ 32.84
(i)	Dehra Dun M. B.	169821	220530	+ 29.86
(ii)	Dehra Dun Cantt.	33637	43566	+ 29.52
(iii)	Clement Town Cantt.	11898	15450	+ 29.85
(iv)	Raipur	5209	13464	+158.48
2.	Haldwani-cum-Kathgodam	52205	77300	+ 48.07
3.	Kashipur	33457	51773	+ 54.74
4.	Rudrapur	25173	34658	+ 37.68
5.	Rishikesh	17694	29145	+ 65.16
6.	Nainital—U. A.	25167	26093	+ 3.68
(i)	Nainital M. B.	23986	24835	+ 3.54
(ii)	Nainital Cantt.	1181	1258	+ 6.52

Hill Region of Uttar Pradesh

1	2	3	4	5
7.	Ramnagar	17495	26013	+ 48.69
8.	Almora—U. A.	20881	22705	+ 8.74
	(i) Almora M. B	19671	20758	+ 5.53
	(ii) Almora Cannt :	1210	1947	+ 60.91
9.	Jaspur	13186	21242	+ 61.10
10.	Mussoorie—U. A. :	20389	18233	− 10.51
	(i) Mussorie M. B.	18038	16323	− 9.51
	(ii) Landour Cantt.	2351	1910	− 18.76
11.	Ranikhet Cantt.	13917	18190	+ 30.70
12.	Pithoragarh	11942	17657	+ 42.86
13.	Kotdwara	11457	17048	+ 48.80
14.	Pauri	8878	13607	+ 53.27
15.	Kichha*	—	13606	—
16.	Virbhadra*	—	12607	—
17.	Tehri	5480	12249	+123.52

1	2	3	4	5
18.	Bazpur*	—	11366	—
19.	Kalagarh*	—	10701	—
20.	Uttarkashi	6020	10043	+ 66.83
21.	Chamoli-Gopeshwar	6354	9709	+ 52.80
22.	Sitarganj*	—	9697	—
23.	Srinagar	5566	9171	+ 64.77
24.	Vikashnagar	7066	9001	+ 27.38
25.	Tanakpur	6003	8818	+ 46.89
26.	Joshimath	3852	8610	+ 43.13
27.	Khatima*	—	8443	—
28.	Lansdowne Cantt.	6670	8106	+ 21.53
29.	Gadarpur*	—	6315	—
30.	Chakrata Cantt.	6105	5217	− 14.55
31.	Majra*	—	4928	—

Hill Region of Uttar Pradesh

32.	Sultanpur*	—	4769	—
33.	Bageshwar	4314	4368	+ 1.25
34.	Karanprayag*	—	3772	—
35.	Narendranagar	2390	3596	+ 50.46
36.	Gauchar*	—	3284	—
37.	Bhowali	2193	3212	+ 46.47
38.	Lalkuan*	—	3155	—
39.	Kaladhungi*	—	3112	—
40.	Dharchula*	—	3086	—
41.	Bhimtal*	—	2871	—
42.	Badrinathpuri (snow-bound)	—	2576	—
43.	Lohaghat*	—	2530	—
44.	Dwarhat*	—	2333	—
45.	Muni-ki-reti	1126	2264	+101.07

1	2	3	4	5
46.	Dogada	1696	2176	+ 28.30
47.	Barkot*	—	2072	—
48.	Didihat*	—	2044	—
49.	Champawat*	—	1072	—
50.	Devaprayag	1527	1701	+ 11.39
51.	Rudraprayag*	—	1331	—
52.	Bhatwari*	—	1157	—
53.	Nand Prayag*	—	1103	—
54.	Kirtinagar*	—	736	—
55.	Bah Bazar	580	529	− 8.41
56.	Kedarnath*	—	120	—

*Treated as urban for the first time in 1981 census.

Source: Census of India, Part X-A.

of the total population of this region lives in urban areas, the total urban population is 2.43 lakhs.

In Garhwal region there are 34 urban centres of different sizes. Among them 3 are in Uttarkashi, 5 in Tehri-Garhwal, 7 in Chamoli, 11 in Dehra Dun and 8 are in Pauri-Garhwal district. In the whole Garhwal region there are two urban agglomarations (U. As.) which includes Dehra Dun M. B., Dehra Dun Cantt., Clement town (Cantt.) and Raipur C. T. in Dehra Dun and Mussoorie M. B. and Landour Cantt. in Mussouri. Dehra Dun is they only class I town not only in the Garhwal region but in the entire U. P. Himalaya. There is no class II town, while the only town of Class III category is Rishikesh (in Dehra Dun district), class IV towns are 8 in number (2 each in Pauri and DehraDun District and one each in Tehri and Uttarkashi District). Class V towns are 6 (2 each in Chamoli, Pauri-Garhwal and Dehra Dun District) and 16 class VI towns (2 in Uttarkashi, 5 in Chamoli, 3 in Pauri, 5 in Tehri and 1 in Dehra Dun) are the main Towns in Garhwal Region.

Growth rate of urbanization during 1971—81 in Garhwal Region varies from one district to another. It is 120.32% in Uttarkashi, 135.79% in Chamoli, 95.5% in Tehri-Garhwal, 37.12% in Dehra Dun and 86.70% in Pauri-Garhwal. In 1971 there were only 20 urban centres in contrast to 34 in 1981. There are 11 M. B., 11 N. A., 5 Cantt, 4 T. A. and 3 C. T. in the entire Garhwal Region. The decennial growth rate of urban centres was 70% during 1971—1981.

3

Development of Tourism in Hill Region of Uttar Pradesh

INTRODUCTION

In the heart of the Himalayas, touching Tibet in the north and the great Indo-Gangetic plain in the south, the hill region of Uttar Pradesh the "Paradise on the earth and the most glorious temple of Nature" occupies a unique position on India's tourist map. Thus the concept of tourism is not new for this region. It has been practising here for the last 5000 years or so. Generally travellers in the past were merchants, scholars or curious way farers, but in India especially in U. P. Himalaya, it all began with pilgrims and pilgrimage. The ancient Aryans designated it 'Dev Bhumi' and used to travel this region to seek divine knowledge. In this respect many references can be seen in different ancient epics such as Ramayan, Mahabharata and Puranas. The great souls and brilliant minds like founder of Jyotirmath, Adi Shankaracharya, Buddhist monk Kasyapgotra, Great Chinese traveller Hiuen Tsang, Guru Gorakhnath, Guru Govind Singh, have travelled these mountains in their holy quest (Bhatt, Madan Chandra, 1973, pp. 52-56). The mighty ranges and towering peaks of the region, with their unparalleled beauty and grandeur have given birth to doctrines and philosophies, explaining the mysteries of nature. It is in this region where Lord Krishna spent thousands of years in meditation (Sharma, P. Mahadhar, 1974, p. 77). So it is clear that before developing in its present form, tourism has passed through a very long period.

GROWTH OF TOURISM : HISTORICAL AND SPATIAL PERSPECTIVES

From the account given above it is fully clear that tourism has a long and chequered history. It started here with the peopling and settling process of the region itself. Its' early format was mostly religious where as in modern times it has assumed the form of an industry, economic and socio-cultural activity. The salient characteristics of these historic trends of tourism development can be described in four phases :

(i) Development of tourism in ancient period,

(ii) Development of tourism in medieval period,

(iii) Development of tourism during British period,

(iv) Development of tourism in post-Independence period.

(i) Development of Tourism in Ancient Period

The period, from the advent of Aryans upto the eleventh century A. D. when Muslims just started entering India, is full of religious fervour and cultural renaissances. This long period of ancient history witnesses an unprecedented growth of religious tourism due to emergence of Brahmanical society, which is responsible for the institution of pilgrimage ritual and Hindu way of life. This region became the sanctum sanctorum of India and pilgrims and devotees from all over India reached the holy shrines of this region, some of which later on developed into flourishing sacred cities. The Ashram of Nar and Narayan is situated on the mountains at the bank of the river Alakhnanda near Badrinath where Raja Janmajai had come for meditation. This is the

90 *Himalayan Environment and Tourism*

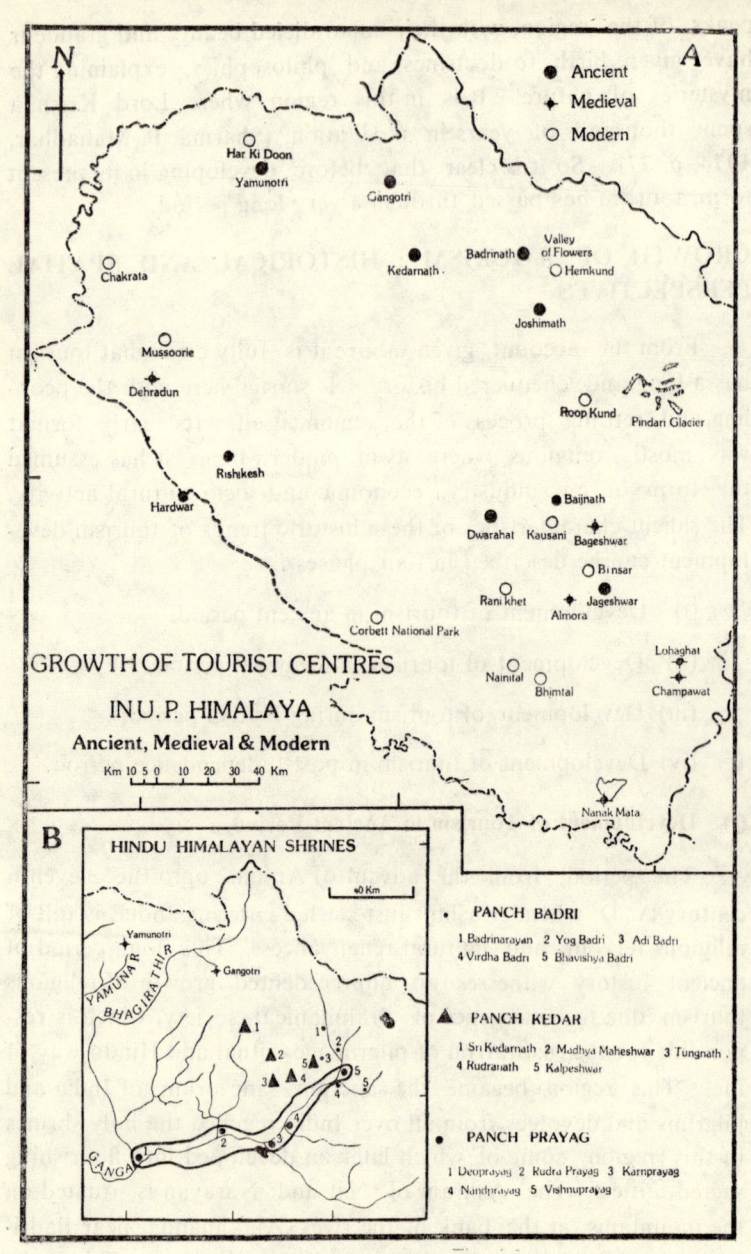

GROWTH OF TOURIST CENTRES IN U.P. HIMALAYA
Ancient, Medieval & Modern

- ● Ancient
- ✦ Medieval
- ○ Modern

Locations shown: Har Ki Doon, Yamunotri, Gangotri, Chakrata, Kedarnath, Badrinath, Valley of Flowers, Hemkund, Joshimath, Mussoorie, Dehradun, Roop Kund, Pindari Glacier, Rishikesh, Hardwar, Dwarahat, Kausani, Baijnath, Bageshwar, Binsar, Ranikhet, Jageshwar, Almora, Corbett National Park, Lohaghat, Nainital, Bhimtal, Champawat, Nanak Mata

B — HINDU HIMALAYAN SHRINES

PANCH BADRI
1. Badrinarayan 2. Yog Badri 3. Adi Badri
4. Virdha Badri 5. Bhavishya Badri

PANCH KEDAR
1. Sri Kedarnath 2. Madhya Maheshwar 3. Tungnath
4. Rudranath 5. Kalpeshwar

PANCH PRAYAG
1. Deoprayag 2. Rudra Prayag 3. Karnprayag
4. Nandprayag 5. Vishnuprayag

Fig. 3.1

place where Lord Brahma imparted religious instructions to the sage Bhardwaj (Charak Sanghita, I). So it is clear that the entire U. P. Himalaya was the major religious centre for Hindus in ancient time. However, from the 6th century B. C. to the 7th century A. D. this region was not only a Hindu pilgrimage centre but also a Buddhist centre. This is the place where armies have rarely penetrated ; Chinese pilgrims seeking the land of Buddha, Hindus the source of the sacred Ganges and the hidden mountain Kailash, have left the impress of their faith in shrines and temples (Spate O. H. K. & Learmonth, 1967, p. 368). Some of the religious centres which were developed in that time are as follows (vide Fig. 3.1A).

1. Yamunotri

Yamunotri (31°1'N Lat.—78°1'E Long.) lying at an elevation of 4421 m in Chamoli District offers the tourists an enchanting flavour of the religious shrine with its majestic natural beauty. The snow-clad Yamunotri peak stands on the western flank of the great peak of Bandar Poonch and forms the watershed of Hanuman Ganga and Tons river. Elevation of this peak is 6315 m from the mean sea level.

The main attraction of this region is the temple dedicated to the Goddess Yamuna. This temple was constructed by the Tehri Naresh Sudarshan Shah in the year 1839. It is situated from six km. of Yamunotri glacier - the source of the great river Yamuna.

The temple of Yamunotri is surrounded by many hot sulphur water springs used for cooking and bathing by the pilgrims. Surya Kund is the most important pool among these hot springs. Near the Surya Kund there is a rock called Divya Shila which is worshipped before puja offered at Yamunaji. From here one can see the glitter of the morning sun on the snow-clad peaks and wide panoramic view of the mountains.

2. Gangotri

Gangotri (30°58'10"N Lat.—78°54'30"E long.) is situated at the altitude of 3140 m from the mean sea level in the District of

Uttarkashi. Gangotri temple dedicated to the Goddess Ganga, is situated at the confluence of the Assi Ganga and the Bhagirathi, This is the place where Goddess Ganga first descended upon the earth from heaven after the great effort made by Bhagirathi to bring down her at the Srikanth Parvat. Later Pandavas also had come here and performed the great 'Deva Yagya' in atonement for the death of their kinsmen in the epic battle of Kurukshetra. The temple of Goddess Gangaji was constructed by Gurkha Commander Amar Singh Thapa earlier in the 18th century. Later it was damaged badly by heavy snowfall. After some years this temple was reconstructed by the King of Jaipur.

'Gaumukh'—an icy cave, another holy shrine, is the real source of Ganga (Bhagirathi). It is 18 km. away from Gangotri. Path to Gaumukh is hard and hazardous and one has to go there on foot.

This area has the best Pine and Deodar forest in all over Asia, full of rich wild-life, with musical sound of cataracts and sweet twitter of colourful 'moral' which serves as a paradise both to the pilgrims as well as to the holiday makers.

3. Kedarnath

Kedarnath (30°44'15"N Lat.—79°6'33"E Long.) is located at the confluence of Mandakini, Chhir Ganga, Madhu Ganga, Saraswati and Swarg Rohini, at an altitude of 3581 m from the mean sea level in the District of Chamoli. The temple of Sri Kedarnath is dedicated to Lord Shiva and one of the twelve Jyotirlingas of Lord Shiva. This temple was constructed by Pandavas in atonement for their sins after the great battle of Mahabharat and reconstructed by Adi Shankaracharya in the 8th century A. D. According to Tribhuvan Narayan's monument this temple was constructed in 1076 Samvat or 1019 A. D. (Apigraphia Part I, pp. 235-36). It is believed that Adi Shankaracharya died here in very young age of 32. This temple stands on a platform of loose and unconsolidated glacial till material. Only 4

Gabala Dev Temple Near Datu Village (Pithoragarh District, Height 10,140′)

km. north from the temple there is a place called 'Swargrohini.' It is believed that from this place Yudhishthir ascended directly to go to the heaven.

4. Badrinath

Badrinath (33°44'N Lat.—79°31'E Long.) is one of the four most sacred places (Char Dhams) of Hindus. It is situated at the confluence of Rishi Ganga and Alakhnanda at an elevation of 3122 m from the mean sea level in the District of Chamoli.

The temple of Badrinath is dedicated to Lord Vishnu. It is an ancient belief that Raja Janamjai had come here for meditation. It is a religious laboratory of Hindus. Even before the time of Lord Krishna, pilgrims from every corners of India worshipped at the shrine of Lord Badri Narayan to wash away their sins, attain "Moksha' and get beyond the wheel of 'Sansara'.

Badrinath - bound pilgrims pass through the famous 'Panch Prayagas'—Dev Prayag, Rudra Prayag, Karn Prayag, Nand Prayag and Vishnu Prayag-situated all along the river Alaknanda (vide Fig. 3.1B). The natural beauty and tranquility of Badrinath provides such a transcendental moods that one can feel the spiritual peace as he enters the region.

5. Jogeshwar

It is famous for its celebrated temple of Lord Shiva, which is one of the twelve Jyotirlingas. The temple is situated in a beautiful narrow valley, 34 km. north from Almora and surrounded by magnificent deodar and monarcha. This temple was constructed by Katyuri Kings who rivalled the Chalukyas in south in the 7th century A. D. This centre is well known for its ancient sculptures.

6. Joshimath

Joshimath is one of the ancient Himalayan shrines and winter seat of 'Rawal Sahib' (the head priest of the Badrinath shrine).

It is situated in Chamoli district 250 km. from Rishikesh at an altitude of 1874 m from the mean sea level.

Jagat Guru Shankaracharya built a temple in the 8th century A D which is one of the four 'maths' constructed by him. The other three maths are - Shringerimath (Rameswaram), Sharda math (Jagnnath Puri), Gobardhan math (Dwarka).

7. Dwarahat

Dwarahat is situated at a distance of 89 km. from Ranikhet on Karn Prayag road. It is famous for its cluster of 55 ancient temples which are divided into eight distinct groups, constructed in the Indo-Aryan, Maru Prathihara or Nagar type. It is observed that this town was the capital of the Katyuri Kings who ruled here in the time of Maurya Dynasty (3rd century B C).

(ii) Development of Tourism in Medieval Period

Medieval period, when Muslims were ruling over India, has not brought any marked change in tourism development in U. P. Himalaya. The early Muslim period was an era of set-back to tourism. Most of the Muslim rulers were interested only in expansion of their kingdom, so they did not give any respect to religious sentiment of the people.

The later medieval rulers especially the Mughals blessed with rare asthetic sense, built a number of forts, places, monuments, mosques and tombs etc. in different parts of Uttar Pradesh. But the Himalayan segment of Uttar Pradesh being the core area of Hindu culture and on account of its isolation from the plains could not attract their attention. As such no new places of tourist interest could be developed in this region during this period nor any improvement could be made upon the old ones.

However, some of the centres which are of utmost tourist attraction today were developed during the period by Sikhs and Hindus (vide Fig. 3.1A). They are discussed as follows :

1. Dehra Dun

Dehra Dun situated in the heart of Doon valley (31°19'N Lat.—78°2'E Long.), is by far the most beautiful piedmont town of Uttar Pradesh. It was established as a residential centre some times in 1676 A. D. by a Sikh leader, Ram Rai. However, it was later developed as a major centre by the later Gorkha rulers-the last ruler being Gen. Bal Bahadur Singh Thapa. It was in the British period that the tourism acquired its present status.

2. Almora

Almora (29°3'N Lat.—79°40'E Long.) is among the important towns of Kumaun region. It is situated on a five km. long horse saddle-shaped ridge at an elevation of 1646 m, 90 km. from Kathgodam railway terminus. It was founded by Raja Baldeo Kalayan Chand in 1563 A. D. This beautiful town is surrounded by a circle of hills, each with a little temple on top. The four surrounding hill ranges, Banari Devi, Kasar Devi, Shyahi Devi and Katarmal are covered with thick, calm and unravaged forest with colourful valleys, while towering above are immense, gigantic glaciers and glistering peaks.

3. Champawat

At a distance of 76 km. from Tanakpur rail road, the ancient capital, Champawat (1615 m), from where the Chand dynasty ruled hold ruins of a past glory. There are present many monuments of Chand King, forts were constructed by Chand Rajas in the 14th century.

4. Lohaghat

Situated some 62 km. from Tanakpur rail road, Lohaghat is the ancient town famous for its scenic charms. It's name was given by the Cariste Assyrians who were dropped from Babylon by the Persians. Reaching India, they settled in the valley of Champawat calling it Kummuh, the name of their ancestral homeland. But this place came to light when Swami Vivekananda, fascinated by its calm and scenic beauty established the Advaita Ashram at Mayawati towards the turn of the last century. In this rapture he exclaimed 'This is the land of dreams of our forefathers, in which was born Parwati—the mother of India...the father of mountains where Rishis lived, where philosophy was born...These Himalayas stand for renunciation and the grand lesson we shall ever teach unto humanity will be renunciation'.

5. Nanakmata

Nanakmata (28°50′N Lat.—79°49′ E Long.) is situated in the foothill zone of Shivalik in Nainital district. It is a famous Sikh centre often called the 'Nankana Sahib' of Uttar Pradesh. With the erection of Nanak Sagar Dam here, this has evolved as a new growth centre for outdoor recreation.

6. Bageshwar

Bageshwar (29°50′15″ N Lat.—79°48′52″ E Long.) is a religious centre in Almora district. It is situated at an altitude of 975m at the conflunce of Sarju and Gomti rivers. It is a pilgrim centre with 15 shrines and the ancient temple of Baijnath, built in 1450 A. D. that gives the town its name. In the month of January, thousands of pilgrims converge here to Uttargayani fair to have a dip in the holy waters on the confluence and worship God Shiva.

7. Baijnath

Baijnath is situated 71 km. from Almora on the bank of Gomti river at an elevation of 1125 m. There are temples not only of Shiva, Parvati and Ganesh but also of Chandika, Kuber, Surya, Brahma and Goddess Kali. These temples were constructed by Chand Kings in 12th and 13th century A. D.

At a distance of 3.5 km. north, there is situated Koteki-Mai where a life-size superably sculptured statue of Vishnu presides over the beautiful old temple artistically pleasing both the soul and eye.

(iii) Development of Tourism during British Period

This was one of the most important periods as far as the tourism is concerned as it brought many remarkable changes to tourism in the hill region of Uttar Pradesh. In this period for the first time the entire hill region of Uttar Pradesh was considered as an area where several tourist centres could be developed. British rulers developed a new pattern of township in the Kumaun Hills. In fact it was the summer seat of U P Government and English people's cool corner.

Thus it can not be ruled out that Britishers were the main people who have developed and set the pace of the modern tourism in this region. After the establishment of Nainital and Mussoorie as health and recreational resorts, road connectivity gave birth to many other pleasure and leisure resorts such as Almora, Ranikhet, Kausani, Chakrata, Bhowali, Bhimtal etc. Some of the major tourist centres which were developed during the period are as follows :

1. Nainital

The lake town of Nainital (27°24′ N Lat. —79°20′ E Long.) is one of the most important hill resorts of the entire U P Himalaya. The main attraction of Nainital is its beautiful lake, at an elevation of 1938 m and 35.4 km. north from Kathgodam railway terminus. The lake is surrounded by majestic mountain peaks and ridges on three sides. It was discovered by Mr. M. P. Barron in the year 1839, and at present it has been developed as a unique lake resort with various tourist services.

2. Mussoorie

It is a famous summer hill resort of U. P. Himalaya mostly for the holiday makers. Mussorie (30°27′ N Lat.—78°6′ E Long.) is situated in the district of DehraDun at an altitude of 2005 m. It was explored by Captain Young during one of his hunting missions on the mountains in the year 1827.

Mussoorie is famous for its magestic natural scenary. The shining snow-clad peaks, beautiful Doon valley, singing water falls, dense deodar and pine forest and pleasing natural odour within themselves provide a treat to the holiday-makers.

3. **Ranikhet**

Ranikhet (29°40′ N Lat.—79°33′ E Long.) is situated at an elevation of 1829 m in the district of Almora. It was discovered and built entirely by the Britishers in the year 1869. The most striking feature of Ranikhet is that one has not to climb the hill to enjoy and see the glimpses of Himalayas. It is the only hill resort in the entire U. P. Himalaya where all roads are motorable.

4. **Kausani**

Kausani (29°52′ N Lat.—79°37′ E Long.) is situated at an elevation of 1890 m, about 52 km. away from Almora. Mahatama Gandhi, during his three week stay at Kausani was deeply moved by its enchanting beauty and bracing climate. He wondered why people go to Switzerland when there is a Kausani. It is from here that we may take clear view of a number of snow-clad ranges and peaks.

5. **Binsar**

Binsar (29°42′26″ N Lat.—79°47′44″ E Long.) is another tourist resort in Almora district. It is situated at an elevation of 2412 m from mean sea level. With its scintillating scenic beauty it is an ideal spot for holiday makers.

6. **Pindari Glacier**

Pindari is perhaps the most easily accessible of the 16 glaciers of Kumaun region, providing a paradise to the trekkers from all over India. The glacier is situated at the base of Nanda Devi and Nand Kota peaks 45 km. from the last bus terminus Kapkot, at an elevation of 4265 m from mean sea level. It is over 3.22 km. in length and 457 m wide.

Development of Tourism 99

7. Valley of Flowers

The Valley of Flowers covering an area of 8785 hectares (30°71′N Lat.—79°7′ E Long.) is one of the most beautiful spot in the entire U. P. Himalaya. It is situated at a height of 3657 m. The attraction of this valley is the abundance of its flowers extending to over 1000 varities (Smythe, F. S., 1932, p. 16). It was discovered by F. S. Symthe in the year 1931 during his Kamet expedition.

8. Hemkund Sahib

It is a holy shrine of Sikhs situated at a height of 4320 m, 20 km. from the last bus terminus Govind Ghat. Its very name Hemkund denotes the presence of a tank of snow which is referred to in Guru Granth Sahib. A reference has been made in 'Guru Granth Sahib' that in one of his previous births, Guru Govind Singh had meditated on the shores of a lake surrounded by seven snow-covered peaks. It is also believed that millennia before Rishi Medhasa of Durga Sapta Shati of Markandeya Purana had come here for penance and King Pandu of Hastinapur had practised Yoga.

9. Chakrata

Chakrata (30°32′20″ N Lat.—77°54′3″ E Long.) is a quiet hill station situated on two hills—Chakrata and Kalina at an elevation of 2135 m in the district of Dehra Dun. It was developed as a military cantonment area by the British army officers in the early seventies of the 19th century. Later it developed as a recreational resort because of its astounding natural beauty with dense conifers forest which is full of rich animals-panther and bear etc.

10. Bhimtal

It is another lake resort in the district of Nainital at an altitude of 1371 m. The lake which is named after one of the Pandavas' brother, is the largest in the district, even larger than Nainital. Bhimtal some 22 km. away from Nainital is known for its robust majesty and the main attraction of this lake is small islet in the middle of the lake.

11. Roop Kund

Roop Kund lies in the west of Trishul peak of Himalaya at the height of 5250 m from sea level in Chamoli district. This place came to the lime light in 1944 on account of the breaking of ice on a massive scale. A number of human sculps were discovered from under the cover of ice. It is gathered that they might have been covered with ice some thousand years ago. There are a number of stories prevalent about this occurrence. It is believed that some Hindus in order to ascend the heaven deliberately gave away their lives. But till now we have not been able to gather sufficient proofs to give any explanations of this story. Because of excessive height this place could not be developed as a tourist spot. Only few tourists visit the place by comming hereby trek route.

12. Corbett National Park

Corbett National Park is situated between (29°25' to 29°39' N Lat. and 78°44' to 79°7' E Long.) at an elevation of 700 to 1500 m above from sea level in Nainital and Garhwal districts. This park is famous for it tigers. It is one of the fifteen tiger reserves in India. Established in 1935, it was known as Haily National Park. It was in 1957 that the Park was rechristend as the Corbett National Park in the memory of Jim Corbett-the famous hunter.

(iv) Development of Tourism in Post-Independence Period

Post-Independence period can be termed as golden era so far as the development of moderen tourism is concerned. After independence, commercialization of tourism his brought many striking changes in it and it has proved as a major source of earning foreign exchange. Tourism was given a big boost in the country by setting up India Tourism Development Corporation Ltd. (1965) and a separate Ministry of Tourism. In fact after independence, development and promotion of tourism became the integral part of country's regional economic policy and planning.

In Uttar Pradesh, tourism development programme was initiated in 1956 with the 2500th anniversary of Lord Buddha which was celebrated in a big way. The State Govt. in collaboration with the Centre have implemented many programmes in the field of administrative, accommodation, transport and entertainment infra-structure.

It is during the plan periods that tourism could make a strong base in the regional economy of Uttar Pradesh Himalaya. Different Five-Year Plans provided a number of incentives to the growth of tourism. New avenues were added and created in almost every sector of tourism economy. Accommodation, transport, travel, recreation, marketing, souvenir trade etc. all are being developed and modernised. Tourism out-lays in various plans have gradually increased (vide Table 3.1).

In the field of accommodation, several types of residences such as star type, luxury hotels (in Dehra Dun, Mussoorie, Nainital), low income group accommodation, tourist bungalows, rest houses, 'dharamshalas', Pilgrims sheds, holiday homes, youth hostels, tourist huts, log cabins etc. have been constructed both by government and private agencies.

Transport and communication systems have also been developed due to heavy tourist demand. Many luxury buses, tourist cars, ordinary buses have been provided in the region to tourists and pilgrims. Rishikesh and Badrinath pilgrim centres have been connected with State Highway.

Besides, Government has been developing many new tourist centres for further development of tourism in the region. Nanaksagar Dam has been constructed (1962) near Nanakmata - the famous Sikhs Centre in Nainital district. Apart from, many wild life sanctuaries have been developing at different places such as

Govind Pashu Vihar sanctuary, Nanda Devi sanctuary, Motichur sanctuary and Malan sanctuary:

TABLE 3.1

Plan-outlay for the Development of Tourism

(in lakhs of Rs.)

	Plan-Period	Year	Uttar Pradesh	Hill Region
1.	First Five-Year Plan	1951-56	1.00	0.5
2.	Second Five-Year Plan.	1956-61	19.00	10.00
3.	Third Five-Year Plan	1961-66	22.00	14.00
	Annual Plans	1966-69	15.18	8.00
4.	Fourth Five-Year Plan	1969-74	115.00	72.50
5.	Fifth Five-Year Plan	1974-78*	378.00	200.00
	Annual Plans	1978-79	280.00	175.00
		1979-80	150.00	100.00
6.	Sixth Five-Year Plan	1980-85	1500.00	750.00
		1980-81	268.25	132.42
		1981-82	286.05	129.68
		1982-83	316.25	140.54
		1983-84	359.00	170.00
		1984-85	484.00	250.00
7.	Seventh Five-Year Plan	1985-90	5000.00	2500.00

Source : Department of Tourism, Govt. of Uttar Pradesh.

*The Fifth Five-Year Plan (1974—79) was cut short by one-year during the Janata Govt.

Development of Tourism

Thus, it is clear that tourism in the Himalayan Region of Uttar Pradesh has had a long and un-interrupted history. Tourism started as a Hindu sacrament in the ancient period, at present it

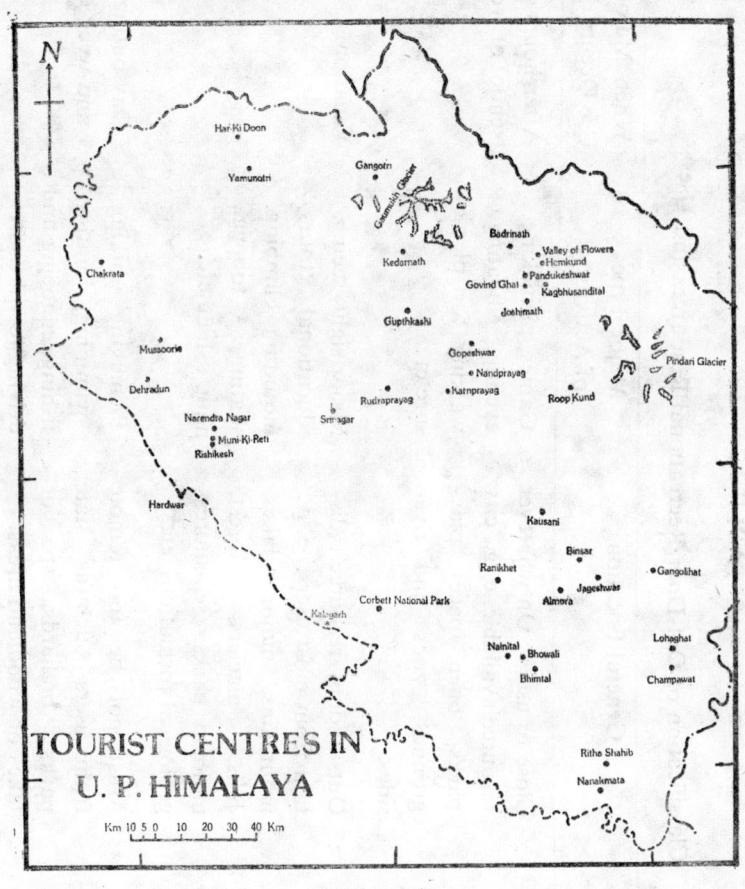

Fig. 3.2

has blossomed into a full-fledged industry earning much needed foreign exchange for the country.

RECREATIONAL RESOURCES IN U P HIMALAYA

Tourism is a multi-dimensional and complex phenomenon. In U. P. Himalaya, there are a number of factors which are res-

TABLE 3.2
Classification of Out-Door Recreational Resources and Uses

Types of Recreation Area	General Location	Major Type of Activity	When Major Use Occurs
User oriented	Close to users : On whatever resource available, e.g., city parks, open spaces, playgrounds, zoos and river sides.	Games, picnicking, cycling, boating, walking for pleasure etc.	After hours (school or work).
Resource based	Outstanding resource : distant from most users, e.g., mountains, major lakes, hills, glaciers, forest, national parks, sea-shores, geological formations etc.	Major sight seeing, educational, tours, mountain climbing, skating, tobogganing, fishing etc.	Vacation.
Intermediate	Must not be too remote from users such as state parks, orchards, spa or lakes or woodland areas.	Picnicking hiking, swimming, hunting, fishing, canoeing and driving for pleasure.	Day outings and week ends.

Development of Tourism

ponsible for the development of tourism in this area, such as geology, land forms, river system, climate, flora and fauna, religious shrines etc., which can be supposed as the basic elements of tourism. A particular element in a specific place attracts tourists towards that place. Recreational resources have been classified in a number of ways. Marison Clawson (1971) has prepared a three-tier classificatory scheme of recreational resources mostly based on the use, distance and time (vide Table 3.2). The table fully illustrates the nature, magnitude and type of interaction between the users and the recreational resources. The resource based recreational areas as conceived by Clawson involves the movement of people from the place of their residence to the place where these resources exist. Thus these areas indicate much spatial imbalance. The recreational areas of Uttar Pradesh Himalaya may conveniently be placed under this category. The development of tourism in such areas needs a throughly worked-out plan.

Some of the basic components of tourism that enhance the attraction of U. P. Himalaya are discussed here at some length :

(i) Aesthetics of Geology and Physical Landscapes

The aesthetics of geology and natural elements of the landscape always remain a major resource for tourism or out-door recreation. The lure of the mountains has attracted mankind since ages. The hill region of Uttar Pradesh, where the Himalaya stands majestically with its glittering snow-clad peaks, furrowed ridges, rippling streams, foaming torrents, lakes, smiling valleys is paramount tourism resource and capable of stimulating tourist activity. In the words of Smythe "Unimaginative is he who can gaze upon the Himalaya from the lower foot hills or the plains, and not sympathise with the simple, child like adoration of the Hindu for the eternal reservoir of snow, the gods of which despatch Mother Ganges to minister to their needs" (Smythe, F. S., 1932, p. 28).

In this region tourists can enjoy the beauty of glorious sunrise and sun-set and the grand Himalayan panorama from the ridges of Mussorrie, Ranikhet, Almora, Kausani. That's why these centres have developed as out-door recreational resorts.

The lake district of Nainital with its belt of lakes (25 km. long and 4 km. broad) is an outstanding hill region with the development of several tourist amenities. Apart from the main lake Nainital, other lakes such as Bhimtal, Naukuchiatal, sattal and lake basins of Khurpatal and Sukhtal also attract large number of tourists in season. In Garhwal Region Diurital lake lying some 16 km. to the north of Ukhimath has not been developed properly as a recreational resort but it can prove a good tourism resource in years to come.

(ii) Rivers and Their Aspects

Rivers, as source of water, have attracted mankind to their banks from ages past. In India rivers have immense religious significance. Hindus sought them religiously as 'sacred mother and goddess' (Markandey Purana, LVIII-30). Fortunately most of the sacred rivers of Hindus have their source in U. P. Himalayan glaciers. Bathing in these rivers was prescribed as an important outdoor religious activity. It is believed that the water of these sacred rivers (Ganga and Yamuna etc.) clean our body and soul and bring them into communion with God and their water honoured the dead whose ashes they have consigned in these rivers (Markandeya Purana LVIII-30).

In U P Himalaya Ganga, Yamuna and Kali are major river systems, while other minor water bodies like lakes, tanks, hot and mineral water springs (Taptkund-Badrinath, Gupt Kashi, Surya Kund—Yamunotri, Shashradhara-Dehra Dun) also have great attraction for tourists and pilgrims. The rivers of U. P. Himalaya along their mountainous course, command imposing natural scenary with deep gorges, transverse valleys, natural terraces and spurs etc.

The legendary river Bhagirathi can be seen emerging from the ice-cave of Gaumukh at Gangotri. Bhagirathi is considered to

Development of Tourism

be the main source of Ganga-though the Alaknanda, the Dhauli, the Pindar and the Mandakini have also been considered as good resource rivers (Bose, S. C., 1968, p. 362). Alaknanda, rising from the twin glaciers of Bhagirath Kharak and Satopanth, flows past to the holy shrine of Badrinath, while Mandakini rising from Chorabari glacier (Kedarnath peak) flows past another Hindu shrine of Kedarnath. The Pindar Ganga rises from the famous Pindari glacier which attracts thousands of trekkers. Ganga's major tributary Yamuna rises from Yamunotri glacier and is torrently rapid with her more turbulent tributary Tons. The Yamuntori shrine is near its source with its geysers and hot springs. All these rivers sculptured Himalayan landscape into beauty.

(iii) Floral and Faunal Attributes

Flora and fauna both have been considered as good resource of modern tourism. The greenary of forest and wild cries of animals always attracted the mankind. As far as U. P. Himalaya is concerned it is very rich and prosperious in floral and faunal resource syndrome.

The forest of Uttar Pradesh Himalaya shows diversity in composition. In the high hills, the main trees are chir, fir, deodar while in the sub-mountains, prominent trees are sal, sain, haldu, semal etc. A galaxy of flowering and shade trees have been planted along 'Parikrama' or pilgrim routes by State Government. Apart from these 'the Valley of Flowers' with it numerous and rarest flower plants is an object of wonder particularly to the western tourists. According to F. S. Symthe, "The wonders of the valley are its flowering plants. You find here different branches of the same plant yielding flowers of different colours and varying fragrance. All these, coupled with the fauna, combine to make a superb and harmonious ensemble".

Wilderness of the forest is the home of wild life and they are potential tourism resource. Uttar Pradesh Himalaya has a colourful and fascinating wild life-majestic tigers and elephants in the sub-mountain region while in the Alpine zone we have some of the rarest animals found in India such as monal, brown bear, snow leopard, musk-deer, snow trout etc. This region has also the wealth of numerous colourful birds and fishes in hill rivers, streams and ponds. The famous 'Jim Corbett National Park' is located in Nainital and draws large number of tourists to see tigers. Besides this three sanctuaries have been developed for the preservation of wild-life. They are—Motichur Sanctuary (Dehra Dun), Malan Sanctuary (Landsdowne) and Nanda Devi Sanctuary. A zoo has been proposed to be established also in Uttar Kashi district.

TABLE 3.3

Wild Life in U. P. Himalaya

Wild Life Zone	Important Wild Animals	Sanctuaries/National Parks
1. Upper Himalaya Zone.	Snow leopard, Brown and black bear, Bharal, Thar, Serow, Muskdeer, Goral, Sambhar, Monal, Chukor, Partridges, Snow trout and many kinds of birds.	1. Govind Pashu Vihar, 953.12 sq.km.
2. Lower Himalaya Zone.	Elephant, Tiger, Panther, Sloth bear, Swamp deer, Hog deer, Spotted deer, Blue bull, Four horned antelope, Peafowl, Junglefowl, Partridges, Kaleege, Pheasant, Porcupine etc. and many kinds of birds.	1. Corbett National Park Kalagarh and Ramnagar Forest Block 528.8 sq. km. 2. Motichur Sanctuary, Dehra Dun 89.56 sq. km. 3. Malan Sanctuary 84.12 sq. km.

Source : Ministry of Forest, Govt. of Uttar Pradesh, Lucknow.

(iv) Climate as a Resource of Tourism

Climate is a vital tourism resource. It has always been a key factor in any tourism resource inventory. A number of phenomena mostly connected with weather and climate like sun-rise, sun-set, mid-night, moon-night, sun-bath, cool breeze-land or sea, snowfall, winter games, summer morn etc. have become the catch words of modern tourism. Tourists' peak and off periods in many region are mostly related to weather conditions. Obviously tourists seek besides other things, a sparkling bracing weather. In U. P. Himalaya, cool hill resorts attract large number of tourists during summer season. In the month of April, May and June when other parts of the state have hot and scorching weather, in U. P. Himalaya climate remains rather cool, soothing, pleasant and healthy. It is in this season that heavy tourist rush can be seen in the hill resorts of Nainital, Almora, Kausani and Mussoorie.

During to winter season some of the hill resorts attract number of tourists to see the glamour of snow-fall. Auli near Joshimath has been set up as the first winter sport centre in U. P.

(v) People-Anthropological and Ethanic Character

"O, Wonder.
How many goodly creatures are there here !
How beauteous mankind is !
O, brave new World,
That has such people in't !"

—W. Shakespeare

Tourism shows an interesting relationship with cultural anthropology—study of primitive or folk cultures, and for exotic ancient culture, a tourist might move for long-haul travels (Wahab, S. E., 1971, p. 19). That which appears to be a common place, incogruous and grotesque in our way of life, becomes an object of tourist's curiosity (Schanche, Don, A., 1972, p. 45).

People in different parts of the world are unique in their physical appearances, dress, food, manner and ideal. In the case of U. P. Himalaya they are due potential tourist resource. The folk-lore and folk dances of Kumaun and Garhwal play significant role in attracting people in these regions. Some of the the famous folk dances of this region are—Ramola, the exorcist dances, chhapeli, the courtship dance, chancheri dance, the joyous-jhora, chholiya dance, the Thali jadda etc.

Tribal life of U. P. Himalaya, with all its colourful customs, rituals and taboos is quite facinating. Tribes like Bhotias, Jaunsaries, Tharus, Bhoxas have always something of novelty and fun in their way of life to interest even home tourists.

POTENTIAL RECREATIONAL AREAS

On the basis of natural (mountains, rivers, caves, lakes etc.) and man-made (fishing, boating, yachting, hunting facilities) tourist resources and their management problem, the Outdoor Recreational Resource Commission U.S.A. (1962) has classified the total recreational areas into six categories :

1. High density recreational areas

    (high degree of facility development involving heavy investment).

2. General out-door recreational areas (involve more extensive and less crowded use).

3. Natural environment areas.

4. Unique natural areas.

5. Primitive areas.

6. Historical and cultural-religious sites.

Development of Tourism

TOURISM TYPOLOGY
IN U. P. HIMALAYA

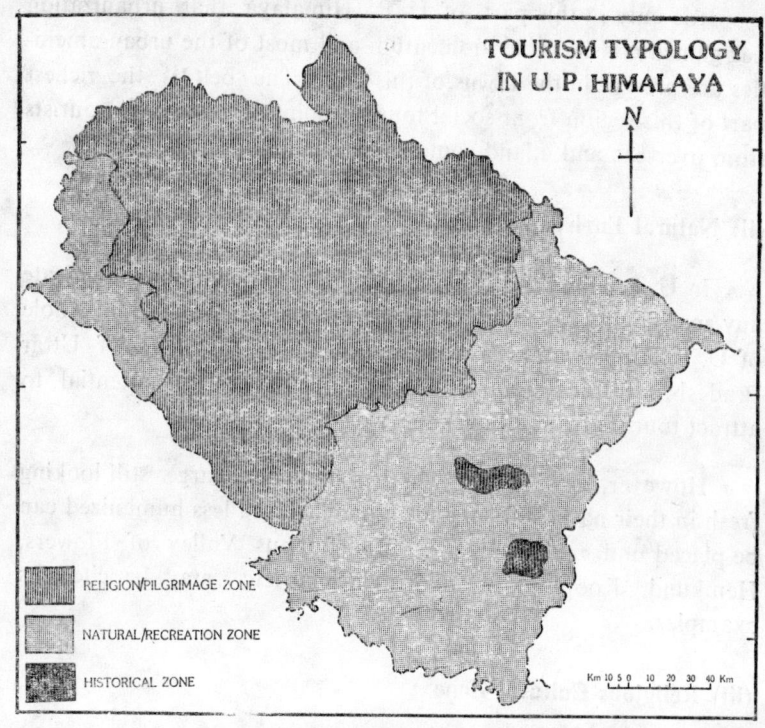

RELIGION/PILGRIMAGE ZONE
NATURAL/RECREATION ZONE
HISTORICAL ZONE

Fig 3.3

But in the case of U. P. Himalaya the entire recreational areas can be divided only into three recreational zones :

(i) High density recreational zone.

(ii) Natural environment recreation zone.

(iii) Religious-cultural zone.

(i) High Density Recreational Zone

In U. P. Himalaya, Nainital and its environs (Bhimtal, Bhowali, Khurpatal, Sat Tal etc.) and Almora-Ranikhet-Kausani belt of Kumaun region; and Dehra Dun-Mussoorie belt in Garhwal region come in the high density recreational areas. These recreational belts draw thousands of tourists during summer season every year.

It is only in this part of U. P. Himalaya that urbanization has gained considerable momentum and most of the urban amenities are present in the towns of this belt. The belt is the richest part of this region from social tourism point of view where tourists from overseas and inland come in greater number.

(ii) Natural Environment Zone

In U. P. Himalaya it is very difficult to delimit and delineate any specific natural environmental zone as it includes the whole of U. P. Himalayan area, because the entire hill region of Uttar Pradesh is full of natural beauty and has much potential to attract tourists from all over the world.

However, those areas whether tiny and large still looking fresh in their natural form and grandeur and less humanized can be placed under this category. The famous Valley of Flowers, Hemkund, Roopkund, Pindari glaciers etc. may be cited as examples.

(iii) Religious-Cultural Zone

U. P. Himalaya particularly the Garhwal region is par excellance a religious and cultural tourist zone of Hindus. The entire Garhwal region is called 'Tapovan.' It is believed that this is the place where at every step Lord Shiva is present. In the entire region there are two separate religious belts, one is Yamunotri-Gangotri and the other is Badri-Kedar belt. These holy shrines draw large number of Hindu pilgrims from all over country and foreign trekkers. According to Hindu mythology- Gangotri is the place where for the first time Goddess Ganga descended upon the earth from heaven. Kedarnath is the place where Pandavas came after the battle of Mahabharat and established the temple of Shri Kedarnath. According to another belief, Lord Shiva after fleeing from Pandavas took refuge here in the form of buffalo and dived into the ground, leaving the hinder part at the surface. The other four parts of God are worshipped in associated shrines—Tungnath (arms), Rudranath (face), Madhya Maheshwar (belley) and Kalpeswar (head) (Poddar, H. P., 1957, p. 615). At Kedarnath 'Swarg-rohini' is the place from where Pandavas left for their last journey for self immolation and Badrinath is one of the four sacred 'dhams' of Hindus.

Another belt consists of Rishikesh and Hardwar religious centres. Here the river Ganga first time enters the plains after finishing her hill journey. This region is also called the Gateway' of Himalayan shrines. Tourists from all over the world come here and they find these centres interesting for oriental culture, yogic thereapy and for the company of sages and saints who administer spiritual anaesthesia to their matter-afflicted souls. From Rishikesh different routes go towards every Himalayan shrines - Gangotri, Yamunotri, Badrinath, Kedarnath and to other religious centres of U. P. Himalaya. Hardwar is considered to be one of the seven most sacred cities* in ancient India (Skanda Puran, 6/68). Its renowned ghats and Har-ki-pauri are the major attractions of the city both for the pilgrims and recreational tourists.

TOURISM ORGANIZATION IN UTTAR PRADESH

The subject of national tourism is more or less the state concern though the Central Government plays a key role in the development of inland tourism too, together with foreign tourism. Tourism taken in the modern context as an industry or as a form of human recreational behaviour is of recent origion in India. It started relatively quite late in the developing countries. In Uttar Pradesh the programme for tourism development was started in 1956 with the 2500th anniversary of Lord Buddha which was celebrated in a big way. The reconstruction and rennovation of the places related with Lord Buddha were at the root of initiating the

---

* Kashi (Varanasi), Kanchi (Conjeeveram), Maya (Hardwar), Ayodhya, Dwarka, Mathura and Avanti are the seven most sacred cities.

promotion of tourism in Uttar Pradesh. In different **Five-Year Plans** a number of measures were taken to develop the infra-structure of tourism both in plains and in the hill regions of the state. The Himalayan region of Uttar Pradesh being somewhat more distinct, rich, beautiful and sacred has caught our imagination in a big way. As such the tourist industry in this part is being developed on a massive scale. It is being considered as the main vehicle of regional development.

For the sake of administration, policy making and effective implimentation of the programmes of tourism in Uttar Pradesh a detailed and systematic organizational network is at work (vide Table 3.4).

There is a full-fledged Department of Tourism headed by a Minister of State rank. Its main function is to formulate policies and programmes and give direction for the development of tourism in the State. The Directorate of tourism with Director at its head is the main implementing authority. Besides, there is a U. P. State Tourism Development Corporation whose main function is commercial. As regards the Hill Region of Uttar Pradesh, it has some special provision for its development. There is a separate department of Hill Development and Hill Development Corporation responsible for the total development of the eight Himalayan Districts of Uttar Pradesh. At regional level too there are two different Divisional Development Corporations namely—Kamaun Division Development Corporation and Garhwal Division Development Corporation. All these different agencies are engaged some way or the other in a number of promotional works relating with tourism directly or indirectly.

The development of tourist infra-structure to preserve and maintain the historical, religious, natural and cultural places, to create better facilities for accommodation, transport, fooding and recreation for tourists and to hold seasonal fairs, rallies and

TABLE 3.4

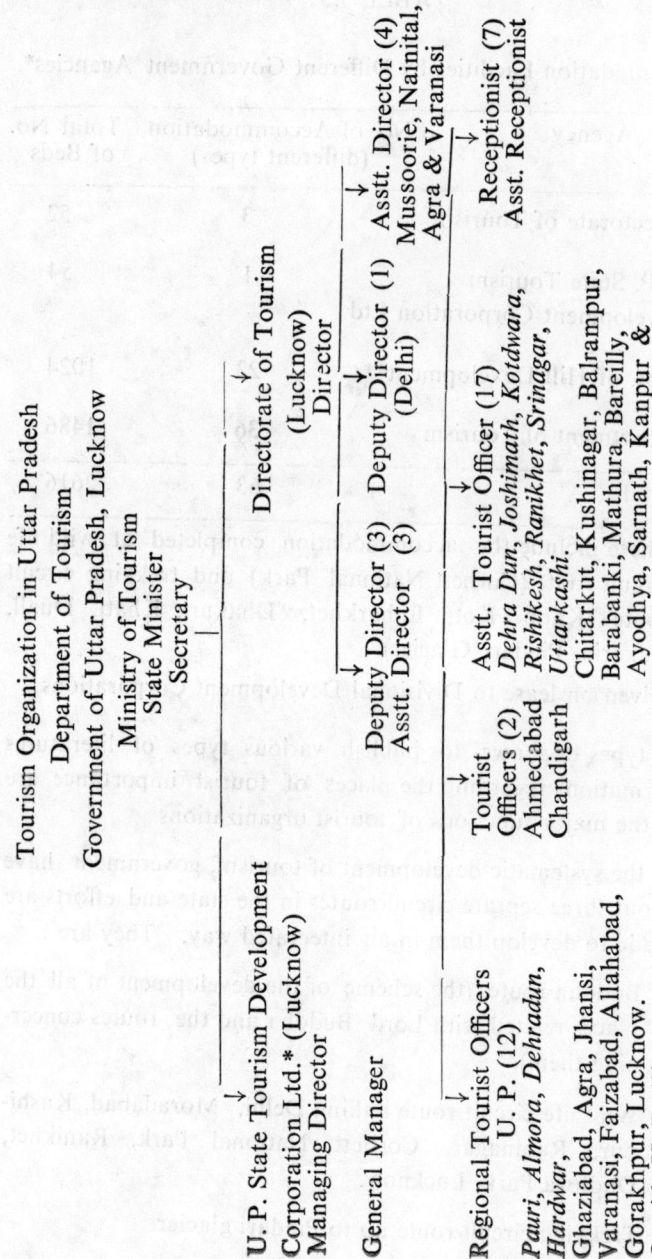

Tourism Organization in Uttar Pradesh
Department of Tourism
Government of Uttar Pradesh, Lucknow
Ministry of Tourism
State Minister
Secretary

```
                         │
         ┌───────────────┴───────────────┐
         ↓                               ↓
U.P. State Tourism Development    Directorate of Tourism
Corporation Ltd.* (Lucknow)            (Lucknow)
Managing Director                        Director
         │                               │
         ↓                               ↓
General Manager              Deputy Director (1)   Asstt. Director (4)
         │                        (Delhi)          Mussoorie, Nainital,
         │                                         Agra & Varanasi
         ↓
Deputy Director (3)    Asstt. Tourist Officer (17)    Receptionist (7)
Asstt. Director (3)    Dehra Dun, Joshimath, Kotdwara, Asst. Receptionist
         │             Rishikesh, Ranikhet, Srinagar,
         ↓             Uttarkashi.
Tourist                Chitarkut, Kushinagar, Balrampur,
Officers (2)           Barabanki, Mathura, Bareilly,
Ahmedabad,             Ayodhya, Sarnath, Kanpur &
Chandigarh             Mirzapur.
         │
         ↓
Regional Tourist Officers
U. P. (12)
Pauri, Almora, Dehradun,
Hardwar,
Ghaziabad, Agra, Jhansi,
Varanasi, Faizabad, Allahabad,
Gorakhpur, Lucknow.
Outside U. P. (3)
Bombay, Chandigarh, Madras.
```

* Its main function is commercial.

TABLE 3.5

Accommodation Facilities by Different Government Agencies*

Sl. No.	Agency	No. of Accommodation (different types)	Total No. of Beds
1.	Directorate of Tourism	3	52
2.	U. P. State Tourism Development Corporation Ltd.	1	54
3.	Dept. of Hill Development**	23	1024
4.	Department of Tourism	36	1486
	Total	63	2616

* These include the accommodation completed at wild life circuit route (Corbett National Park) and trekking circuit route (Kaop Kot, Loharkhet, Dhakuri, Khati, Duali, Fukaria, Pindari Glacier).

** Given on lease to Divisional Development Corporations.

different types of shows, to publish various types of literatures and informations regarding the places of tourist importance are some of the major functions of tourist organizations.

For the systematic development of tourism, government have marked out three seprate circuit routes in the state and efforts are being made to develop them in an integrated way. They are :

1. Buddha route (the scheme of the development of all the places related with Lord Buddha and the routes concerning them).

2. Wild life circuit route linking Delhi, Moradabad, Kashipur, Ramnagar, Corbett National Park, Ranikhet, Dudhwa Park, Lucknow.

3. Trekking circuit route up to Pindari glacier.

Out of these three, Corbett National Park (wild life circuit route) and the trekking circuit route completely lie in the study region. A number of accommodation facilities have been provided on these routes.

The detailed account of different types of accommodations with their bed capacity arranged by various government agencies in the hill region of Uttar Pradesh is shown in Table 3.5.

4

Tourism in Kumaun Region–Case Profiles and Studies

TOURISM AND TOWN

The development of tourism has taken different shapes and magnitude in different environmental situations. The open country-sides and wide ranging sea coasts have always been the key resources for tourism. In the developed countries of the west space, beauty, quiet, wild life-all these attributes of country-side are being preserved cautiously for the public enjoyment. In England, Spain and other European countries a holiday maker often desires the peace of nature for the refreshment of his body and mind. Just for the sake of relief from stress and strain of modern life many turn to the country sides for rest and refreshment at week end. Urbanites in great number are being enticed to the countryside. Outdoor activities and holidays are becoming popular in the west for hunting, shooting, pony trekking etc. in country side. Considerable use is made of the countryside for educational and academic purposes too. The concept of 'second homes' has largely developed in these regions because of increased family income, more leisure time and a wish to escape from the drudgery of daily urban routines.

From tourism point of view the sea and the coast have always been regarded as one of the most potential resorts. For the most of the western countries the coast line is and will continue to remain as their main national play-ground. The magical qualities of oceans, infinite varieties of coastal scenery and activities related with sea water have been fascinating man from the beginning of human civilization. England, Spain and France etc. have a number of sea resorts having immense tourism resource potentials. A beginning has been made in India too where Goa-Bombay coast is attracting a large number of tourists every year.

However, in this age of industrialized urbanization and urbanized industrialization the format of travel and tourism has assumed a totally new dimension. Modern urban centres of varying size and shape besides their normal social and economic functioning also perform a number of activities related to recreation and pastime. Tourism towns are of relatively recent growth. It is not very easy to define tourism towns as they vary widely in their character, function and size. They may be quite large with varieties of amenities or they may be just small nuclei with some basic objects for attracting tourists. In a number of urban studies dealing with functional grouping of towns a special category of towns is often worked out having activities and services related with tourism. Generally they are termed as resorts/recreational towns. But there is ample debate on the use and misuse of these technical terms. Some of the writers use recreational and resorts as synonyms. But there are others who keep resort towns altogether apart from other towns which have tourism based on extra-recreational grounds, such as religious, educational and historical/cultural etc. In this study we have normally used 'tourism towns' for all those urban centres related with tourism in one way or the other. Resorts or recreational towns are taken to be merely a sub-group within the broader group of tourism towns.

All such towns whether mountains centres or watering places have certain characteristics in common :

1. They mainly depend for their existence upon their ability to offer a different and distinct environment.

2. They seldom possess well developed central place activities or manufacturing industries etc. Industries whatsoever are mostly light and house-hold. A considerable proportion of working population is engaged in some sorts of tertiary occupations.

3. A further distinct feature of such towns is a marked seasonal rhythm of activities and employment with a high proportion of causual work.

In U. P. Himalaya mostly the towns become moribund in winter when there are practically no tourist arrivals. Here summer and autumn are the active seasons when life returns to the towns.

4. Towns specializing in tourist activities or depending on them are generally small in size.

5. Lastly tourism towns are required to provide a number of facilities and amenities to induce all sorts of tourists.

Out of the various criteria taken for town classification today, sites and functions play the most important role. It is the factors of sites that determine the morphology of towns. In the Himalayan region this factor becomes much more significant where linear and irregular patterns with zig-zag roads and unevenly scattered houses are the commenset feature. On the basis of sites, the towns of U. P. Himalaya may broadly be grouped into four categories :

(*i*) *Foot Hill or Gate Towns* : Mostly rail or road-heads from west to east like Dehra Dun, Hardwar, Rishikesh, Kotdwara, Ramnagar, Kathgodam and Tanakpur are placed in this group of town. They are locally known as 'dwar' (meaning gate).

(*ii*) *Spur or Ridge Towns* : These towns on account of their real mountainous location and healthy climate have become important tourist centres of U. P. Himalaya, Mussoorie, Ranikhet, Almora, Chakrata are good examples.

(*iii*) *Valley or Basin Towns* : The largest number of the towns of this region are located in valley bottoms over somewhat flat surface. Dehra Dun (Doon valley), Nainital (Naina lake basin), Joshi-math (Alaknanda basin) may be cited as examples.

(*iv*) *River Towns* : Such towns are located mostly at confluences or river terraces. Five Prayagas, Uttar Kashi, Srinagar etc. are good examples.

These locational aspects are fully manifested in the functional morphology of most of the Himalayan towns. The characteristic feature of these towns is their tertiary sector which is dominated by 'other services'. The commercial activities are developed to a considerable degree mostly in large towns. However, the transport activities are clearly localised in 'gate-towns.' Recreational functions dominate highly in the functional structure of a number of hill towns. Mussoorie and Nainital are the best examples. Tourism functions are also the characteristics of all the religious or pilgrim towns of U. P. Himalaya. Dehra Dun may be cited as the best example of multifunctional towns in the entire region. Besides performing administrative functions some towns are also specialised in educational and defence activities too.

The classification of towns based on tourism required a number of considerations. However, broadly a two-fold divisions may conveniently be made which are follows :

1. Centres which have developed purely and simply as tourism towns. They are nothing more, nothing less but nothing else. Most of the towns of our study region might well be placed within this group.

2. Towns which have developed tourist industry as supplementary or complementary to their normal urban functions. Dehra Dun may clearly be put into this second category.

The establishment and successful growth of tourist centres has been either due to historical accidents or due to physical/natural attractions. So far as the U. P. Himalaya is concerned here every place or area is both attractive as well as significant from religion point of view. However, the towns of U. P. Himalaya may broadly be categorised into four main group :

(i) Religious/Pilgrimage Towns

Tourism in Himalaya as in the case of India as a whole is basically religious. These religious centres become much more important as they are located in attractive mountain surroundings. Hardwar (Saharanpur district), Badrinath, Rishikesh, Kedarnath, Karnaprayag, Joshimath, Devaprayag, Dwarahat, Baijnath, Bageshwar are the main towns devoted solely to religious tourism.

(ii) Scenic/Recreational Towns

Such centres are the main planks of tourism in the modern sense. Many resorts grew up because of the attractions of their local natural scenario-mountains, lakes, waterfalls, unique geological formations, pleasant weather, typical flora and Fauna etc. Subsequently they developed a number of other attractive features such as sporting facilities and other amenities. Nainital, Ranikhet Almora, Mussoorie, Chakrata, Bhimtal, Bhowali—all these developed as centres of tourism as a result of their location in areas of outstanding Himalayan scenic beauty.

(iii) Historical/Cultural Towns

Such types of centres are of a more transient character. Tourist seldom visit these centres. However, these historic towns with their fortifications and other ancient monuments have a great fascination for many. Champawat, Dwarahat, Jageshwar, Tehri are such towns.

(iv) Educational Towns

Like historical these centres are also very few and far between. Dehra Dun, Srinagar, Pantnagar may be placed in this group.

In short, tourist centres in our study region are either basically religious or scenic and recreational or both simultaneously. Considering these characteristics, in all nine towns were selected for detailed studies. Out of these three Nainital, Almora and Ranikhet recreational/scenic resorts are taken from Kumaun region. Among the rest five towns Dehra Dun, Mussoorie, Rishikesh, Badrinath and Kedarnath lie in Garhwal region and the other one Hardwar in Saharanpur district of Meerut Division. Barring Mussoorie and Dehra Dun all these towns are basically centres of pilgrimage. Mussoorie is a typical European style hill resort and Dehra Dun has more or less a cosmopolitan outlook. It is a normal central place town. Besides the centres defined as towns some other spots and areas have also been taken for our study that have attractions to a wide range of tourists. Such as Corbett National Park (Kumaun Region), Valley of Flowers, Gangotri, Yamunotri (Garhwal Region) etc.

METHODOLOGY

As it has already been mentioned in the very outset (Preface), town profiles and tourist trend analyses are mostly based on primary data generated through author's field survey and direct contact with tourists in the region. For selecting towns and to collect classified informations about them a series of field surveys with the help of prepared schedules and questionnaires were conducted in a systematic and phased manner. First of all a general 'reconnaissance' survey was made of the entire region in order to get introduced with the region and have general informations about its geography, routes, towns, different other places of interest and the people. This was just a preliminary survey to have first-hand informations about the U. P. Himalaya. This initial and the first phase of survey lasted about 35 days in 1983 from May 15th to 20th of June. The author toured the whole Kumaun (985 km. including 52 km. trek) and Garhwal region and most of their towns.

The informations and insight acquired through the survey as well as the study of all basic possible literature on the region both helped a lot in selecting the specific towns and spot/areas for detailed study. Every care was taken in selecting the centres so that they might truly represent all the basic tourism characters of the region—its antiquity, importance, religion, recreation, culture, beauty, size and impact.

After selecting Nainital, Almora, Ranikhet and Corbett National Park (Kumaun region) and Dehra Dun, Mussoorie, Hardwar (Saharanpur District), Rishikesh, Badrinath, Kedarnath Gangotri, Yamunotri and Valley of Flowers (Garhwal region) for making detailed studies, the second phase of field survey was initiated. One schedule for towns, and two questionnaires one for getting informations from management of different types of hotels and the other for interviewing the tourists were prepared· In making the schedules and questionnaires every attention was given to the limited tourist time and ease of communication.

Only the basic questions in simple language requiring minimum time in the answer were incorporated. They were prepared in both the languages—Hindi and English.

Kumaun Himalaya was taken for the second systematic survey. It lasted from 20th of May to 5th of June during 1984. Detailed and classified informations were collected about Nainital, Almora and Ranikhet with the help of town schedules.

The third leg of field survey covered the whole of Garhwal region. It was conducted in 1985 from Sept. 23rd to October 17. The total itinerary covered some 1132 km. including 145 km. on trek. Detailed informations about Dehra Dun, Mussoorie, Hardwar, Rishikesh, Badrinath, Kedarnath, Gangotri, Valley of Flowers were gathered with the help of schedules and questionnaires.

The fourth and the last trip was to Hardwar in April, 1986 during Kumbh fair. The Kumbh at Hardwar facilitated the author in meeting with people of different shades and colours from every part of the country. Really it was an unique occasion for the author to have a new insight into tourism behaviour at a pligrim centre.

In all these surveys some 1165 tourists were contacted and interviewed for getting informations regarding their tourism behaviour. All possible care was taken in seeking interview with the tourists—their limited time, mood and comfort were given top priority. All these informations were later on systematically arranged, tabulated and analysed to have a clear view of the state of affairs regarding tourism in the region. However, with the constraints of time and specially resources available for field research to the author, only a small number of tourists could be contacted for interview and thus the data generated are not enough and variable for any closer analysis, mostly they have been converted into percentage to show the behavioural trends.

NAINITAL

(i) Introduction

Nainital is one of the most beautiful hill-resorts not only in U. P. Himalaya but also in India. This hill resort has been developed around the famous lake 'Naini'—a gem in a perfect wild setting. It is surrounded by the majestic hill ranges and covered by dense forest. Nainital, with all its attractions provides a fine opportunity to enjoy the mystery of Mother Nature to all kinds of tourists. P. Barron, a seasoned traveller confessed about its beauty—'It is by far the best site I have witnessed in the course of a 1,500 mile trek in the Himalayas'.

Thus Nainital has occupied a unique position on India's tourist map and overflows with domestic as well as international tourists in season.

(ii) History and Development

The lake which is the main attraction of Nainital was discovered by P. Barron in the year 1839. Professionally Barron was an English businessman engaged in sugar trade in Shahjahanpur. Once, while hunting along with his brother-in-law in Haldwani he lost his way. As he was straying on the hills to find out his way back, he entered Bhimtal by chance, and there he was informed by the native people about the existence of another lake in the hills nearby. Barron's passion and eagerness to locate the place was so strong that he explored the lake in a very short time. So enamoured was Barron with the beauty of the lake that he decided to establish an European colony on the shores of the lake.

The first account of Nainital appeared is the issue of 'Englishman Calcutta' announcing the discovery of a lake in the vicinity of Almora in the year 1841. Barron wrote his travelogues in the 'Agra Akhbar' (1838-40) under the pen-name 'Pilgrim'. About Nainital he wrote :

"An undulating lawn with a great deal of level ground interspersed with occasional dumps of oak, cypress and other beautiful trees, continues from the margin of the lake for upwards of a mile, up to the base of magnificent mountain standing at the further extreme of this vast amphitheatre, and the sides of the lake are also bounded by splendid hills and peaks, which are thickly wooded down to the water's edge. On the undulating ground between the highest peak and the margin of the lake, there are capabilities for a race-course, cricket ground etc. and building sites in every direction for a large town."

In 1842 Barron asked a contractor to build a dozen bungalows beside the lake. The first house to be built on the fairytale greenary of the lake was his—he called it 'Pilgrim Cottage.' It is still as new and fresh as it was 140 years ago. Later Mr. Lushington (then commissioner) planned a bazar, now known as Tallital. After the takeover by the East India Company and later by the

British Government, development of Nainital as a hill resort came up rapidly. The Government House, the Secretariate, lodges and offices all were constructed in a very short period and it became the summer headquarter of the Britlsh Government. The period from 1869 to 1900 A. D. witnesses hectic building activity going on here. Most of the hotels, public buildings, lodges, bungalows have been constructed around the pear-shaped lake and Nainital has blossomed into a unique hill resort with varied tourist services.

Origin of the Lake

The main attraction of Nainital town is the lake 'Naina.' The story about the origin of this lake is very interesting and mysterious according to Indian mythology. It is said that Parvati daughter of the King Daksha married Lord Shiva against the wishes of her father. King Daksha, to embarras and insult both his daughter and son-in-law, held a great 'yajna.' Every body was invited except the couple. However, Parvati went to her father's house at her own will but she could not get any respect there. Parvati fumed at this insult leapt into the raging flames before the horrified eyes of her father. Lord Shiva himself retrieved the half charred body and took it tenderly in his arms. On the way back to Mount Kailas, her eyes dropped into the lake giving it the name 'Naina', the Sanskrit word for eyes and 'Tal' for water. A temple was put up to the Goddess Naina Devi, a name given to Parvati.

In Manasa Khanda of the Skand Purana, there is a different tale about the lake's origin. Here the lake is mentioned as 'Tri-Rishi' sarovar, named after the three rishies—Atri, Pulastya and Pulaha, who came to Gager range now called Naini peak (formerly known as Cheena peak) during their pilgrimage. The thirsty sages unfortunately found no water, so they remembered the Holy Manasarovar which inspired them with zeal to dig a large pit. Almost miraculously it was filled with fresh water from Mana. The lake got the name 'Tri-Rishi-Sarovar.'

But scientifically rather geologically the origin of the lake is associated with two theories—(a) that they are due to glacial action, (b) that they are hollows of denudation for the most part by landslips.

(iii) Location and Extent

Nainital town (29°24′N Lat. and 79°29′E long.) is situated on the extreme southern part of the lesser Himalaya Zone at an altitude of 1938 m. from the mean sea level. The total area of the town is 14.32 sq. km., stretching from the end to end of lake, with total population of 26093 (1981).

Kathgodam, 'the gateway of Kumaun hills' is 35 km from Nainital. It is the nearest railway terminus from Nainital, while the nearest airport Phoolbagh in Pantnagar is 72 km from Nainital town. Private taxies, delux buses, Kumaun Motors Owners Union Ltd. (KMOU) and Uttar Pradesh State Roadways Transport Corporation (UPSRTC) buses for Nainital are always available in Kathgodam as well as in Pantnagar.

Nainital's peripheral tourism-zone extends up to Malvatal to the east, where Bhimtal, Sat tal and Naukuchia tal, as adjunct to Naini, have fairly developed tourist amenities. In fact, the entire range of 20 to 25 km area is confined with mountain scenary and pleasant cool weather.

(iv) Physical-Natural Scenario (Tourism Resource)

Nainital has a number of recreational resources which have turned it into a superb hill resort. The most powerful recreational resource of Nainital is its natural scenic beauty which draws thousands of holiday-makers and nature lovers around it. In addition, the bracing climatic condition and rich floral-faunal life give physical comfort as well as mental peace to the tourists. Let us have a glance on these recreational resources one by one :

(a) Space Scenary and Landscape

The town of Nainital is matchless in its space scenary and landscape charms. The surrounding hill ranges and the overlooking peaks give it the added charms of wilderness. Human eyes are too weak to comprehend fully the divine beauty of the place and lips are too feeble to describe what they see. One can perceive this precious gift of Mother Nature only with his body and mind.

Nainital Lake

The celebrated lake 'Naina', the key resource of the resort, has made this town an outstanding tourist centre. This lake is surrounded by seven lofty peaks—Cheena peak (2610 m), Kilbury (2528 m), Laria Kanta (2481 m), Deopath and Camels Back (both 2435 m), Dorothy's Seat (2290 m) and Snow View (2270 m) which give it a panoramic view.

Nainital is the prettiest among the 66 lakes of Kumaun. At an elevation of 1938 m from the sea level, the lake is 1370 m in length and 360 m in width. The maximum depth of the lake is 28 m and minimum is 6 m. The circumference of the lake by road is 3624 m. The lake is divided in two parts—Mallital and Tallital (upper and lower lake).

In the absence of a shore line and sunny beaches in the state, the placid water of the lake serves as a 'toy-substitute'. One who loves sailing can enjoy the pleasure of yachting on the lake. The elegant 'Nainital Yacht Club' established in 1890 is the highest yacht club in the world. It has yachts specially designed to cope with the mountain winds. The lake has promoted yachting in India through this club. Every year Zonal and National races are held here.

Boating on the crystal clear water of the lake has its own charm for every tourist. Though the Boat House Club is exclusive, a number of boats can be hired at fixed rates at the Tallital or Mallital.

The water of the lake is very good and bluish-green in colour and well adopted for drinking purposes. In the lake itself there is a sulphur spring opposite to the Smuggler's rock in the depth of 18.5m and another outside it near the Tallital bazar, which has been found with curative property.

In the day time the limpid beauty of rippling water of the lake presents a panoramic view when Sun shines directly on the bluish green water. At times, it appears as if the golden sun rays are engaged in playing hide and seek. The reflection of hills in the water makes it more beautiful in the day. As the evening proceeds and Sun sinks behind the mountains, the lake turns into an enchanting fairly land. The quivering dance of full Moon in water, the stars and the multicoloured light all around the lake combine to create a fantasy on the lake. Boating in the lake is very pleasant during night. The lake with all its charm and beauty compete favourably with the Windermere of England and the Lucerence of Switzerland.

(b) Flora

In every hill resort flora always play a significant role in drawing tourists from hustle and bustle of congested urban areas. Nainital too is covered with almost every type of foot hill flora. During spring time the entire valley presents a panorama of natural beauty against the backdrop of gorgeous hills. The greenary of the town definitely leaves a soothing effect on the tourists' mind. The trees of Chir and Deodar around the lake and sweet chirp of forest birds beckon the tourists her charming beauty.

(c) Climate

Nainital, unmatched in climatic comforts, is a super hill resort in Uttar Pradesh. When the plains burn with the scorching heat of the blazing sun in the month of April, May and June, Nainital makes it own climate with moderate temperature (maximum 26.7°C and minimum 10.6°C) and adequate amount of relative humidity, approaching ideal conditions for human comfort. The sparkling bracing quality of weather makes it a tourism

The Magnificent Lake of Nainital

merchandise. Three months of summer constitute the peak period when more than 60 thousand tourists arrive Nainital.

(v) Adjoining Tourist Attractions/Spots

Apart from these major recreational resources there are some minor recreational spots around and nearby the Nainital town. One can enjoy them during their visit to Nainital. They are so near to the town that the visit to all these places is almost included in the visit to Nainital itself. It hardly needs any extra-plan and tourage can be performed only through the local means of transport or sometimes on foot. Normally they require 2 to 4 hours time. And all these spots have hardly any facility except that of tea stalls. They are as follows :

(a) *Naina Peak* (*Cheena Peak*) : It is one of the surrounding peaks, some 5.64 km from the lake. The height of the peak is 2611 m. On a clear day, a view of the wide range of the snow-clad Himalays can be had from this peak.

(b) *Laria Kanta* : It is also one of the surrounding peaks, 5.61 km away from the lake. From this peak one can see the glorious view of surrounding suburban lake region.

(c) *Snow View* : It is situated on Sher-ka-Danda at an altitude of 2270m just 2.4 km away from the main town and most easily accessible.

(d) *Lands End* : It is 4.08 km away from the main town at an elevation of 2118 m. Tourists can enjoy the magnificent view of Khurpatal and the terraced fields from here.

(e) *Hanuman Garhi* : It is an ecstatic spot famous for its glorious sun-set and the Hanuman temple which has turned it into a pilgrim centre as well.

(f) *State Observatory* : Just near the Hanuman temple at Hanuman Garhi, U. P. Government Astronomical Observatory and Satellite Tracking Centre is situated. A large number of enthusiastic tourists go there during their visit to Hanuman Garhi.

(g) *Khurpa Tal* : It is one of the most beautiful lakes in Nainital district lying some 10 km from Nainital town. This lake is loaded with various types of fishes easy to catch. It provides a paradise to anglers.

(h) *Naina Devi Temple* : This temple is situated at the eastern corner of the lake and dedicated to the Godness Naina Devi, a name given to Parvati. Beside the Goddess Naina, the temple is also dedicated to the Goddess Nanda, the favourable Goddess of the last rulers of the Chand dynasty of Kumaun. It is said that Nanda was the sister-in-law of a Chand princess who was killed by a wild buffalo on her way to her-in-laws. Since then she was worshipped as a Goddess.

All these additional but charming tourism resources have made Nainital an ideal hill station for all types of tourists—the serious and peace loving, the curious, the religious the pleasure seeking, the sight seeing, the sport loving, the comfort wishing and the lust wandering.

(vi) Morphology of the Town

Nainital blessed with perennial charming natural beauty and health giving climate is the most popular hill resort in U. P. Himalaya. Though it has been developed as a recreational centre particularly for holiday makers, some other factors also motivate people towards Nainital. Nainital has always been known for its public schools founded by Furopean missionaries. But beginning from its origin up to modern development it has reputation as a recreational centre par excellance and continuous tourist flow has changed not only the economy of the town but its impact can be seen on the functional morphology of the town too.

Although the functional classification of this sort of town is somewhat difficult, Nainital has highly developed a tourist service Zone. The segregation of functional Zone of this town also does not follow any definite pattern but it is clear that all the functions are concentrated around the lake. In fact the morphology of the town is very much affected with the presence of the lake.

Tourism in Kumaun Region

At the southern end of the lake a chain of luxury and star hotels, cottages, boarding houses, restaurants, tourist bungalows are situated in the midst of pine and oak trees, from east to west, which provide good shelter and accommodations to the tourists. The north end of the lake is called Mallital and the south end Tallital; both ends have well laid-out shopping centres with beautiful luxury shops and stores. Both these ends are connected by the beautiful Mall, the another important tourist core.

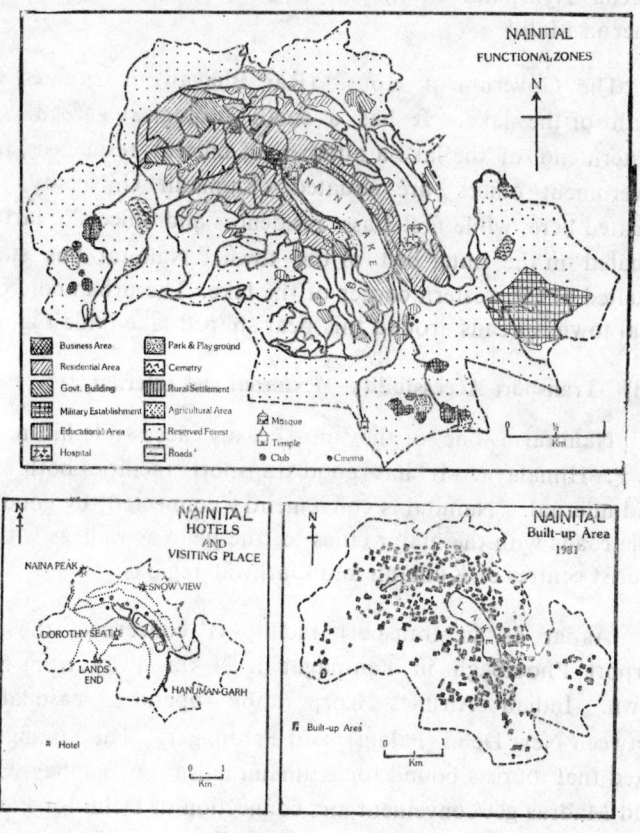

Fig. 4.1

For sports loving tourists, the grounds conventionally known as 'flats' situated at north-eastern end of the lake afford ample space for various games and sports. Many tournaments of hockey, football, cricket, kho-kho are held here. A semi-circular amphitheatre skirts the ground for the convenience of the spectators. The famous Nainital Yacht Club is situated at the Tallital end of the lake.

There are four sets of roads, running at different levels on each side of the lake previously known as the Mall and the Cheena Ayarpalta Mall, the Upper Ayarpatla Mall and the 'Cheena Mall.'

The Government House (Raj Bhavan) is situated to the south of the lake. It has a small Zoological garden. At the western end of the lake a number of official residences, hostels, government offices are situated. Kumaun University is also situated here, while first-class residences and officers' quarters are situated in the outer belt of the town. Nainital bus station is situated at the western corner of the lake. The urban core of Nainital town spreads around this pear shaped lake (vide Fig. 4.1).

(vii) Transport Accessibility—External and Internal

Nainital is one of the most easily accessible hill resorts in U. P. Himalaya. It has good transport facilities both external and internal. Nainital is conveniently connected by goodmotorable roads with the major cities of the plain as well as with other tourist centres of Kumaun and Garhwal regions.

As far as air transport facility is concerned, the nearest airport Phoolbagh in Pantnagar is 71 km away from Nainital town. Indian Airlines Corporation operates seasonal flights between New Delhi (Palam) and Pantnagar. The timings are so fixed that tourists bound for Kumaun hills from Bambay, Calcutta and Madras get convenient air connection in Delhi for Pantnagar to enable them to reach Nainital the same afternoon. From Pantnagar an air coach carries the passengers to Nainital in two hours. The drive from Pantnagar to Nainital through green forests, fields and orchards of Tarai is very pleasant and sportive.

Tourism in Kumaun Region

Kathgodam at the foot hills is the nearest railway terminus of the North Eastern Railway which is only 35.4 km from Nainital town. It is directly connected with Agra, Lucknow and Bareilly by regular train services. Tourists from other centres have to change from the broad gauge to meter gauge line at one of the above stations. The U.P.S.R.T.C. (Government Roadways) also provide direct bus services to Nainital from Delhi, Dehra Dun, Hardwar, Meerut, Moradabad and Lucknow.

TABLE 4.1

Distance and Bus-Service Frequency from Nainital to Some Important Places

Sl. No.	Place	Distance (km)	Frequency (per day)
1.	Bhowali	11	14
2.	Jeolicot	17	20
3.	Bhimtal	22	8
4.	Ramgarh	26	3
5.	Haldwani	40	20
6.	Ranikhet	59	3
7.	Almora	66	3
8.	Bareilly	141	2
9.	Pithoragarh	188	2
10.	Delhi	340	6
11.	Lucknow	399	—
12.	Hardwar	417	1
13.	Dehra Dun	458	1

Major Routes and Conducted Tours

(a) Delhi to Nainital :

Delhi to Bareilly by broad gauge, from Bareilly to Kathgodam by meter gauge on train and from Kathgodam to Nainital by road on bus or taxi. Or Delhi to Moradabad by broad gauge on train and Moradabad to Nainital by road.

(b) Bombay to Nainital :

Bombay to Mathura (broad gauge) and Mathura to Kathgodam (meter gauge) by train. From Kathgodam to Nainital by road.

(c) Calcutta to Nainital :

Calcutta to Lucknow (broad gauge) and Lucknow to Kathgodam (meter gauge) by train. From Kathgodam to Nainital by bus or taxi.

(d) Madras to Nainital :

Madras to Mathura and Mathura to Kathgodam by train through broad gauge and meter gauge respectively. From Kathgodam to Nainital by road.

Enough transport facilities are also available from Nainital to Almora, Bhimtal, Kathgodam, Pithoragarh, Ranikhet, Lucknow, Ramnagar, Bareilly, Dehra Dun, Hardwar, Rampur etc. The U. P. S. R. T. C. and K. M. O. U. Ltd. buses provide regular services to the entire Kumaun and Garhwal regions. Apart from these transport facilities, regular conducted to tours are organised by some 20 travel agencies. Six of them are run by Government or agencies recognized by it and the rest are private. According to a survey of ten travel agencies including Kumuan Mandal Vikas Nigam, the seven package tours conducted by them are as below* :

Tour No. 1 Kausani (2 days)

Covers-Bhowali, Kainchi Temple, Almora Kausani (N/H), next day Kalika Temple, Golf Link, Ranikhet and Chaubatia Garden.

---

*Some minor variations may be seen in the package tour programmes conducted by different agencies.

Tour No. 2   Ranikhet (Full day)

Covers—Bhowali, Kainchi Temple, Ranikhet, Kalika, Golf Link, Chaubatia Garden and Bhimtal.

Tour No. 3   Sat Tal (Full day)

Covers—Bhowali, Ramgarh, Ghorakhal, Bhimtal, Naukuchiatal, Sat Tal and Hanuman Temple (Hanuman Garhi).

Tour No. 4   Bhimtal (Half day)

Covers—Bhowali, Ghorakhal, Bhimtal and Naukuchiatal.

Tour No. 5   Corbett National Park (2 days)

Covers—Corbett Museum at Kaladhungi, Ramnagar, Dhikala (N/H) and back via Kathgodam.

Tour No. 6   Binsar (2 days)

Covers—Bhowali, Kainchi Temple, Almora, Binsar and next day back via Ranikhet.

Tour No. 7   Badrinath (5 days)

Covers—Kainchi Temple, Ranikhet, Dwrahat, Adi Badri, Karanaprayag, Gwaldam, Baijnath, Kausani and back to Nainital via Almora.

As far as local conveyances for sight seeing in surrounding tourist spots are concerned boats, ricksaws, dandies, ponies, city buses, rope way and private taxies are available almost every time. To some spots tourists can go even on foot if they like.

(viii) Accommodation

Nainital has reasonably good accommodation facilities. The galaxy of hotels along the lake, boarding houses, bungalows, cottages, lodges, dharamshalas in the midst of pine and oak trees provide good shelter and accommodation to the tourists.

In Nainital there is only one 3-star hotel 'Sherwani' while ten hotels are with western comforts (Belvedere, Grand, Metropole,

Royal, Swiss etc.) and more than 35 hotels are of Indian style. Apart from these, there are more than 35 lodging houses and 4 Government Estate accommodations of different institutions such as-Nainital Club premises with 78 rooms Secretariate premises with two blocks, Brooke Hill premises with 56 rooms and Oak Park premises with 46 rooms. Four holiday campuses, managed by Kumaun Mandal Vikash Nigam, Nainital, four inspection houses (Hydel, U. P. Jal Nigam, P. W. D., Telegraph and Telephone deptt.) and six dharamshalas are also there for tourists.

Rate charges of these hotels are not fixed and different hotels have different rate charges. Hotels of European style charge Rs. 60 to Rs. 100 for single bed room and Rs. 120 to Rs. 220 for double bed room while for the entire suite they charge Rs. 200 to Rs. 250 per day. Hotels of Indian style have comparatively low rate charges. In an Indian style hotel for a single bed room it ranges from Rs. 15 to Rs. 55, for double bed room Rs. 30 to Rs. 120 and for a suite Rs. 100 to Rs. 160 per day. Rate charge of government accommodation ranges from Rs. 8 to Rs. 20 per day and for a person not on duty it ranges between Rs. 10 to Rs. 100. Rate charges of holiday homes range between Rs. 25 to Rs. 40 for single bed room and Rs. 50 to Rs. 90 for double bed room. Dharamshalas and lodging houses are rather cheap. But except western type hotels and some of the Indian style hotels most of the accommodations do not provide modern furnitures and good cuisine facilities.

Nainital faces an accommodation crisis during the peak season in May and June when more than 5000 tourists arrive here every day. During the peak season it needs more less expensive and moderately priced hotels and hostels.

(ix) Other Recreational Amenities

Apart from sight-seeing, several other recreational amenities are also present for tourists in Nainital. For the amusement seekers there are three cinema houses (Ashoka, Capital, Vishal) where English and Hindi films are regularly shown. The club interested people can join the Boat House Club, Nainital Club, Nainital Mountaineering Club, Gymkhana Club, Rotary Club, Lions Club etc., where they can spend their time easily. Television and Videos are also available in the town for entertainment of the tourists. But here the T. V. transmission is not very clear and continuous.

Tourists can gather general informations from U. P. government tourism offices (Tourist Bureau and Asstt. Director Tourism) at Nainital and may seek help from guides.

(x) **Tourism Characteristics : Trends and Analyses**

Every hill resort has two seasons in general. Similarly Nainital has two popular tourist cycles : (a) The Summer cycle (May-June), (b) The Autumn cycle (Sept-Oct).

In the months of May and June when mercury shoots up in the plains, Nainital gets too busy in dressing her 'tourism shop'. The hotel, cafe and restaurant owners, the porters, the taxi-drivers, the coolies all look forward for a good business. The second half of May and the first half of June constitute the peak period when more than 60 thousand tourists arrive to get relief from scorching heat of the plains. Sports lovers from all over India come here for polo, hockey, football, golf, fishing and above all yachting. For 100 years till 1947, the U. P. Secretariat used to move up to the Summer Capital, Nainital for six months. After 1947, the Government carried on the practice but only for two summer months, later in 1963 that was discontinued and now only the Governor comes and stays in May/June with frequent trips to Lucknow.

The second tourist cycle is associated with autumn festival. In this season mostly those tourists gather here who normally do not like to visit Nainital during the summer season due to high-cost holiday. Young fun-seekers who do not like the noise pollution of the serene Himalayas during summer, come back to the hills when the rains have given them a fresher, greener and brighter look. Enthusiastic tourists enjoy the month long autumn festival, a revival of the British tradition of fun and gaiety.

The problem of measuring tourism is difficult and rather a complex task as it involves various types of relationships in reference to socio-economic and space-time aspects. To understand general characteristics of tourists in Nainital a detailed field-survey was conducted meticulously. Several informations with specific purposes were acquired through questionnaires, filled up by the tourists. Some 112 tourists were interviewed separately in their leisure time and recreational mood for clear expressions, during the survey period.

TABLE 4.2

Tourist Arrivals in Nainital

Sl. No.	Years	Tourist Arrivals (Nos.)	Variation (Nos.)
1.	1978	444094	
2.	1979	487711	+ 43617
3.	1980	479770	− 7941
4.	1981	512703	+ 32933
5.	1982	485303	− 27400
6.	1983	500720	+ 15417
7.	1984	575211	+ 74491
8.	1985	525000	− 50211

Source : Data collected from the toll barrier of Nagar Palika of Nainital.

According to the analysis of all informations, some salient characteristics of tourists' behaviour come to the fore. They may be summarised as follows (vide Fig. 4.2) :

(a) Profession of Tourists

As regards to profession-wise distribution of tourists in Nainital, about 50% of the tourists were Government employees, followed by those engaged in education including students, their share was 21.4%. Some 17.8% tourists were businessmen and the rest 10.7% tourists had engaged in other professions such as-lawyers, farmers, doctors (private practice), self-employed persons etc.

TABLE 4.3

Profession-wise Distribution of Tourists

Sl. No.	Profession	Actual Number of Tourists	Percentage
1.	Service	56	50
2.	Education	24	21.4
3.	Business	20	17.8
4.	Others	12	10.7

(b) Purpose of Visit and Duration of Stay

In other tourist centres, it is not very easy to classify the purpose of visit into different groups, because most of the tourists have more than one reason. But in the case of Nainital, as it is a resort with majestic natural beauty and bracing climate, pleasure and holiday making are the most important reasons for visit. The percentage of tourists coming to Nainital for religious or academic purposes were very low.

Being asked about the duration of their stay in the town, majority of tourists replied that they would like to stay just two to four days in this pleasure-trip to enjoy the natural beauty of Lake and the town. They would also like to see the nearby scenic spots during their stay in Nainital.

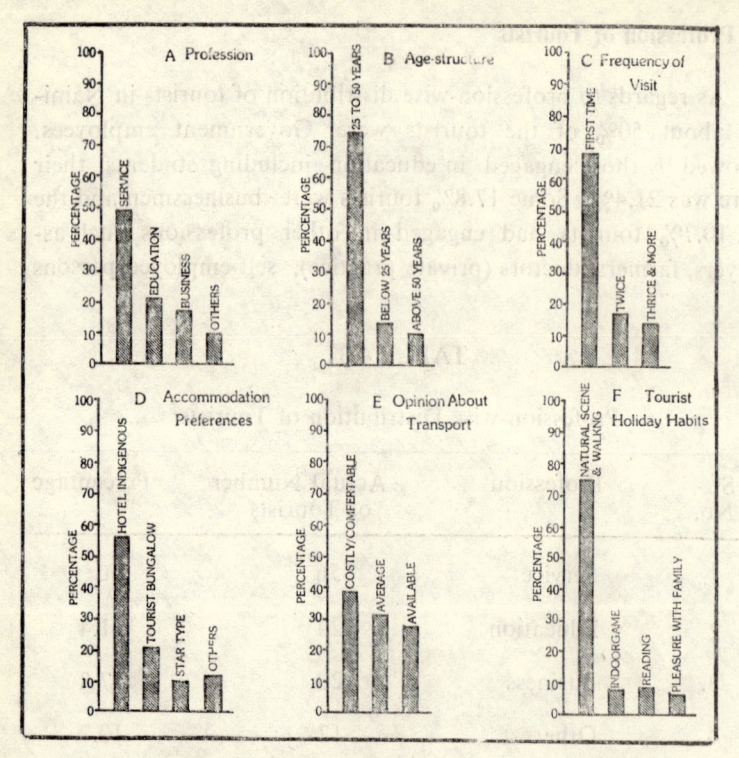

Fig. 4.2 Tourist Trends in Nainital

(c) Age-Structure of Tourists

As Nainital is a recreational resort, most of the tourists come here for recreation and holiday-making, thus majority of them are young or middle-aged. In the survey it has been found that

TABLE 4.4
Age-Structure of Tourists

Sl. No.	Age-Group	Actual Number of Tourists	Percentage
1.	25 to 50 yrs	84	75.0
2.	Above 50 yrs	12	10.7
3.	Below 25 yrs	16	14.3

75% tourists were in the age-group of 25 to 50 years. Tourists below 25 years accompanied their elders mainly to help them. Their percentage was 14.3%. Some 10.7% tourists were above 50 years. They had come with their family to regain health or to change air, certainly not seeking for recreation.

(d) Preference for Accommodation Types

In the entire survey it was noticed that majority of tourists preferred indigenous types of accommodations. Their percentage was near about 57%. Some 21.4% tourists liked to stay in tourist bungalows. If bungalows were not available, they preferred indigenous hotels. About 10.7% tourists from upper class liked star type hotels with western comforts and facilities and other 10.7% tourists liked to take shelter in rather cheap accommodations, such as-dharamshalas, lodging houses. Mostly the Government employees liked to stay in dak-bungalows, whether they were on official visit or on un-official tour.

TABLE 4.5

Preference for Accommodation Types

Sl. No.	Type of Accommodation	Actual Number of Tourists	Percentage
1.	Hotel-Indigenous Type	64	57.2
2.	Tourist Bungalow	24	21.4
3.	Hotel-Star Type	12	10.7
4.	Others	12	10.7

(e) Previous Experiences

During the survey when it was asked if they had visited this town ever before. About 68% tourists replied in negative, while 14% tourists answered that it was their second visit to the town. About 17.8% tourists replied that they had visited this town more than three or four times. Being asked 'why they are visiting this town again and again' majority of tourists replied that divine beauty of this town and lake itself invite them repeatedly.

TABLE 4.6

Frequency of Visit

Sl. No.	Frequency	Actual Number of Tourists	Percentage
1.	For the First Time	76	68.9
2.	Twice	16	14.3
3.	Thrice and more	20	17.8

(f) Tourists' Holiday Habits

Nainital is unique in its natural beauty, thus sight-seeing and enjoying the majestic view of surrounding areas and boating on the bluish-green water of lake are the most important means of recreation for holiday makers. Some 75% tourists enjoy these means of recreation during their visit to Nainital. Tourists mostly youths and sports lovers (8.9%) have shown their interest in games like table tennis, chess and yachting. Some tourists (8.9%) replied that they liked just reading books in their room. During the personal conversation with the tourists, 7.1% of them confessed that they enjoyed the company of their family members most.

TABLE 4.7

Holiday Habits of Tourists

Sl. No.	Holiday Habit	Actual Number of Tourists	Percentage
1.	Sight-seeing and walking	84	75
2.	In-door games	10	8.9
3.	Reading	10	8.9
4.	Pleasure with family	8	7.2

(g) Shopping Pattern

When tourists have been asked about their shopping—"what they would like to purchase in Nainital ?" near about 80% tourists have shown their interest in woolen cloths and candles of different shape, while 15% tourists were not interested in shopping at all, they come just for recreation. Some tourists (5%) have expressed their intention in buying photographs of scenic beauty of Nainital, particularly of lake and its surrounding areas.

(h) Tourists Opinion and Comments

About external and internal transport facility, mostly tourists have opinion that it is costly as compared to the other hill resorsts. About 39% tourists had opinion that the external transport in Nainital was more expensive than the internal. They find it rather un-comfortable particularly the old people. Above 32% tourists find it just about mean, while 28% tourists have expressed their satisfacation over external and internal transport facility. But majority of tourists have the opinion that transport should be improved in the entire Kumaun region.

TABLE 4.8
Tourist Opinion about Transport Facilities

Sl. No.	Items	Actual Number of Tourists	Percentage
1.	Costly and comfortable	44	39.3
2.	Average	36	32.1
3.	Available	32	28.6

About accommodation facility majority of the tourists said that it was just average, but they also stated the problem of accommodation in the peak season specially in the earlier half of June. In general, most of the tourists have found it satisfactory but somewhat little expensive.

Regarding 'food,' tourists have varied opinion. Tourists from high income group find it satisfactory both in quality as well as in cost. But tourists from low income group find it easily available in a number of hotels and restaurants but expensive. This contradiction in the opinion is probably due to the variation in purchasing capacity. When asked about the general problems during their visit and stay in Nainital, mostly people expressed their dis-satisfaction over collecting taxes at toll barrier by Nagar Palika in the way. They suggested that it either should be abolished altogether or be included in the fair itself. Though majority of tourists have found the local people very co-operative and good in their behaviour, they complained about the agents and businessmen specially who come from the plains because of their bargaining and cheating. Tourists have been cheated by the hotel agents, taxi-drivers and coolies quite often. About 90% tourists have expressed their satisfaction over the behaviour of the guides and information given by the Tourist Bureau.

In general, majority of tourists said that their visit to Nainital was very pleasing and they were returning home with plenty of everlasting happy memories in their mind. In fine, it can be said that with all its modern facilities, hospitality and cosmopolitan outlook, Nainital has the ideal atmosphere of a twentieth century holiday resort and tourists get worth of their money here.

ALMORA

Almora is the most important and beautiful hill-resort of Kumaun Himalaya after Nainital. Surrounded by a circle of hills it combines a rapturous view of the snow-covered peaks of Himalaya. Almora has basically been developed as a recreational centre, but it is less commercialised as compared to Nainital.

(i) Historical Background

Almora, once the capital of Kumaun was founded by Raja Baldeo Kalyan Chand of the Chand dynasty in 1563 A. D., when he shifted his capital from Champawat (in Pithoragarh distt., 135 km from Almora). It is said that once Raja Kalayan Chand had come for hunting in Almora. As the king was chasing a hare, it suddenly turned into a tiger at first and finally it disappeared. The king was very surprised at this. He came back to the counsellor and said about his encounter. Tne counsellor convinced him that it was a good 'omen' (sign) and he should shift his capital here immediately. Raja Kalyan Chand did so subsequently. Since then it was the permanent capital of Chand dynasty until they lost the battle against Gorkhrs. In 1773 they engaged in a war with Rohillas. The Rohillas were defeated and driven out by the Britishers but in the next battle with much stronger opponents- the Gorkhas from Nepal, they were defeated. From 1790 to 1815 Almora was under their rule. The deposed Chand King finally sought the help of the British, who after the Nepalese-Siguali war of 1816 forced the Gorakhas out and in return they got a large part of Garhwal including Almora.

(ii) Location and Extent

The location of Almora is on the north-western part of the Kumaun hills in lesser Himalaya at an elevation of 1560 m to 1646 m from the mean sea level. The town of Almora is situated on a 5 km long horse saddle-shaped ridge, which is mentioned in *Skand Purana* as "a sacred mountain situated between the two rivers Kaushika (Koshi) and Shalmali (Suyal)."

The total area of the town is 8.03 sq. km with the population of 22705 (1981). It is 90 km away from the nearest rail head Kathgodam while the nearest air-port Phoolbagh in Pantnagar (Nainital distt.) is 127 km from Almora. Nainital is only 67 km from here. Nainital-bound tourists can easily visit Almora by bus or taxi.

(iii) Physical-Natural Scenario

With all its natural beauty and grandeur, Almora provides a perfect spot for sober and mature tourists, particularly for naturalists, scholars, artists, poets and trekkers. Poets like Tagore and Pant found the region inspiring for verse-writing. Mahatma Gandhi also wrote his Geeta commentary here at Kausani.

(a) Space Scenary and Landscape

The town of Almora with its unique natural scenary and specific location on a ridge, provides a vital tourism potential. That is the reason it has been called as 'unspoilt child of Kumaun'. The beautiful town is surrounded by the temples of Banari Devi, Kasar Devi, Shyahi Devi and Katarmal, perched on hill tops which have give it more religious outlook than leisure/pleasure resort. The gigantic glaciers and glittering peaks have great attraction for young trekkers from all over the country.

(b) Floral Panorama

The entire town of Almora is covered with thick unravaged forests with beautiful trees. The outskirts have magestic greenary. The slopes of surrounding hills are gorgeously wooded by deodar, and cypress trees. Entire valley is decorated with violet and red flowers and fruits during spring season. Thus in Almora flora have been proved a vital resource of tourism.

Apart from these resources, bracing climate of Almora attracts numerous tourists specially those who come to regain their health after long sickness. The soothing and pleasant climate, tranquility of the atmosphere give them not only physical comport but also mental peace.

(iv) Adjoining Tourist Spots

Surrounding beauty spots have made this town much more significant. Some of them are as follows :

(a) *Simtola* : It is only 3.6 km away from the main town of Almora. It presents an ideal picnic spot to young fun-seekers with its glorious scenic beauty. Once it was a great tea estate.

(b) *Kalimath* : A perfect spot for sight-seeing, only 4.6 km from Almora. With its divine beauty it presents a vision of a picture-postcard with Almora on one side and the snow-clad glittering peaks of Panchchuli on the other side.

(c) *Chital Temple* : It is one of the many temples in Almora in the background of towering peak covered with lovely woods. This tample is dedicated to Lord Golla, only 6 km from Almora.

(d) *Kasar Devi* : An enchanting spot with unmatched beauty evokes foreigners as well as home tourists to settle down here permanently to get relief from the humdrum of present urban life. It is a beautiful old temple of beauteous Goddess Kasar Devi. The temple is situated in an area called Upreti Khola—8 km from the main town of Almora.

(e) *Mohan Joshi Park* : It is another beautiful spot just within hiking distance from Almora. The main attraction is a small park with a V-shaped artificial lake—a fine picnic spot for holiday makers.

(f) *Brighton End Corner* : This spot has been named after a popular sea-side resort of England—'Brighton Beach,' where one can see the glorious view of setting sun. Just 2 km from Almora, it also offers a magnificent opportunity to see both the sun-rise and sun-set in the background of spectacular snow-clad peaks of Himalaya.

(v) **Morphology**

Structurally the town is divided into three distinct zones — (i) Inner Zone, (ii) Middle Zone, and (iii) Outer Zone.

The inner zone of the town is totally built-up area, dominated by walls, gates, forts, temples and buildings of European style. Although Almora is not densely populated and congested town in general, yet this zone is rather congested compared to other parts of the town.

The middle zone of the town comprises rest of the town area, relatively less congested. In this zone mainly government

ALMORA

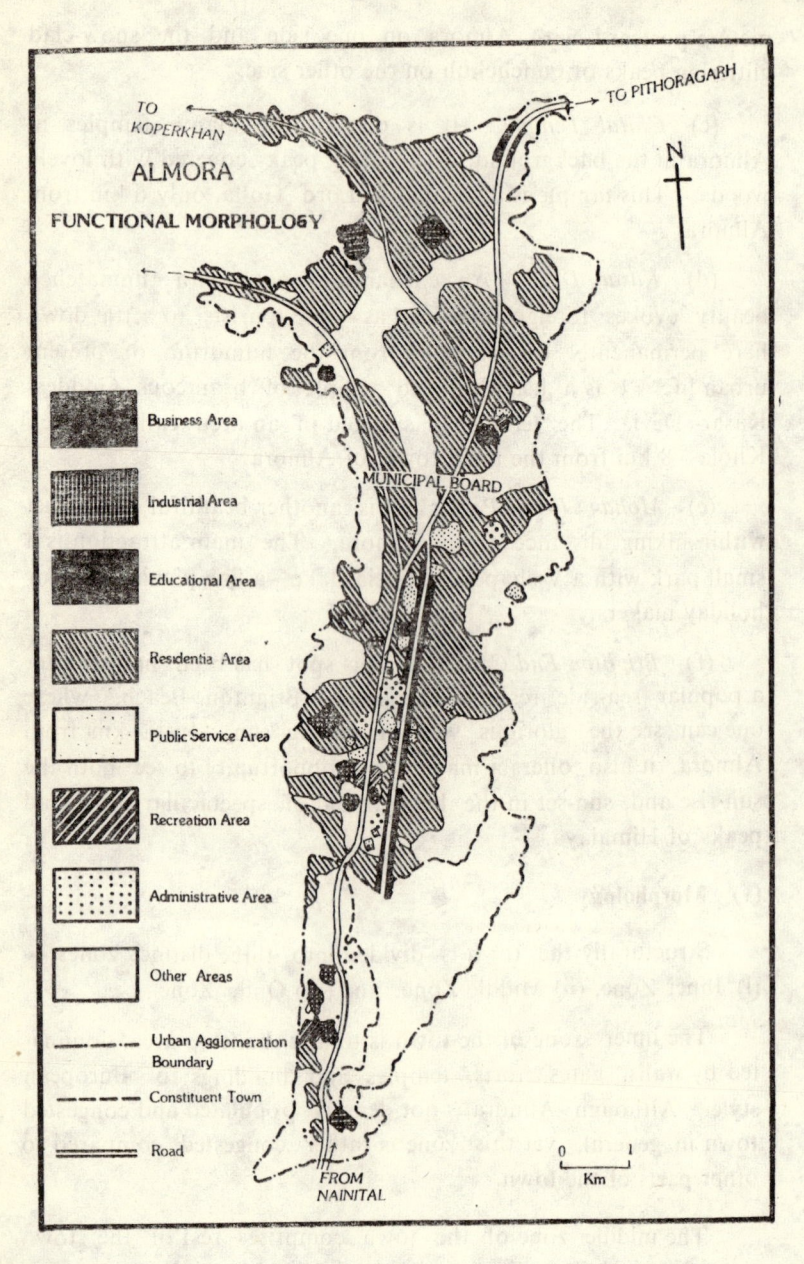

FUNCTIONAL MORPHOLOGY

TO KOPERKHAN
TO PITHORAGARH
MUNICIPAL BOARD
FROM NAINITAL

- Business Area
- Industrial Area
- Educational Area
- Residential Area
- Public Service Area
- Recreation Area
- Administrative Area
- Other Areas
- Urban Agglomeration Boundary
- Constituent Town
- Road

Fig 4.3

offices, institutions, hotels, restaurants are situated. In this zone Cart Road has many tourists' amenities such as dak bungalows, clubs, post and telegraph office, cottages and cantonment area. Both these zones are situated on the crest or on the northern slope of the ridge.

The outer zone of the town is residential area of upper classes and government officials. It is situated below the main ridge to the north-south, specially in Pande Khola, Baldhoti, Dugalkhola, Hiradungi etc.

A road runs almost north and south between western end of the bazar and parade ground. To the south of the main town there is depression occupied by the leper asylum. Beyond that there is a beautiful Granite Hill developed as a recreation spot.

(vi) Transport Accessibility

Almora has very good transport facility both internal as well as external. The town is connected with very good motorable roads with other centres of the region (Nainital, Ranikhet, Kathgodam, Kausani, Bageshwar, Pithoragarh etc.). The nearest

TABLE 4.9

Distance and Bus-Service Frequency from Almora to Some Important Places

Sl. No.	Place	Distance (km)	Frequency (per day)
1.	Kausani	52	6
2.	Nainital	67	3
3.	Kathgodam via Khairana	90	4
4.	Bageshwar	90	3
5.	Kathgodam via Ranikhet	133	2
6.	Bareilly	196	1
7.	Delhi	378	1
8.	Pithoragarh	118	1

air-port is Phoolbagh (127 km) and the nearest rail head is Kathgodam (90 km). U.P.S.R.T.C. and K.M.O.U. Ltd. buses, private taxies, delux buses are always available for Almora. The State High Way No. 37 passes through this town.

For internal transport private taxies and mini-buses are easily available in Almora. Tourists have not to face any problem to visit surrounding scenic spots. Conducted tours are not arranged by travel agencies separately for Almora like Nainital, mostly Nainital bound tourists come here.

(vii) Accommodation

Almora did not face any accommodation problem either in general or in peak season because 70% tourists come here from Nainital and they like to stay in Nainital rather in Almora. In fact they come from Nainital and after a brief stop over in Almora they move to other places like Kausani, Pindari Glacier etc. in the routine of their conducted tours. But for those tourists who specially come to Almora for recreation, there is a Holiday Home managed by India Tourism Development Corporation with 18 rooms (18 double bed, 6 four bed and 2 delux), two first class hotels with 23 rooms (15 double bed, 4 single bed and 4 suites) and nine ordinary hotels with 93 rooms (24 single bed, 69 double bed). Few guest houses of departments of Hydel, U. P. Jal Nigam, P.W.D. and Zila Parishad are also there. The total bed capacity of this town comes to about 300.

The rate charge of double bed room is Rs 25, four bed room is Rs 40 and of delux room is Rs 50 per day in holiday home, while it is Rs. 30 for single bed room, Rs. 30 to Rs. 40 for double bed room and Rs. 75 for a suite per day in a first class hotel of Indian style. The rate charge of ordinary hotels are quite low. However these rates tend to change in peak seasons.

In Almora most of the hotels fail to provide modern furnitures, and good food facility and cleanliness. Only holiday home and two first class hotels are able to give modern facilities.

(viii) Other Recreational Amenities

The town of Almora does not provide a wide range of other recreational amenities apart from sight-seeing like Nainital. There is only one cinema hall, one ordinary club and a museum. Although television and video facilities are present but T. V. transmission is not very clear. There is a Regional Tourist Office which provides guides and other informations for tourists.

(ix) Tourism Characteristics : Trends and Analyses

Like other hill resorts of U. P. Himalaya, Almora also has two popular tourist seasons-Summer season (Mid-April to June) and Autumn season (September-October), when tourists in large number come here for recreation. Even those enthusiasts going on different expeditions to Milan/Pindari glaciers, normally pass through Almora.

TABLE 4.10

Tourist Arrivals in Almora

Years	No. of Tourists	Variation in Percentage
1978	294646	—
1879	329975	—1.40
1980	325339	—1.40
1981	335788	+3.21
1982	341019	+1.56
1983	399631	+17.19
1984	301440	—24.57
1985	371251	+23.16

On an average some 947 tourists visit Almora per day. The highest number of tourists come in the months of May and June. Nature-loving tourists mostly come in the months of September and October during autumn. Among the tourists, Bengalis predominate especially in Durga Puja vacation. Locally the autumn is often termed to be the season of Bengali tourists.

In the above two seasons a number of tourists of different age-group and from different social set-up come to Almora not only for outdoor recreation but also for religious purposes and for seeking health. The general characteristics of tourists behaviour such as their profession, income, purpose of visit problem, age etc. have been analysed (vide Fig. 4.4) through the data obtained by sample survey and questionnaires filled by the tourists as well as by personal interview with the tourists in their jovial mood :

(a) **Profession or Tourists**

As far as professions of tourists are concerned, majority of them were found to be government employees, followed by the businessmen and students. The purpose of visit of these students and businessmen was certainly recreation and less educational or commercial. Rest of the tourists were politicians, farmers, and persons having different other professions.

TABLE 4.11

Profession-wise Distribution of Tourists

Sl. No.	Profession	Actual No. of Tourists	Percentage
1.	Service	50	62.5
2.	Business	10	12.5
3.	Education	10	12.5
4.	Others	10	12.5

(b) **Purpose of Visit**

The purpose of visit of tourists need not much explanation. It is clear that large number of tourists come here for recreation and fun as in other hill resorts. But in comparison to Nainital tourists come to Almora even for religious purposes due to surrounding temples. As there is no important educational institution in Almora, very few tourists come here for their academics. However some tourists come here just to meet their friends or relatives.

TABLE 4.12

Purpose-wise Distribution of Tourists

Sl. No.	Purpose	Actual No.	Percentage
1.	Recreational	48	60
2.	Religious	08	10
3.	Academic	04	05
4.	Others	20	25

(c) **Age-Structure of Tourists**

In total survey the middle aged persons between 25 to 50 years were in dominant position. As much as 87.5% tourists belong to this age-group. Tourists below 25 years of age come mostly with their parents. Only 7.5% of the tourists above 50 years of age come here for the changed climate and for seeking health.

TABLE 4.13

Distribution of Tourists by Age

Sl. No.	Age-Group	Actual No. of Tourists	Percentage
1.	Below 25 yrs	04	5
2.	25—50 yrs	70	87.5
3.	Above 50 yrs	06	7.5

(d) **Accommodation Preference**

The survey reveals that 50% tourists in Almora prefer to indigenous type of hotels. Though 37.5% tourists like to take

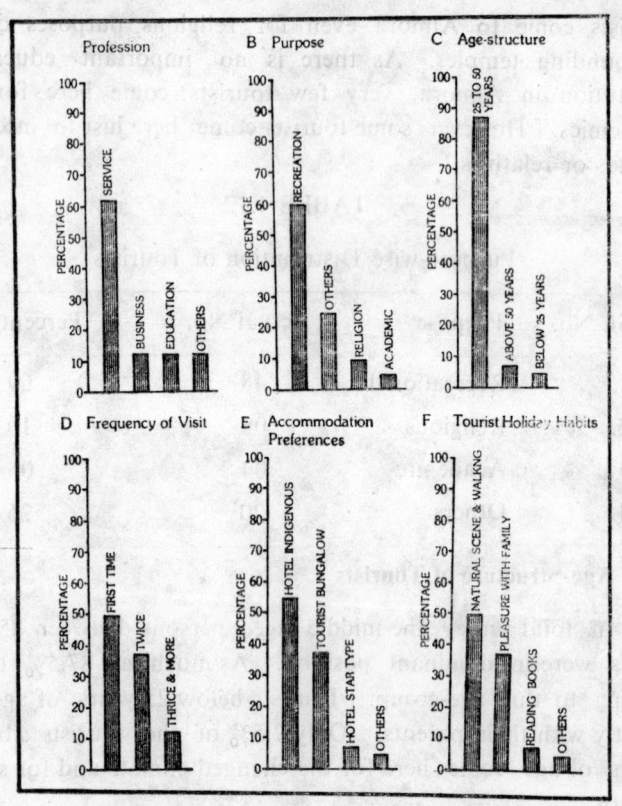

Fig. 4.4 Tourist Trends in Almora

shelter in tourist bungalows, yet they have to stay in hotels because tourists bungalows are not easily available always. Some 5%

TABLE 4.14

Accommodation Types and Tourists' Preferences

Sl. No.	Type of Accommodation	Actual No of Tourists	Percentage
1.	Hotel Star Type	04	5
2.	Hotel Indigenous Type	44	55
3.	Tourist Bungalow	30	37.5
4.	Others	02	2.5

tourists of rich upper class like to stay in hotels with western comfort, but as there is no such hotel of star type, they prefer to first class hotels of Indian style. Very few tourists like to stay in local dharamshalas, while the state government officials stay in dak-bungalows.

(e) Previous Experiences

Having been asked about their previous experiences of this town if they had any, some 50% tourists replied that it was their first ever visit to this town. Some 37.5% tourists were in their second trip while 12.5% tourists confessed that they had visited this at three or four occasions. But these tourists were mostly businessmen and officials. A number of tourists with literary taste (particularly writers, poets, artists, painters) have expressed their willingness to visit this town again and again as they were deeply moved by the beauty and calm in the environ of Almora.

TABLE 4.15

Frequency of Tourists' Visit

Sl. No.	Frequency of Visiting	Actual No. of Tourists	Percentage
1.	First time	40	50
2.	Twice	30	37.5
3.	Thrice or more	10	12.5

(f) Tourists' Holiday Habits

The question put to tourists 'how they keep themselves engaged' in off-time, revealed some interesting facts. Some 50% tourists expressed their liking to enjoy the majestic view of mountains and pleasant weather. About 37.5% tourists enjoyed just company of their family members in the midst of natural beauty and 7.5% tourists of old age have shown their interest in just reading books and magazines. Only 5% tourists liked to spend their time by seeing cinema or playing in-door games etc.

TABLE 4.16

Tourist Holiday Habits

Sl. No.	Habits	Actual No. of Tourists	Percentage
1.	Sight seeing	40	50
2.	Pleasure with family	30	37.5
3.	Reading books etc.	06	7.5
4.	Others	04	0.5

(g) Shopping Pattern

During the survey when tourists were interrogated about their shopping, majority of them denied of having any intention of shopping in Almora. They confessed that in case they had to buy something they would like to do their shopping in Nainital. In fact most of them have done their shopping in Nainital earlier. Only 10% tourists have shown their interest in woolen cloths and articles made of copper at Almora.

(h) Tourists' Opinion and Comments

Lastly the tourists were asked to make their own observations on various aspects of tourism in Almora. Majority of the tourists have the opinion that the behaviour of local hill people is very friendly and co-operative. However they were harrased by the people from outside Almora, particularly from the plains of U.P. They did a lot of bargaining in their dealing and sometimes they cheated the innocent tourists. Some tourists also felt that these people were destroying the art, culture and atmosphere of this town.

Most of the tourists were not satisfied with the transport facility of this town both external and internal. They feel that the transport is somewhat inconvenient and the fare is very high. They were not very happy with the condition of the roads. Some 70% tourists complained about the non-availability of internal transport and suggested that transport system must be improved in the entire Kumaun region.

About accommodation facility, majority of the tourists have the opinion that the standard is just about average. However they found it rather cheaper as compared to other hill stations. Majority of the tourists complained about the non-availability of quality food stuffs. The varieties too were quite limited and there was hardly much scope for choice. Tourists were observed normally to be happy with their visit to Almora. They enjoyed their every moment in the midst of mountains, hoping to return with pleasant memories of this town. Some of them even expressed their desire to come to Almora again during personal conversation.

RANIKHET

(i) Location and Extent

Ranikhet is another significant tourist centre in Kumaun Himalaya. It is the headquarter of Ranikhet tahsil forming part of the Almora district.

The town (29°40′N Lat.—79°33′E long) lies at an elevation of 1829 m above sea level, covering an area of 21.75 sq. km. The town in situated on the north facing ridge of Kumaun Himalaya acting as water parting between the river Ramganga in the north and north-west and the Kosi in the south and south-east.

(ii) History and Morphology of Town

Ranikhet was discovered and developed by the Eastern Command of British Army. In 1869—1872, Lord Mayo-the then Viceroy of India had described Ranikhet as a hill station of heavenly beauty and had regarded it as one of the best hill stations of the world. He was so impressed with its scenic beauty that he proposed to shift his army headquarter from Simla to Ranikhet.

The development of urban settlements in Ranikhet started in very low key in the initial stages. The population was only 3246 in 1901 and any noticeable increase was not observed in the next four decades as the population was only 4894 in 1941. But in later years especially after Independence it has increased remarkably. In 1981 the total population of Ranikhet was 18,190. The population increase which was only 1648 in the first four decades, shot up to 13,296 in the next four decades. At present Ranikhet is the third largest urban centre in the entire Kumaun Division.

It has been noticed in the morphology of Ranikhet that it has two heavy built-up areas on two parallel ridges. The north face of the ridge is the area of clustered settlements close to the main road, while the scattered dwellings and isolated bungalows are confined mostly to the peripheral area. Cantonment area is also away from the main built-up area. In the last two decades many tourist amenities like hotels, motels, restaurants, shopping centres, picnic-spots etc. have developed to provide the better treatments to the tourists. Due to fast growing population and continuous increase in tourist traffic, many commercial and educational institutions, transport facilities alongwith many urban amenities have also been developed. On the basis of its morphological structure this town can be divided into two distinct zones : (i) North Zone, and (ii) South Zone.

The northern zone of this town is in form of residential area of high class and middle class while the southern zone is mostly the tourist service area with many luxury hotels (West View, Norton), Rotary Club and general post office etc.

(iii) Physical-Natural Scenario

Ranikhet has acquired the status of a hill tourist resort due to its picturesque surroundings, the majestic view of snow-clad peaks of mighty Himalayas. It was acclaimed as 'heavanly hill station' by Lord Mayo, the then Viceroy of India. On his visit to Ranikhet, the Prime Minister Jawahar Lal Nehru observed, "I wish more of our people living in plains below would visit the Himalayas...They can have their feel of flowers there and noble trees in primeval forests. They can breathe the free untained air which invigorates and they can return strengthened in body, mind and spirits."

Ranikhet invites all excursionists as well as those who find their greatest pleasure in the company of Mother Nature with all its mystery. Mainly recreation is the key factor in the development of tourism at Ranikhet.

(a) Space Scenary and Landscape

The town of Ranikhet being situated on the two parallel ridges provides the rare opportunity of enjoying devine beauty of sun-rise and sun-set. Tourists do not have to climb the high mountains to see the glimpses of rising sun in the morning as well as setting sun in the evening due to its specific location. Tourists can also enjoy the snow-view and snow field from any spot of this town. When the golden rays of the Sun touch the snow-clad peaks early in the morning, it appears as a master piece of a painter's brush who has painted all the peaks in indigo blue to rose pink colours. But gradually as the Sun starts shining in full bloom and its glittering rays cover the whole range, colour changes into dazzling silver white. With all its surrounding beauty it appears as some thing spectacular.

(b) Flora and Fauna

Flora and fauna are the precious heritage of mountains and always are the important resources of tourism in every hill station. Without these floral beauty and faunal wealth, these mountains would be bare rocks or are only barren hills. It is true in the case of Ranikhet also. The beauty of pine trees standing all around the town with sweet chirp of forest birds and wild cries of animals always create a sensation among tourists.

(iv) Adjoining Tourist Spots

Apart from these natural resources many recreational spots have developed around the town for extra enjoyment of the tourists. Some of them are given below :

(a) *Chaubatia* : As the name implies, four paths are the four fruit gardens with a fruit research centre. Varieties of apples are available here in these fruit gardens for sale in the season. This place is 10 km from the main town.

(b) *Bhaludam* : It is only 3.2 km from the main town. Its main attraction is a small artificial lake which supplies drinking water to the whole town. The lake also provides an opportunity of fishing to the fun-loving tourists.

(c) *Upat and Kalika* : Upat, 6 km from Ranikhet bus station has 9 golf links. This place is a boon to the enthusiastic visitors. Only one km away from Upat is Kalika, the famous temple dedicated to the Goddess Kali. Near the temple, Forest Nursery is another worth mentioning place to see. From here tourists can enjoy both the glorious snow-view on one side and the golf links at Upat on the other side, at the same time.

(d) *Co-operative Drug Factory* : The factory—3 km away from Ranikhet bus-station on the road towards Ramnagar is engaged in various researches and production of Ayurvedic drugs, which are derived mostly from the herbs, being collected from the surrounding mountains.

(e) *Tarikhet* : This place is 8 km from Ranikhet on the motorable road which goes towards Ramnagar. Mahatma Gandhi was associated with Tarikhet for quite a long time during the days of freedom struggle. Gandhi Kuti and Prem Vidyalaya are the main attractions of this place. Gradually it has been developing as a beautiful recreational spot. A planned township is also coming up.

Besides these places of attraction, some other places mostly of religious nature are also there in Ranikhet and tourists can see them if they spare time, such as Hanuman Temple and Jhula Devi Temple on the way to Chaubatia, Shiva Temple, Catholic Church on way to Upper Mall, English Methodist Church, St. Mirton's Church etc.

(v) Transport and Accommodation

Ranikhet is one hill resort in the entire U. P. Himalaya which provides excellent transport facilities, both external and internal, to the tourists. It is connected with good motorable roads with almost every important place. In fact Ranikhet is the only place in the entire U. P. Himalaya where tourists can reach every place by four wheeler. The transport system in Ranikhet was well planned by the Britishers as it was their army headquarter. U.P.S.R.T.C. and K.M.O.U. Ltd. buses are on regular services from and to between Ranikhet and other important tourist centres. During peak season State Government provides extra buses for tourists' ease and comfort. Buses are

TABLE 4.17

Distance and Bus-Frequency from Ranikhet

Sl. No.	Places	Distance (km)	Frequency (per day)
1.	Gopeshwar via Karnprayag	145	2
2.	Kausani	62	8
3.	Nainital	59	6
5.	Almora	50	5
6.	Pithoragarh	169	1
6.	Kathgodam	84	4
7.	Bareilly	190	1
8.	Delhi	361	1
9.	Ramnagar	95	2

easily available from the nearest Railway station, Kathgodam. There are regular and direct bus services between Ranikhet and Delhi, Moradabad, Bareilly, Nainital, Almora and Kausani etc.

As far as internal transport is concerned private taxies, city buses and ponies are easily available for visiting surrounding spots and temples.

Ranikhet does not have to face accommodation problem like the other popular hill resorts in Kumaun Himalaya. Most of the tourists make their visit to Ranikhet in their conducted tour. They start from Nainital and after visiting the entire Kumaun Himalaya return back to Nainital. Their stay is fixed by the travel agents themselves. But for the tourists who do stay at Ranikhet, all the accommodation facilities are easily available. There are three star-type hotels with all the facilities and comfort of western type. Two of them (West View Hotel and Norton Hotel) are two star and the other one (Hotel Moon) is one star hotel. Apart from these about 22 ordinary hotels and three dharamshalas are also there. For government employees respective departments have their own rest houses. Forest Department, P. W. D., Zila Parishad and Jal Nigam have such facilities.

The rate charge of star type hotels ranges between Rs 60 to Rs 80 for single bed, Rs 80 to Rs 120 for double bed and Rs 120 to Rs 150 for a suite, while the charge of an ordinary Indian style hotel is comparatively low. It ranges between Rs 15 to Rs 25 for single bed room and Rs 25 to Rs 50 for double bed room. Govt. rest houses cost only Rs 10 per day but they are only for their employees. Tourists have daily meal facilities both in star type hotels as well as in ordinary hotels, but except in the star type hotels the quality of food is not very good. They do not have even sufficient varieties. Most of the hotels lack in modern furnitures, cleanliness and other facilities. There are about 15 road-side restaurants which provide tourists some breakfast and morning-evening tea.

(vi) Other Recreational Amenities

Tourists have many other recreational amenities apart from site seeing in their free time in Ranikhet. There are two cinema halls and two clubs—Ranikhet Club and Rotary Club. These clubs are well equipped and offer temporary membership even to the tourists. Tourists can enjoy their time in playing tennis, golf and other indoor games. They can also enjoy T. V. and video shows at selected places.

In order to provide general informations to the tourists there is a tourist office of State Government. They can seek all necessary informations about Ranikhet and surrounding centres from here. There are five Banks also for tourists' transactions.

(vii) Tourism Characteristics : Trends and Analysis

Ranikhet being predominantly a tourist spot does not have any popular season in the true sense. Normally the peak and off seasons do not have much significance for Ranikhet as the tourists use to come here throughout the year. But in general tourists like to make their visit to Ranikhet specially during (i) March to June in summer season and (ii) September to October in autumn season.

During summer tourists come from every corner of the country to get some relief from scorching heat of the plains. Some foreign tourists also come here during summer while in autumn bulk of the tourists are Bengalis from West Bengal as well as from other parts of the country. Those tourists also come during autumn who could not afford the high accommodation charge of summer.

The table 4.18 reveals that there are some minor changes in tourist arrivals almost every year though that change is not of much significance. But it is true that tourism has been developed in Ranikhet only after independence, more so in later decades. Tourist arrival, which was limited upto 90 thousands during 1940-50, is now over three lakhs. The ternds of the tourists' behaviour at Ranikhet are discussed below (vide Fig. 4.5) :

TABLE 4.18
Tourist Arrivals in Ranikhet

Sl. No.	Years	Tourist Arrivals	Variation In No.	Variation In Percent
1.	1978	255750	—	—
2.	1979	280662	+24912	+9.7
3.	1980	286427	+ 5765	+2.1
4.	1981	284943	— 2164	—0.8
5.	1982	315756	+30813	+10.8
6.	1983	319587	+ 3831	+1.2
7.	1984	323500	+ 3913	+1.3
8.	1985	335000	+13500	+4.2

(a) Profession of Tourists

As far as the profession-wise distribution of tourists is concerned, the servicemen constituted the major portion of it, their share being 42.8 percent. The next category was of educational group, mostly teachers and students. Their percentage was 28.5. Nearly 14.3 percent tourists were engaged in different types of business, while the rest 14.3 percent tourist were of other professions such as farmers and self-employed persons.

TABLE 4.19
Profession-wise Distribution of Tourists

Sl. No.	Profession	Actual Number of Tourists	Percentage
1.	Service	24	42.8
2.	Education	16	28.6
3.	Business	08	14.3
4.	Others	08	14.3

(b) Purpose of Visit

Regarding the purpose of the visit to Ranikhet by the tourists it has been easily observed that recreation and pleasure were the key factors. Students come here both for recreation as well as for seeking knowledge. Fairly low percentage of tourists come here for religious purposes. A handful of tourists were on their business trip. At the end of the survey it was felt that recreation was the main factor behind all most all the visits to Ranikhet by tourists.

(c) Age-Structure of Tourists

During survey it was observed that majority of tourists visiting Ranikhet belonged to middle age-group, that is, 25 years to 50 years (57.1%). Tourists below 25 years of age often come to help or to give company to their parents and guardians. Tourists above 50 years were mostly businessmen or those who came to regain their falling health.

TABLE 4.20

Age-Group of Tourists

Sl. No.	Age-Group	Actual Number of Tourists	Percentage
1.	25 to 50 years	32	57.1
2.	Above 50	16	28.6
3.	Below 25	8	14.3

(d) Accommodation Preference

From the analysis of the data it becomes clear that the highest percentage (68.7%) of tourists prefer indigenous type of hotel for their stay at Ranikhet. At the same time they expressed their liking for government tourist houses. About 10.7% tourists were found looking after 'dharamshalas' and other cheap accom-

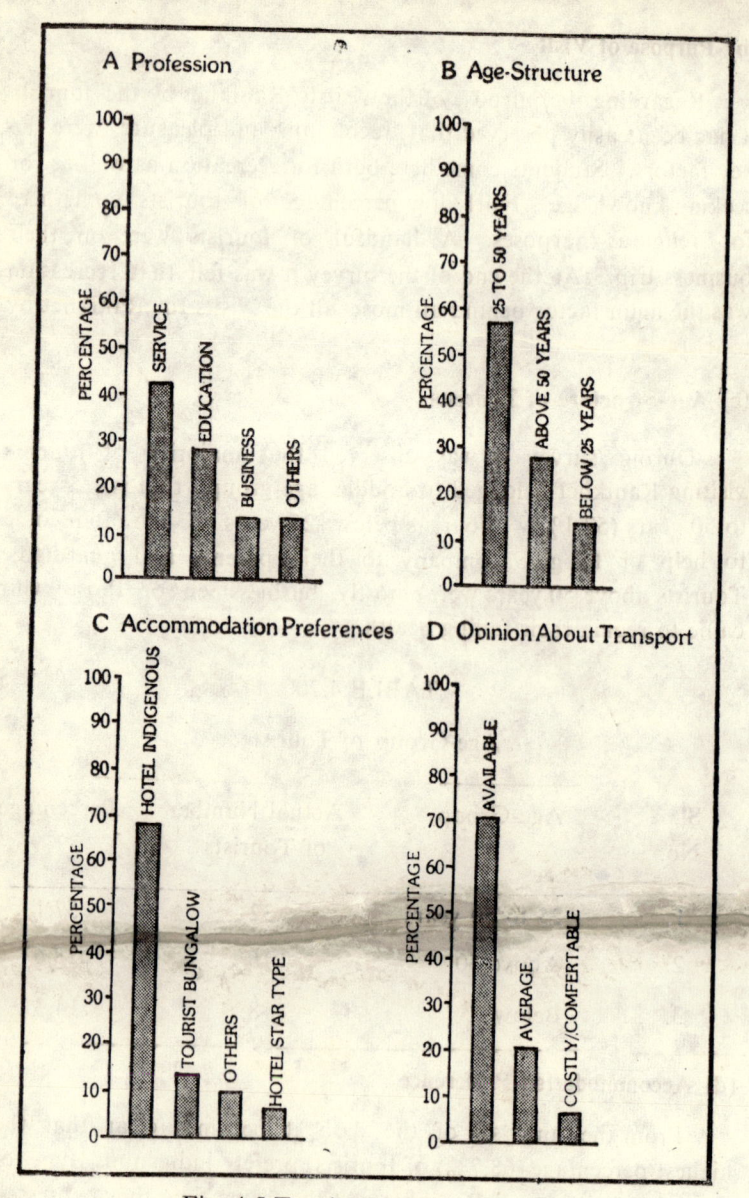

Fig. 4.5 Tourist Trends in Ranikhet

modations. Only 7.2% tourists of higher income group have shown their interest in star type hotels.

TABLE 4.21

Preference for Accommodation Types

Sl. No.	Type of Accommodation	Actual Number of Tourists	Percentage
1.	Hotel Indigenous Type	38	68.7
2.	Tourist Bungalows	08	14.3
3.	Hotel Star Type	04	7.2
4.	Others	06	10.7

(e) **Tourists Opinion and Comments**

Majority of tourists have shown their satisfaction over the transport facilities provided here. They considered it as standard though the rate charge was a bit high. They were generally satisfied with the internal transport also. Though none of the tourists made out complaint about it, yet 80% tourists had the opinion that it could have been made more effective with little effort.

TABLE 4.22

Tourist Opinion about Transport

Sl. No.	Items	Actual Number of Tourists	Percentage
1.	Available	40	71.4
2.	Average	12	21.4
3.	Costly and comfortable	04	7.2

majority of tourists have found the accommodation facilities in Ranikhet of average standard. It does not create any problem though it is somewhat expensive in comparison to the other hill resorts in Kumaun Himalaya except Nainital. But the tourists who had visited the town twice or more have the idea that accommodation is not quite sufficient during the peak season.

As regards the availability of food, tourists of high income group did not have to face any problem. But the tourists of middle income group did not find it quite satisfactory. They realized that transport or food was easily available but it was quite expensive. Tourists of low-income group have shown their interest in preparing their food by themselves.

Overall the tourists were quite appreciative of Ranikhet. They did not have to face any major problem during their stay here. They were satisfied with all the services provided to them They found even the behaviour of the staff of Tourist Bureau very compromising and informal.

CORBETT NATIONAL PARK

"A place of known delight and proven desires".

(—Lord Linlithgow, Viceroy of India (1936-48).

(i) Location and Extent

Corbett National Park (Fig. 4.6), a land of astounding floral and faunal beauty, is situated in the foot hills of U. P. Himalaya. Two third of its area is in Garhwal region and the rest in Kumaun region. The major portion of the park is in Kalagarh (Bijnor) and Ramnagar forest division (Nainital). The park is spread over 520.8 sq.km and lies between 29° 13' 30" to 29° 35' 15" north latitude and 78° 33' to 78° 36' east longitude.

The forest covers a number of more or less parallel ridges from north to south, descending in height towards the plain. The altitude varies from 400 m to 1200 m with undulating topography. The heighest point in the park is 'Kanda', a Forest Rest House

—1210 m from the sea level. The river Ramganga which passes through the park is its main source of water.

(ii) History and Development

This park was established in 1935 as 'Hailey National Park' named after Sir Malcolm Hailey, the then Governor of United Provinces. In the year 1948 it was renamed as 'Ram Ganga National Park', because of the river Ram Ganga flowing across the park. Finally in 1957 it was renamed after the celebrated writer of the famous book "Man Eaters of Kumaun" and the world famous wild life pioneer Edward Jim Corbett as Jim Corbett National Park. On first April 1973, the park alongwith seven other reserves was included under Project Tiger. Among 190 sanctuaries and 20 legally constituted National Parks of India, it has the distinction of being the first and certainly the best wild life centre of India.

(iii) Corbett National Park Resource Conservation and Tourism

The park has earned the name "Land of Roar, Trumpet and Song" due to its rich wild life. Corbett National Park is pretty rich in faunal variety, housing almost all the major groups of animals known to exist in Lower Himalayan region. Upto now, fifty endemic species of mammals, five hundred seventy seven of birds, twenty six of reptiles, seven of amphibians, besides many anthropods and other lower animal groups have been identified from the park area.* The park is famous for its tiger, elephant and birds. Among 1200 species of birds found all over India, more than 750 species are found in this park alone, such as barbet, babbler, bulbul, flycatcher, kaleege, Indian roller, thrush, peafowl, shama, magpie, kingfisher, drongo, jungle fowl, pea fowl, minivet, oriole, falcon, duck, goose, gull etc. The melodious whistle of birds and their colour add the grandeur of the park.

---

* The enumeration of park fauna was undertaken by Northern Station of Zoological Survey of India, DehraDun in 1973.

Among wild animals apart from Indian elephant and tiger one can see the glimpses of panther, spotted deer, cheetal, sambhar, hog-deer, barking deer, wild bear etc. Wild cries of these animals thrill the visitors.

River Ram Ganga passes through the heart of the Park. Crystal clear water of the river is full of fishes like mighty Mahseer, Indian trout and goonch. Angling/fishing is a popular sport on the beautiful Ramganga. Gajral, Sarapduli and Dhikala are favourite resorts of the anglers. The insect fauna, including

TABLE 4.23

Important Wildlife in Corbett National Park

1	2	3	4
Mammals	Reptiles	Birds	Fish
1. Tiger	1. Marsh crocodile (Magar)	1. Barbet	1. Mahaseer
2. Indian elephant	2. Long anouted crocodile (Gharial)	2. Babbler	2. Indian Trough
3. Panther	3. Python (Ajgar)	3. Bee-eater	3. Goonch
4. Sloth bear (Bhaloo)	4. Hamadryad or King cobra	4. Bulbul	
5. Wild bear (Jangali suar)		5. Bunting	
6. Hyena (Lakarbagha)		6. Crow-pheasant	
7. Lare Indian antelope (Nilgai)		7. Dore	

1	2	3	4
8. Four horned antelope (Chausinga)		8. Drongo	
9. Swamp deer (Sambhar)		9. Flycatcher	
10. Spotted deer (Chital)		10. Flower Pecker	
11. Hog deer		11. Tit	
12. Barking deer		12. Hornbill	
13. Garal nemorhaldus		13. Kaleeji Pheasant	
14. Common monkey		14. Kite	
15. Rhesus monkey		15. Lark	
16. Porcupine (Sahi)		16. Minivet	
17. Otter (Udbilao)		17. Munia	
18. Indian ratel (Bijju)		18. Myena	
19. Mangoose (Neola)		19. Nightjar	
		20. Nittawa	
		21. Oriole	
		22. Pealfowl	
		23. Wood Pecker	
		24. Baya	
		25. Chloropsis	
		26. Warbler	
		27. Shama	

Source : Corbett National Park, Department of Tourism, Government of India, October, 1982.

beautiful butterflies, bugs, beetles, bees, moth etc. found in the park are indeed varied and colourful.

The Patli dun, a broad flat valley is the most picturesque area of the park covered with almost every type of foot hill flora. The floral beauty of the park has made it quite distinct and significant. The park about with its a hundred and ten varieties of trees, fifty one varieties of shrubs, thirty three varieties of bamboos and grasses and twenty seven varieties of climbers is indeed very rich in flora. The vegetation is rather a mixed type, comprising deciduous tropical and sub-tropical species.* During spring season it presents a panorama of natural beauty against the background of gorgeous hills. The sprouting 'Sheesham,' scarlet flowers of 'semal', mauve flowers of 'Kachnar', reflecting in the sparkling water of Ram Ganga, coupled with perfumes of blooming flowers, form the main attraction of the park. Sai, Haldu, Amtlas, Ber, Nim, Dhak, Bahera are some of the trees found in the park vicinity. The only indigenous conifer to be found is chir.

TABLE 4.24
Visiting Time of the Park

Months	Animals to be seen (generally)	Weather
November	Tiger and Crocodile	Cool
December	Tiger and Crocodile	Cool
January	Tiger and Crocodile	Cold
February	Carnivora, Deer, Crocodile	Pleasantly cool, night cold
March	All forms of Wild life	very pleasant
April	—do—	—do—
May	—do—	days hot

* Botanical Survey of India, Northern Circle, DehraDun surveyed the flora of Corbett National Park from Nov., 1970 to May, 1971.

Typical Panoramic View at Corbett National Park

Toursim in Kumaun Region 175

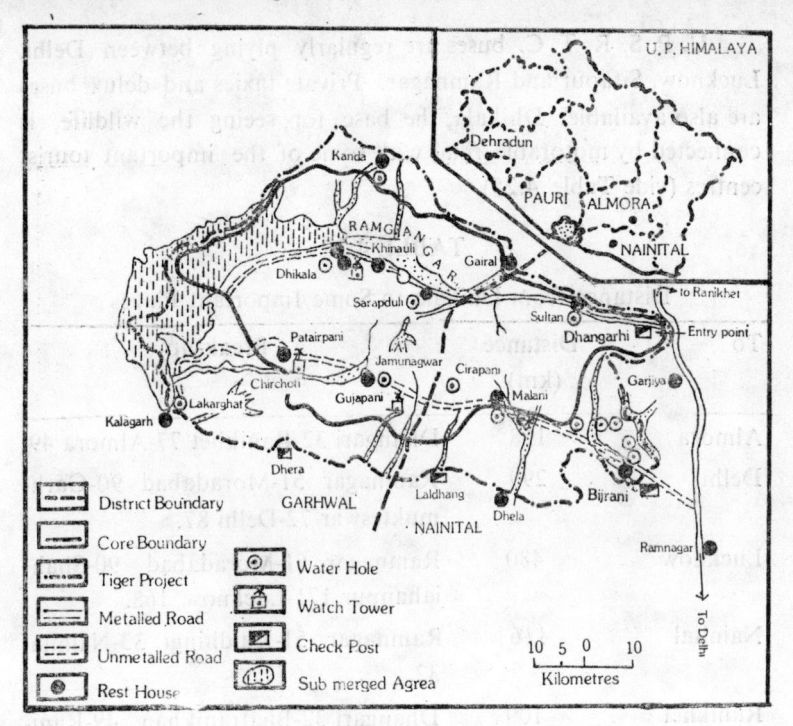

Fig. 4.6 Corbett National Park.

The park can be visited any time between the middle of November and May but the best period is from February to May. It remains closed from the mid June to middle of November.

(iv) Transport and Accommodation

Corbett National Park provides moderately good transport both inside and outside the park, good boarding and lodging facilities and well informed guides. Ramnagar is the nearest rail terminus of North Eastern Railway and obligatory point to reach Corbett National Park.

Tourists from Delhi side have to break their journey at Moradabad and have to catch the meter gauge Moradabad-Ramnagar train. The tourists from Lucknow side have to break their journey and change the train at Lalkuan.

U. P. S. R. T. C. buses are regularly plying between Delhi, Lucknow, Sitapur and Ramnagar. Private taxies and delux buses are also available. Dhikala, the base for seeing the wildlife, is connected by motorable road with some of the important tourist centres (vide Table 4.25).

TABLE 4.25

Distance from Dhikala to Some Important Places

To	Distance (km)	Break-up
Almora	158	Dhangari 32-Ranikhet 77-Almora 49.
Delhi	299	Ramnagar 51-Moradabad 90-Garhmukteswar 72-Delhi 87.
Lucknow	480	Ramnagar 51-Moradabad 90-Shahjahanpur 171-Lucknow 168.
Nainital	116	Ramnagar 51-Kaldhingi 33-Nainital 32.
Ranikhet	109	Dhangari 32-Bhatranjkhan 49-Ranikhet 28.

Tourists holidying at Nainital, Ranikhet and Almora can conveniently reach the Park by buses. At Ramnagar, jeep, taxies, mini-buses are always available for Park. Vehicles may be charted on advance intimation from (1) Wild Life Warden, Corbett National Park, Ramnagar, (2) Kumaun Motor Owners Union, Ramnagar, district Nainital. Good motorable roads enable tourists to move about in the Park. Elephant-ride is also provided.

Dhikala is the main centre providing accommodation facilities to the visitors. Dhikala has 4 suite in the forest rest house, 6 suites in the annexe, 6 suites in the tourist hutment and 6 swiss cottage tents with modern sanitary arrangements, furnishings and fittings. Apart from these, rest houses at Sultan (2 suites), Bijrani (6 suites), Kandha (2 suites), Malani (2 suites), Jherna

(2 suites), Sarapduli, Boxar, Paterpani, Gaujpani and Jamunagwar are also available for short stay. Except Bijrani most of these rest houses have usual basic furnishings (with bed and bath). Catering facility is available only in Dhikala, while no bar facility is there in the park.

(v) Recreation : Uses and Abuses

Though the concept of nature conservation is the central idea in the plan formulations of all sorts of national parks all over the world, tourism punctuated with recreation and education automatically becomes intimately attached with it. Parks every where generate some sorts of tourism activities. But the recreation phenomena should be adjusted with these 'protected areas' in such a fashion that the maximum pleasure, fun and frolic may be obtained without harming the eco-balance of the nature in the park.

TABLE 4.26
Tourist Arrivals in Corbett National Park

Sl. No.	Years	Tourist Arrivals	Variation In No.	In Percent
1.	1974-75	7356		
2.	1975-76	9040	+ 1684	+ 22.9
3.	1976-77	10543	+ 1503	+ 14.3
4.	1977-78	11112	+ 569	+ 5.1
5.	1978-79	9834	− 1278	− 13.0
6.	1979-80	10432	+ 598	+ 6.08
7.	1980-81	11152	+ 720	+ 6.90
8.	1981-82	13445	+ 2293	+20.56
9.	1982-83	18092	+ 4647	+34.56
10.	1983-84	19621	+ 1529	+ 8.45
11.	1984-85	15015	− 4606	−23.47

Corbett National Park is being gradually exposed to human intervention, but as only special class of tourists visit such type of parks, their number is not very large. However, visitors are increasing with the increasing tempo of tourism movement in India. During 1974-75 some 7356 tourists visited the park of which 6527 were native visitors alone, while in 1978-79 this number rose to 9834 including 1085 foreign tourists. The maximum number of park visitors recorded so far (1984-85) were a little more than fourteen thousand, the foreigners' share being less than two thousand. This clearly indicates that the park has failed to generate considerable awakening among the overseas tourists. It is indeed an irony that international tourits who are definitely wild life lovers seem to be quite ignorant about the rich faunal wealth of India. The various records of the park are the best testimony to it. There is hardly any monitoring cell equipped with modern audio-visual aids and relevant litratures and photographs to help visitors in enjoying the park life without disturbing it all the time, and to educate them. Up-to-date and complete inventory of either flora or fauna is also wanting. In order to preserve the park eco-system the accommodation and roads in the park need somewhat restructuring. The roads going through the park often disturb its harmony and peace by frequent on-going vehicles. For the better use of the park for recreation etc, recreation resource capacity of the park should be fully analysed. Some pre-visit educative programmes (literature, film etc.) should be conducted for the tourists coming from different strata, status and age-group of the society.

The Ramganga Multi Purpose Hydel Project which has now come up on the western periphery of the park has somewhat affected the natural environment of the park. With seventy eight sq. km of the park area devoted to the reservoir, much of the precious habitat is now a submerged land causing some loss to the floral and faunal wealth of the park. Cheetal and hog deer are the worst affected mammals. As such all possible measures should be taken to safeguard against the adverse impacts of the project Park milieu in no way should be disturbed and marred

5

Tourism in Garhwal Region-Case Profiles and Studies

INTRODUCTION

Out of the two distinct sub-zones of U. P. Himalaya, the Garhwal region is somewhat newer and lower than Kumaun in the context of socio-economic development. However, the seedlings of religious tourism first germinated in Garhwal Himalaya. The very concept of Hindu religion and philosophy got inertia and impetus in this part of region. Its pilgrimage history is as old as the Hindu civilization itself. Garhwal Himalaya imbraces some of the most ancient and pious shrines of the Hindus, mostly devoted to the various forms of Lord Shiva. Together with the Mother river Ganga, Lord Shiva reigns supreme in the entire Garhwal region. "Out of 550 temples in Garhwal, 350 are dedicated to Lord Shiva and his female form (Atkinson, E. T., 1973 : Vol. II, p. 701). While Shiva is the Lord, protector and friend of the mountain, Ganga is mother and daughter of the mountain. While Shiva is the organ of generation, Ganga the liquid essence of life—the two are never far apart and occur together (Singh, T. V. (Ed.), 1982 : p. 224) and the region is endowed with and enriched in both of them.

From time immemorial tourism in the form of pilgrimage has been an important characteristic of this region. Every bit of land in Garhwal is pious and sacred having the latent potential of religious tourism. The Panch Prayagas, Panch Badries, Panch Kedars (vide Fig. 3.1) and a number of other holy places abound in the Garhwal Himalaya.

Garhwal Himalaya is equally rich in its natural scenario too. The region has beautiful natural environs and varigated scenic landscape. The world famed 'Valley of Flowers,' Hemkund and the origin place of Ganga and Yamuna have hardly their parallels in the world. It may be argued that it is the natural attraction, awe and the reverence for Almighty Nature that led to the development of pilgrim centres here. "In fact Hindu sages and Saynasis had identified sites of exceptional physical attractions through their keen landscape perception which are even today unrivalled in their beautiful setting (Singh, O. P., 1983 : p. 207)."

This way, the whole of Garhwal region is finely embroidered with attractive sites and spots both religious and scenic. In this context the region surpasses Kumaun where most of the attractions trend to lessen after Kausnni. In the northern part of Kumaun the Himalayan beauty is seldom localised.

Out of 31 towns in Garhwal region the three important pilgrim centres—Rishikesh, Badrinath, Kedarnath together with Hardwar (in Saharanpur district) and two resort towns—Dehra Dun and Mussoorie have been taken for some detailed studies. Besides towns, some natural areas like Gangotri, Valley of Flowers have also been incorporated because of their greater importance and relevance to the tourism of the region.

DEHRADUN

(i) Location, History and Development

Dehra Dun is one of the most beautiful and important tourist centres in U. P. Himalaya. At the same time it has been developed as an equally important educational and research centre too.

The town of Dehra Dun (31°19′N lat. and 78°2′E long.) is bounded by the majestic Himalayan ranges in the north and south while by the Ganges in the east and the Yamuna river in the west. Its maximum height above the mean sea level is 640 m, with an area covering about 79.91 sq. km. It is the only class I town in the entire U. P. Himalaya with the population of 293,010 (1981).

Dehra Dun seems to be an ancient town as it has been described in the Purana as a part of Kedarkhand region—the abode of Lord Shiva after whom the hills were christened as Shivalik. It is also said that at this place Rama and Laxman had performed their penance for the killing of the demon King of Lanka-Ravana. This is the place where Drona came in search of peace, it was then called Drona Ashram—the abode of Drona. Here came the five Pandavas to immolate themselves.

Besides its long traditions of Hindu faith and religion, this place had also some imprints of Sikhism. In the 17th century Guru Ram Rai—a religious Sikh leader—his bonafides and legitimacy being doubted by his own men came here and took refuge giving it the present name Dehra Dun (Dehra-Camp and Doon-Valley between the mountains). He ultimately settled here (Walton, H. G., 1929 : p. 222). He arrived on the fifth day after Holi—the event is still annually celebrated by hoisting the 'flag' (Jhanda) on the Guru Ram Rai Gurudwara on the same day.

Dehra Dun is a city symbolic of a pro British culture too. The final phase of its occupation by the Britishers ended with the treaty of Sagauli in 1816 with the Gurkhas in Nepal. From that starts the modern history of the city. Till 1835, the whole area was included in the Presidency of Bengal when it was separated and called North-West Frontier Province.

Due to its lovely natural setting and beauty, it fastly rose as a favourite residential and important educational and defence centre even much before independence. The Indian Military Academy housed here is rated as at par with England's Sandhurst and the United States' West point.

(ii) Morphology of Town

Dehra Dun is the most urbanized town in the entire U. P. Himalaya. Ranging between 9 to 10 kms the city is growing in the shape of a triangle. The base is in the south and east and the apex is in the north-west in the form of Palton bazar. Clock tower is the meeting point of old and new market. It is from here that roads divert in all directions. Both the markets, old and new, have many tourist amenities, such as-shops of high commercial value, restaurants, hotels and cinemas etc. The main business centre lies around the clock tower in the inner zone. The middle zone of the town has many hotels, dharamshalas, banks, other institutions and a part of the zone is residential area of upper class citizens. The outer zone of the town has a number of lime-stone factories, some other important institutions as well as the residences of lower and middle class people (vide Fig. 5.1).

(iii) Tourism Resource Base

Dehra Dun is one of the most advanced and developed hill stations not in U. P. Himalaya but also in entire India. It also appears as a gateway to Mussoorie and other Himalayan shrines. With all its natural surroundings between mountains, the town has been developed in such a way that at present it is not merely a hill station but it is known as a celebrated educational, cultural as well as industrial centre.

Tourism in Garhwal Region

It is a piedmont town, situated in the heart land of the valley between the Greater Himalayan range and Siwalick, bounded by the sacred rivers Ganga and Yamuna. In 1808, when Captain Raper first time visited this spot, it was simply an 'extensive village' (Capt. Raper, 1810 : p. 86). Now the entire complexion of the town has changed and at present it is the only first class town in the entire U. P. Himalaya. The town is very neat-clean

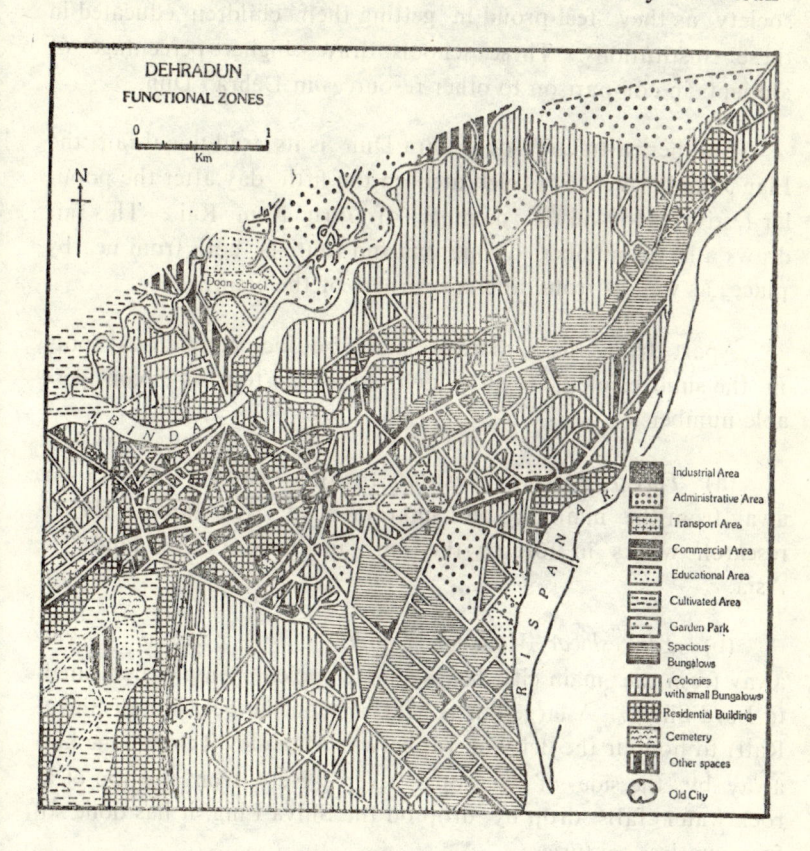

DEHRADUN FUNCTIONAL ZONES

Legend:
- Industrial Area
- Administrative Area
- Transport Area
- Commercial Area
- Educational Area
- Cultivated Area
- Garden Park
- Spacious Bungalows
- Colonies with small Bungalows
- Residential Buildings
- Cemetery
- Other spaces
- Old City

Fig 5.1

and tidy compared to the other hill resorts of Garhwal Himalaya. Its physical setting, pleasant weather, natural and cultural environment have tremendous attractions for excursionists, educationists, researchers and thousands of other tourists from all over India.

Dehra Dun has number of Government and Semi-Government offices such as-the Geological Survey of India, Oil and Natural Gas Commission, Indian Military Academy, Survey of India, Forest Research Institute etc. To-day this town has made its name as a prominent educational centre because of its various English medium institutions. These institutions (specially Doon School) have special attraction for the higher class people of society as they feel proud in getting their children educated in these institutions. These schools draw higher percentage of students in comparison to other resources in Dehra Dun.

Another attraction of Dehra Dun is its traditional fair 'the Flag Jhanda' which is celebrated on the fifth day after the popular festival Holi in the memory of Guru Ram Rai. This fair draws a large number of pilgrims and tourists both from nearby places as well as from different corners of the country.

Apart from these, there are many outdoor recreational spots in the suburbs of the town which attract the tourists in considerable number :

(a) *Forest Research Institute* : This institute is only 5 km away from the main city on Chakrata road. It is famous for its research works in forestry-the only institution of its kinds in Asia.

(b) *Tapkeshwar Mahadev Temple* : This place is 4.5 km away from the main city, having some ancient temples dedicated to Lord Shiva. A large fair is held here on the occasion of Shiva Ratri to honour the deity of Tapkeswar Mahadev Temple-one km away by the side of a seasonal river. Here, from the top of a rock water falls drop by drop on the Shiva Ling, it has done so far countless centuries.

(c) *Robber's Cave* (*Guchchu Pani*) : This place is an ideal picnic spot for tourists. It is one of nature's phenomena mysterious to understand. This is a stream, the water of which suddenly disappears from sight, a few metres away it re-appears again as a gushing stream. This place is about 8 km away from main town. Local buses, taxies and auto-rickshaws are available up to Anarwala village and from there one and a half km is to be covered on foot.

(d) *Tapovan* : This place is famous for an actient temple. It is believed that during the days of Mahabharata Drona Acharya and legendary Kuru prince did penance in the forest retreat. It is 6 km away from the main city. Regular bus services as well as private taxies are easily available upto 4 km on Raipur road. The rest 2 km is to be covered on foot.

(e) *Laxman Siddh* : This place dedicated to the saint Swami Laxman Siddh-a famous modern Indian Saint-is surrounded by dense forest. It is a very good picnic spot also. Though this place has not any shops or houses, still devotees and tourists come to pay homage in large number. This place is 12 km away from the main city on Rishikesh road. Private taxies and buses are available only upto 9 km. Rest of distance is to be covered on foot.

(f) *Sahastra Dhara Fall* : This waterfall is very popular among tourists visiting Dehra Dun because of its natural beauty and sulphur springs. The water here is very useful for curing polio and a number of other diseases. This beautiful place is about 14 km away from the main town and tourists can easily go there on bus or taxis, which is easily available at resonable 'rate. P.W.D. and tourist guest houses providing only lodging facility, are available here. Some fashionable cafeteria are also there specially around Sahastra Dhara.

Besides these, there are a number of other spots and places of tourist interest-some quite near and some little far. Indian Institute of Petrolium, Guru Ram Rai Gurudwara (Jhanda Mela), Chandi Devi temple and fair in Rajpur (11 km from Dehra Dun in route to Mussoorie), Malsi Deer Park, Dak Patthar are some of noteworthy places.

Chakrata-famous for the panoramic view of the Himalaya is somewhat far from Dehra Dun (92 km). The Tiger Fall here is the most picturesque and is among the highest in the state.

(iv) Transport Accessibility and Accommodation

Dehra Dun is one of the most easily accessible hill resorts in the entire U. P. Himalaya. It is connected by regular and direct bus services with almost all important centres of Northern India such as Delhi, Agra, Ambala, Chandigarh, Simla as well as with Nainital, Pauri, Uttarkashi, Mussoorie, Rishikesh and many other centres in Garhwal and Kumaun region. A number of buses of various types plying in between these places provide good and effective services to the public in general and to the tourists in particular.

Regular bus services are always available from Dehra Dun to Dak Patthar, Mussoorie, Chamba, Gopeshwar, Nainital and Uttarkashi etc.

TABLE 5.1

Distance and Bus-Frequency from Dehra Dun to Neighbouring Places

Sl. No.	Place	Distance (km)	Frequency (per day)
1.	Mussoorie	35	45
2.	Rishikesh	43	15
3.	Dak Patthar	45	5
4.	Paonta Sahib (Himachal Pradesh)	51	3
5.	Kalsi	52	5
6.	Hardwar	54	20
7.	Chakrata	94	4

Tourism in Garhwal Region

There are several travel agencies which arrange conducted tours of entire Garhwal region. Some prominent travel agencies are-Chugh Travels, Kumar Trading Company, Lopan Travels, Nijhawan Travel Service, Trans-World Tours etc. They are ticketing agents of Vayudoot also.

Dehra Dun is the last terminus of Northern Railway and has good rail connections with Delhi, Lucknow, Varanasi, Calcutta, Amritsar and Bombay etc. The nearest Airport (Jeoligrant) is 27 km away from the main town. For internal transport city buses, autorickshaws and Tongas are easily available. Garhwal Mandal Vikas Nigam arranges regular conducted tours for nearby tourist spots. Starting from Tourist Office it covers a number of places like Malsi Deer Park, Shahanshahi Ashram, Tapkeshwar Temple, Forest Research Institute and Sahastradhara etc.

In Dehra Dun, accommodation is not a problem to the tourists in any case, though rate charges are quite high during summer. It has sufficient number of hotels of every standard. There are 35 ordinary and star luxury hotels and 4 dharmshalas. Apart from these about 12 guest houses of different departments are also available for the officials.

The rate of western type luxury hotels ranges between Rs 35 to Rs 100 for single bed room, Rs 45 to Rs 200 for double bed room and Rs 80 to Rs 300 for four-bed room. The rates of Indian style hotels are comparatively lower. It ranges between Rs 15 to Rs 30 for single bed room, Rs 20 to Rs 50 for double bed rooms. Dharamshalas are quite cheap. Its charge ranges between Rs 2 to Rs 20 per day. The charge of Government guest houses ranges between Rs 4 to Rs 15 per suite. All the luxury hotels have provisions for running hot and cold water, channel music, telephone, money exchanging facility, dry cleaning, bar, doctors on call etc.

(v) **Tourist Trends and Analyses**

Dehra Dun has reputation as a good relaxation, outdoor recreational and educational centre. And of course it is the biggest tourist centre in U. P. Himalaya. The town receives, tourists, excursionists, educationists from every corner of the country throughout the year.

During summer this town attracts businessmen, traders, trainees of different kinds and a large number of tourists who use to come here only for recreation and fun, while the months of October and November are the popular seasons for students who often come here on their educational tour from various institutions.

TABLE 5.2

Tourist Arrival

Years	Tourist Arrival (No.)	Variation in %
1980	437280	—
1981	440000	+0.6
1982	578080	+8.7
1983	496455	+2.2
1984	507965	+2.3
1985	525000	+3.4

During survey at Dehra Dun only 75 tourists could be personally contacted, interviewed and interrogated. The inferences drawn from the analysis are as follows (Fig. 5.2) :

(a) **Profession and Purpose-wise Distribution of Tourists**

As far as the profession-wise distribution of tourists is concerned, the highest percentage is constituted by the educational group (37.3%). They were mostly students who came to seek admissions in various schools and the researchers from various disciplines. The next category of tourists were businessmen, their share being 30.7%. Nearly 23.7% tourists were servicemen. They were either on their official tour or had come just for recreation. Rest of the tourists were related with some other professions, as doctors, lawyers etc.

TABLE 5.3

Profession-wise Grouping of Tourists

Sl. No.	Profession	Actual Number of Tourists	Percentage
1.	Service	17	22.7
2.	Education	28	37.3
3.	Business	23	30.7
4.	Others	07	9.3

The professions of tourists are clear indications of their purpose of visit to Dehra Dun. The main purpose of nearly 60% tourists were related with their academics but recreation was also a vital factor. The purposes of a large number of tourists (33.3%) was only recreation and pleasure. A handful of tourists also came here for some religious purposes. Rest 4% tourists had some other purposes.

TABLE 5.4

Purpose-wise Distribution of Tourists

Sl. No.	Purpose of Visit	Actual Number of Tourists	Percentage
1.	Recreation	25	33.3
2.	Religion	02	2.7
3.	Academic	45	60.3
4.	Others	03	4.0

(b) **Age-Structure of Tourists**

In survey it has been found that middle aged tourists have their largest share (69.3%) in total arrivals at Dehra Dun.

Tourists below 25 years of age were mostly students and their share was 20%. Some of them had come with their parents or relatives. Tourists of 50 years and above were mostly businessmen, their percentage being 10.7.

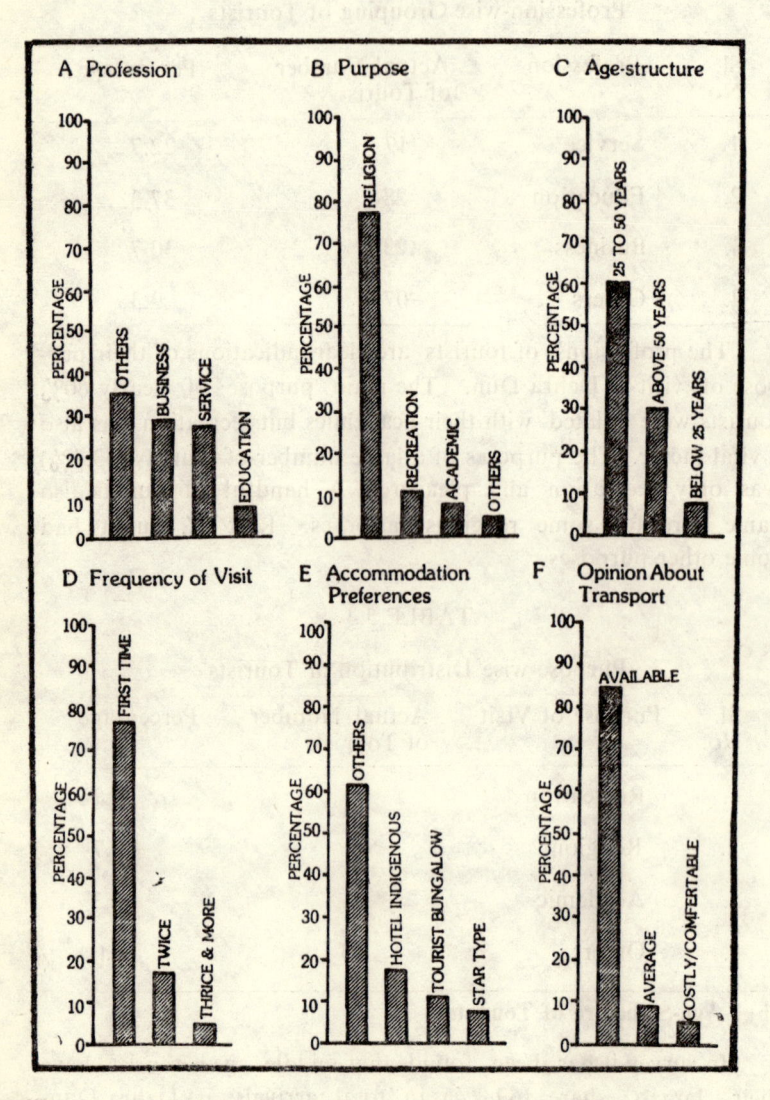

Fig. 5.2 Tourist Trends in Dehra Dun

TABLE 5.5
Age-Structure of Tourists

Sl. No.	Age-Group	Actual Number of Tourists	Percentage
1.	Below 25 years	15	20
2.	25 to 50 years	52	69.3
3.	Above 50 years	08	10.7

(c) Previous Experiences

When tourists were asked about their previous experiences of this town, nearly 80% of them have confessed that it was their first visit to Dehra Dun. Nearly 10.7% tourists were on their second trip of the town. A considerable number of tourists (9.3%) had visited this town at more than two or three occasions.

TABLE 5.6
Frequency of Visit to the Town

Sl. No.	Frequency	Actual Number of Tourists	Percentage
1.	For the first time	60	80
2.	Twice	08	10.7
3.	Thrice & more	07	9.3

(d) Accommodation Preference

In survey majority of tourists have shown their liking for the indigenous type of hotels. They gave the second preference to tourist bungalows. About 13% of tourists have shown their special interest in star type hotels as they can afford the high cost. Only 17% tourists were interested in other types of accommodations such as dharmshalas, tent houses and other cheap accommodations.

TABLE 5.7

Preferences for Accommodation Types

Sl. No.	Types of Accommodation	Actual Number of Tourists	Percentage
1.	Hotel Star type	10	12.3
2.	Hotel Indigenous	38	50.7
3.	Tourists Bungalow	19	25.3
4.	Others	08	10.7

In survey it was felt that the selection of accommodation types was directly related with the income of tourists.

(e) Tourists' Opinion and Comments

About 87% of tourists have expressed their satisfaction over the transport facilities in Dehra Dun. Some tourists (9%) have found it of average standard and felt that internal transport should be made more effective. Only 9% tourists have found transport facilities both external and internal as comfortable, easily available and effective, but a bit costly.

TABLE 5.8

Tourist Opinion About Transport

Sl. No.	Items	Actual Number of Tourists	Percentage
1.	Available	65	86.7
2.	Average	5	6.7
3.	Costly and comfortable	2	2.6
4.	No comments	3	4.0

Majority of tourists had the opinion that accommodation facility of the town was not very satisfactory. Hotels at Dehra Dun are either of high standard and therefore more expensive or sub-standard type which do not encourage the average tourists.

Tourism in Garhwal Region 193

As regarns food etc. majority of tourists found it easily available but at the same time they also opined that it was somewhat costlier.

When tourists were asked for their overall opinion about their visit to Dehra Dun and if they had any problem during their stay in the town, majority of them complained against the non-co-operative behaviour of local public. They have shown their anger over the higgling and bargaining practised by the local transport agents. Some of the tourists have complained about high rates of auto-rickshaws and private taxies. The behaviour of the owners were not very good with the tourists. Few tourists were cheated by the hotel agents too.

A number of suggestions were put forth by them. They suggested that drinking water and cafeteria should be made available at every picnic spot. They felt greatly that a bridge should has been constructed between Dehra Dun and Sahastradhara over Jhandu Nala. Suitable bathing ghats are required at Sulphur tank. Some tourists suggested that roads of municipal area were not upto the mark and they must be improved.

In general tourists were satisfied with their visit of Dehra Dun and they had very much enjoyed their stay in the city.

MUSSOORIE—'QUEEN OF THE HILLS'

Mussoorie, one of the most popular hill stations of Uttar Pradesh, is famous for its inherent scenic beauty and gaiety of social life. The town is commonly known as 'the Queen of the Hills' because of its fairy land atmosphere.

The town of Mussoorie looks like a horse-shoe shaped foot hill (30°27'N lat.—78°06'E long. at) the elevation of 2005 m above sea level in the lesser Himalayan zone in the district of Dehra Dun. The total area of this town is 67.65 sq. km with the population of 18,233 (1981).

(i) History and Development

The history of this town is not more than 150 years old. In 1827, Captain Young came here for the first time, accompanied by a hunting party. He spotted the area, now known as Landour Bazar, which was first developed as a military station but gradually became an integral part of this hill resort.

Captain Young, responsible for founding Mussoorie, fell in love with the spot he had strayed into. Besides its scenic stanch and splendour, the weather was bracing and the climate salubrious. The situation of the locality offered immense possibilities. In the year 1827 itself the first building came up in the area to be used for the summer sojourn. The structure is still there now as the premises of Mullingar Hotel. Almost instantly the stream of visitors began to pour in and buildings appeared in sporadic outbursts all over the hill. The architecture was Elizabethan English type. All most overnight a bit of Alpine Europe had been transplanted in India and new hill-station was born. Among the first of the elites to join the caravan were the Indian Maharajas who contributed immense palaces on the hills, built to look like the country seats of British aristocracy.

In the early days, the only access was 11 km trek from Rajpur either on horse back or on a 'dandi' carried by porters. The rigours of the journey were quickly forgotton on reaching the idyllic spot. However in 1920 the first car arrived from Dehra-Dun. The connecting motor road was completed almost as soon as the motor car made scene in India. Coiling like a snake the road rises from 640 m to an altitude of 2005 m within an hour and half.

(ii) Tourism Resource and Recreational Amenities

Mussoorie is one of the most popular hill stations in northern India famous for its inherent natural scenic beauty and gay social life. The spirit of gaiety pervades everywhere in the 64.25 sq. km area making the town a good mixer. The town is surrounded by beautiful peaks, valleys, magestic waterfalls and lush green forest mostly of deodar and pine trees. Encircled by hills, and overlooking the Doon Valley, the gay summer resort is mantled in snow for winter bursts. Snowfall in Mussoorie has always been the 'hot shot' for the adventure-loving tourists.

Other attractions of the town are its various winter and summer sports/tournaments/shows arranged by many clubs and organizations. The Happy Valley Club arranges tennis tournament in its spacious tennis courts. Billiard rooms are in Picture Palace, while two skating rinks are in Kulri bazar and Library bazar which give an opportunity of skating to the sports-loving tourists. The season lasts from March 15 to October 31st. The famous polo ground holds an annual polo tournament. A beauty contest elects 'The Queen' who reigns Mussoorie all through the season.

The rink stages a boxing tournament while at the Savoy there is a Dog Show every September. The best ball rooms are at the Savoy and Hackman's hotels. All these sports/events create terrific sensation among enthusiastic tourists. An annual autumn festival is also arranged by Mussoorie Club which attracts a number of tourists.

Apart from these major attractions there are several easy to reach beauty spots in and around Mussoorie which have special charms for the tourists, nature loving and seeking sylvan bliss. Some of them are described below :

(a) *Gun Hill—'Erstwhile time keeper of the town* : This second highest peak of Mussoorie is 400 m away from the main town. The maximum height of this peak is 2143 m from mean sea level. On a clear day, tourists can enjoy the magnificent view of Kedarnath, Badrinath, Nandadevi and Bander Punch from this hill top. Tourists can easily reach here only in two and half minutes by rope way trolley. Swinging high above the hills in areal ropeway, one gets a wide angled view of snowy Himalayan peaks and down below the winding serpentine valley. An up hill road also goes upto Gun Hill, starting from the fashionable Mall. About the name of this hill it is said that in earlier days a fun was used to be fired from this hill at 12 O' clock (noon) to denote the time. Though in later years this practice was discontinued and the gun removed, yet the ghost of the name still clings to the Gun Hill top, now there is a reservoir that feeds the town.

(b) *Municipal Garden* : This beautiful garden, 4 km away from the Mall, is full of flowers, valvety lawns, deodar and pine trees with an artificial lake. There is a Children Park-a plateau about 3 km away from this garden, noted for its excellent views of both the Himalayas and the Doon Valley.

(c) *Lal Tibba* : This is the spot where Captain Young stayed first time in the Doon valley. Lal Tibba, the peak of Landour or Depot Hill is at an altitude of 2,438.4 m. It seems to be the highest point of Mussoorie. It is only 5 km away from the main town. From this point, with the aid of an electric operated binocular, one can get a bird's eye view of Gangotri, Kedarnath, Chaukhamba, Nandadevi and Srikantha peaks.

(d) *Mossy Falls* : This spot is only 6 km away from the main town. This picturesque place around the Mossy waterfall is one of the most beautiful picnic spots near the city.

(e) *Camel's Back Road* : It is an ideal place for horse riding. The road which provides the opportunity of horse riding starts from Kulri behind the skating hall and ends at the Library bazar. From this road, a foot path goes to Bhilaru pumping station, an interesting place to visit. The Hawa Ghar is one of the several resting places on this road, curving round a mountain looking like a camel's back. The fashionable western style shops are in the Mall, Kulri and Library bazar, while the Indian style bazar is in the area around Landour.

(f) *Kempty Falls* : Kempty falls, the prettiest spot in Mussoorie, is about 15 km away from the main town, on the

Fun and Frolic in the Colourful Company Garden at Mussoorie

Mussoorie-Chakrata road which attracts hundreds of tourists every day. Gushing out of the mountains the majestic water fall splits into five distinct falls one on the top of the other. The highest one is over 12.2 m. Tourists can visit this water-fall only on Wednesday, Saturday and Sunday as on the other days of the week it is diverted and used for irrigation. There is a fashionable restaurant and a Forest Rest House.

Apart from site seeing a number of other recreational amenities are also present in Mussoorie for tourists. The infectious holiday spirit has resulted in establishments that cater to the every whim of pleasure-seeking society, be it dancing, riding, theatre and cinema going, skating and sporting events etc. There are six picture halls (Capital, Rialt, La Anjuman, Picture Palace etc). Mosts of the hotels have T. V., Radio, record player and video facilities for the tourists. Tourists can enjoy fishing in Agler valley, Yamuna river after getting permission from D.F.O., Yamuna Division Mussoorie. The river is full of different types of fishes like Mahseer, Malli etc. Skating facilities are available at the rinks (Kulri Bazar), Jayson Roller (the Mall) and at skating rink (below Hackman's Hotel). There are several clubs as Rotary Club, Mussoorie Co-operative Club, Lion's Club etc.

Apart from these recreational amenities there are other facilities too for the tourists. There are six Banks where tourists can get their traveller cheques cashed. There are four hospitals and several private clinics. For religious minded tourists there are a number of temples in and around the town as Arya Samaj, Sanatan Dharam Mandir, Luxmi Narain Mandir in Library bazar ; Jain Mandir in Landour Bazar and Tibetan temple in Happy Valley. For Muslim tourists there are mosques in Library, Kulri and Landour bazars. For Sikh tourists there is Gurudwara at Landour bazar and for Christian tourists churches are there in Library, Landour and Kulri bazars.

Even for the tourists coming here for in-depth study of either nature or man (human group) there is ample territory to tread upon. The hill folk of Mussoorie are simple and hardy, living in tiny villages scattered over the surrounding hills. Cheery and honest, their main occupation is agriculture. Their house are built of cut rocks, roofed with heavy beams strong to stand the winter snows.

(iii) **Townscape**

This town was developed basically as a picnic spot and summer resort for the Britishers at first but at present perhaps Mussoorie is the most beautiful recreational centre in entire U.P. Himalaya. The morphology of the town (Fig. 5.3) can be understood by dividing the town into three distinct zones :

(a) *Inner Zone* : The inner zone of the town is in the form of tourist service zone. This zone provides many tourist amenities as fashionable shops, cinema houses, skating rinks, many restaurants such as-Royal Cafeteria, Kwality, Neelam etc. and many luxury and ordinary hotels (Hackman's, Grand, Roxy, Silverton, Himalaya etc.) and clubs. There are two main markets lying in this zone :

1. *Library Bazar* : This market is situated near Library but stands on the Mall road. There are many western type luxury hotels as Savoy Hotel (4 star) and others. Many fasionable shops, restaurants, banks, cinema houses are also there.

2. *Kulri Bazar* : This market is situated in the eastern side of Mall road which goes upto Camel's Back. This market is also full of several tourist amenities-cinema halls, shops, banks, telephone exchange, golf rinks etc.

(b) *Middle Zone* : The middle zone is of different educational institutions, government offices and retail shops. A part of this zone is residential area also with parks and play arounds.

(c) *Outer Zone* : The outer zone of the town is mainly the area of surrounding picnic spots and tourist centres as Municipal Garden, Happy Valley, Camel's Back etc. Some important

Serpentine Breedle Path Between Dehra Dun and Mussoorie

Tourism in Garhwal Region

institutions are also there in this zone like—L.B.S. Academy, Modern school etc. Residential area of this zone is found in rather scattered form.

(iv) Transport and Accommodation

The town is connected by good motorable roads with every major centre of tourist interest in this region. Roadways and private buses along with private taxies provide regular services from Mussoorie to other places.

TABLE 5.9

Distance from Mussoorie to other Important Places

Sl. No.	Place	Distance (km)
1.	Dehra Dun	35
2.	Tehri	72
3.	Chakrata	81
4.	Barkot	96
5.	Hardwar	103
6.	Saharanpur	107
7.	Delhi	290

The nearest railway station Dehra Dun is about 35 km from Mussoorie in the south. From here buses and taxies are easily available for Mussoorie. The nearest Airport (Jeolly Grant) in Saharanpur district is about 60 km away from Mussoorie. For internal transport buses and taxies are easily available at Masonic bus stand and Library bazar. Hand-pulled rickshaws, ponies and horses are available for local transport. Rope-way trolley system is available between the Mall and Gunhill.

Mussoorie has very good accommodation facilities as compared to other hill resorts of U. P. Himalaya. There are about 75 hotels, 8 dharamshalas, 6 guest houses of different government departments and 6 tourist bungalows. There are 6 one- star and two-star hotels and more than 20 hotels are of western style with

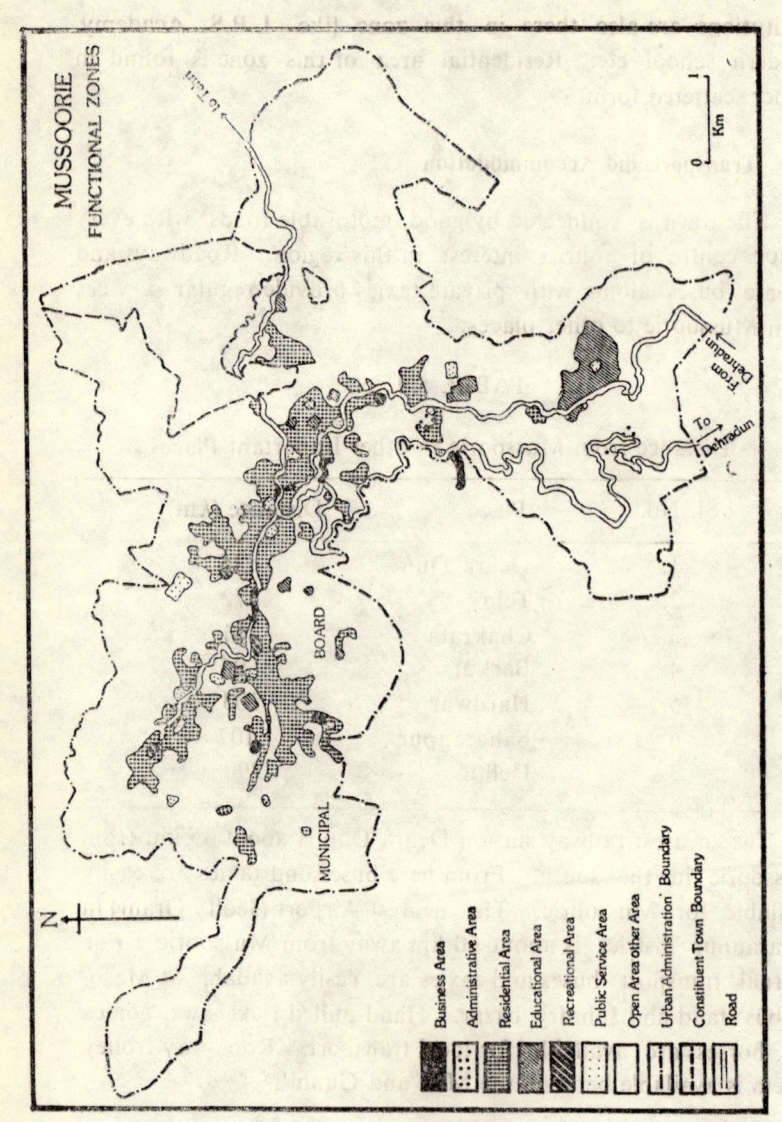

Fig. 5.3

all the modern facilities. The charges of luxury hotels range between Rs. 150 to 200 for single bed room, Rs. 200 to Rs. 250 for double bed room and Rs. 250 to Rs. 315 for a suite.

The charge for Indian style ordinary hotels ranges between Rs. 25 to Rs. 75 for single bed room, Rs. 50 to Rs. 150 for double bed room during peak season, while in the off-season charge ranges between Rs. 10 to Rs. 25 for single bed room and Rs. 15 to Rs. 50 for double bed room. The dharamshalas are comparatively cheaper. It costs Rs. 5 to Rs. 15 per day. Rates of government inspection houses range between Rs. 10 to Rs. 15 for Indian tourists and Rs. 25 to Rs. 30 for foreign tourist.

For catering and cuisine there are as many as 50 restaurants and hotels. More than 40 residential hotels provide different types of cuisine as Chinise, Continental and Indian etc. Some of the hotels arrange taxies and buses also for the tourists.

(v) **Tourist Trends and Analyses**

Mussoorie is easily accessible throughout the year. In summer, tourists come here to get relief from the scorching heat of plains. In winter they come to see the clear sky, when Mussoorie provides an ideal setting for viewing the Himalayan panorama. But majority of tourists make their visit during summer in May and June and the minimum number of tourists come in the months of December and January. The winter tourists come here mainly to enjoy the 'snow fall'. Autumn festival of Mussoorie draws a large crowd during October-November and winter sports/tournaments also attract enthusiatsic tourists.

TABLE 5.10

Tourist Arrivals in Mussoorie

Sl. No.	Year	Tourist Arrivals	Variation (No.)	(%)
1.	1981	724756	—	—
2.	1982	770717	+ 45961	+ 0.6
3.	1983	827069	+ 56352	+7.3
4.	1984	872105	+ 45036	+5.4
5.	1985	948799	+ 76684	+8.8

The tourist trends observed from the analysis of data gathered during field survey at Mussoorie are as follows (vide Fig. 5.4):

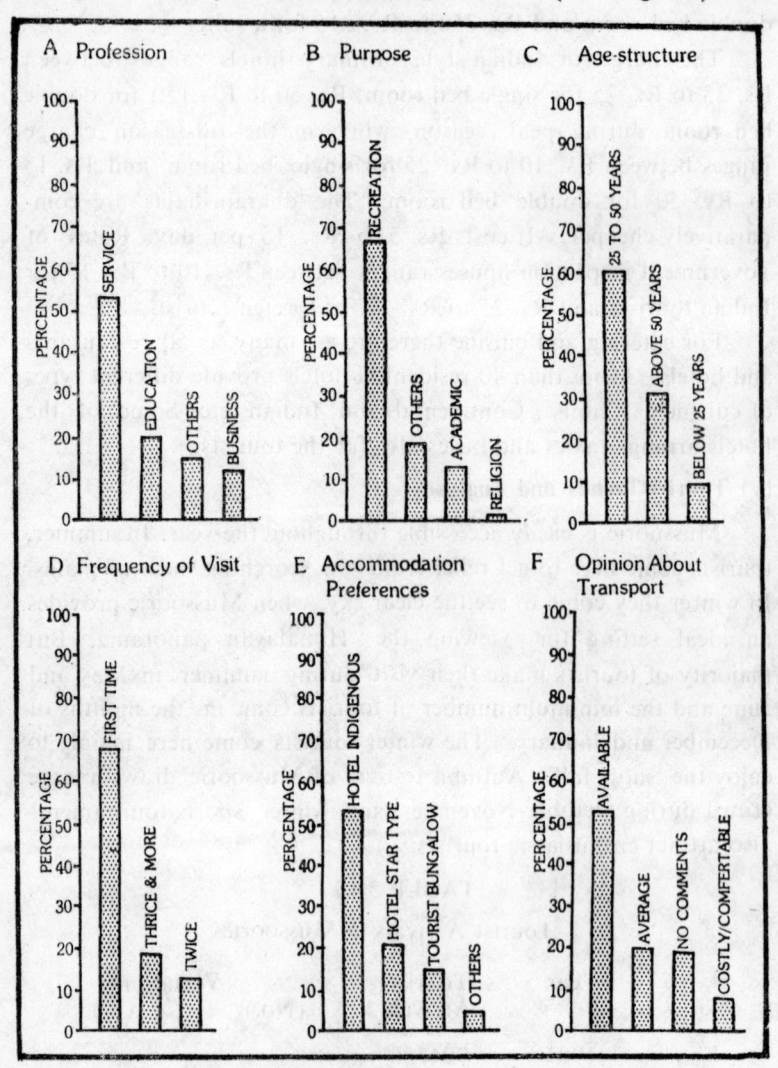

Fig. 5.4 Tourist Trends in Mussoorie

(a) Profession of Tourists

As regards the profession-wise distribution of tourists visiting Mussoorie, the service men constituted the highest percentage.

Their share was over 53 percent. The next category was of educational group mostly students and teachers. Their share was about 20%. Nearly 14 percent tourists were of several other professions such as doctors, engineers and lawyers, etc. Only 12 percent tourists were businessmen.

TABLE 5.11

Profession-wise Distribution of Tourists

Sl. No.	Profession	Actual Number of Tourists	Percentage
1.	Service	40	53.3
2.	Education	15	20
3.	Business	9	12
4.	Others	11	14.7

(b) Purpose of Visit

When tourists were asked about their main purpose of visit of this town, more than 66 percent tourists confessed that their purpose was purely recreation and pleasure. A handful of tourists (18%) had come with some other intentions such as business or meeting with their friends or relatives. About 13.3 percent tourists had come in connection of their academics. Very few tourists (1.3%) were found with religious purpose.

TABLE 5.12

Purpose-wise Grouping of Tourists

Sl. No.	Purpose of visit	Actual Number of Tourists	Percentage
1.	Recreation	50	66.7
2.	Religion	01	1.3
3.	Academic	10	13.3
4.	Others	14	18.7

(c) Age-Structure

It was noticed in survey that the middle aged tourists were in the dominant position in total arrivals at Mussoorie. Their percentage was 60. About 30 percent tourists were above 50 years of age, mostly they had came as head of the family. Some of them were businessmen also. Some tourists of the age group were on their way to Himalayan shrines. Only 9.3 percent tourists were below 25 years. They came only with the senior members of family. Some of them were students also.

TABLE 5.13

Age-Group of Tourists

Sl. No.	Age-Group	Actual Number of Tourists	Percentage
1.	Below 25 years	7	9.3
2.	25 to 50 years	45	60
3.	Above 50 years	23	30.7

(d) Previous Experiences

When tourists were asked about their previous experiences of this town, nearly 68 percent tourists replied that they were on their first visit to Mussoorie. About 13.3 percent tourists were visiting this town for the second time and only 18 percent tourists had visited this on more than two or three occasions. Mostly they were sports lovers.

TABLE 5.14

Frequency of Visiting the Town

Sl. No.	Frequency	Actual Number of Tourists	Percentage
1.	For the first time	51	68
2.	Twice	14	13.3
3.	Thrice or more	10	18.7

Tourists, who had come for the first time in Mussoorie had gathered most of the informations about this town from the nearest Tourist Bureau.

(e) **Accommodation Preference**

Majority of tourists have shown their likeness for indigenous types of hotels, their share being over 53 percent. About 26 percent of tourists showed their interest in star type hotels. Only 14 percent of tourists were interested in tourist bungalows. In the case of non-availability of tourist bungalows they gave preferences for the indigenous type of hotels. Nearly 5 percent tourists of lower income group were interested in cheap accommodations as tent houses, dharamshalas etc.

TABLE 5.15
Preferences for Accommodation Types

Sl. No.	Type of Accommodation	Actual Number of Tourists	Percentage
1.	Hotel Star Type	20	20.7
2.	Hotel Indigenous Type	40	53.3
3.	Tourist Bungalow	11	14.7
4.	Other Types of Accommodation	04	5.3

(f) **Tourists' Opinion and Comments**

About 53 percent tourists expressed their satisfaction over the transport facilities, both external and internal in Mussoorie. Some tourists (20%) found it just of average standard, while about 18.7 percent tourists did not make any comment about it and only 8 percent tourists felt that it was easily available and comfortable but it was a bit expensive.

TABLE 5.16
Tourists' Opinion About Transport Facilities

Sl. No.	Opinion about Transport	Actual Number of Tourists	Percentage
1.	Available	40	53.3
2.	Average	15	20.0
3.	Costly and comfortable	6	8.0
4.	No comments	14	18.7

About the availability of food, majority of tourists did not face any problem, however the items were generally costly. When tourists were asked for their overall opinion about their visit of Mussoorie, most of them did not make complaints. However some had few suggestions that provisions should be there for foreign currency to be easily cashed and local handicrafts should be properly developed to meet the need of outside tourists. Tourists have shown their interest in the local festivals. They were reported to be satisfied with the behaviour of local people, shopkeepers and government employees. A Very low percentage of tourists complained against the non-co-operation of goverdment workers and cheating by hotel agents.

In general, majority of the tourists enjoyed their visit of Mussoorie, they were satisfied and have shown their intention of coming here again.

HARDWAR - 'GATWAY TO GOD'

Hardwar happens to be gateway of all Himalayan shrines of Uttarakhand-Badrinath, Kedarnath, Gangotri Yamunotri etc. The location of this town is on the right bank of the holy Ganga at the foot hills of Shivalik in Saharanpur district at an elevation of 292.7 m above from sea level. The total area of this town is about 42.01 sq. km, with the population of 145946 according to 1981 census.

(i) Historical Background

This town has a good name as a pilgrim centre since 'Pauranick age'. In 'Purana' it was named as 'Mayapuri'. The celebrated Chinese traveller Hiuen Tsang has also made a mention of this town in his book. It was known as 'Gangadwar' and 'Tapovan' in ancient time and even before it was known as 'Kapilsthan'. It is said that the ancestor of Raja Bhagirath were burnt to ashes by the curse of sage 'Kapil Muni'. For their salavation, Bhagirath performed austerities and brought down Ganga from heaven.

This is one of four pilgrim centres in India where after every twelve years 'Kumbh' is held. Other centres are Prayag (Allahabad), Ujjain and Nasik. Millions of Hindus take holy dip in the sacred water of Ganga seeking emancipation from the worldly sins during Kumbh.

About the origin of 'Kumbh' fair it has been said that in Pauranic era, when 'Amrit Kalasha' was recovered from 'Samundramanthan', a tense war was going on between Devatas and Asuras for its possession. There was every possibility of getting hold of it, rather forcibly by Asuras as they were more powerful than the Devatas. So its safety was entrusted to Devata Brahaspati, Surya, Chandra and Shani. These Devetas ran away with the 'Amrit Kalasha' to hide it from Asuras. On learning this conspiracy of Devetas, Asuras turned furious and chased them. During this chase Devatas and Asurars went round the earth and it lasted 12 days and nights. During this chase Devatas put 'Amrit Kalasha' at four different places i.e., Hardwar, Prayag, Ujjain and Nasik. To mark this memorable holy event Kumbha is celebrated in every twelve years at these places. It is also said in other Puranic legends that an actual fight took place between Devatas and Asuras resulting in 'Amrit Kalasha' being broken, out of which Amrit fell down at above four places.

The astrological date of Kumbh at Hardwar falls when Venus and Jupiter coincide with Acquarius and Sun and Moon are on the Aries and Sagittarius respectively. This was the position in April, '86 and thus Kumbh was celebrated at Hardwar.

(ii) Places of Tourist Interest and Pilgrimage in and around Hardwar

There are many pilgrim centres as well as other places of tourist interest in and around Hardwar :

(a) *Har-Ki-Pauri* : It is the most sacred bathing ghat at Hardwar. About this ghat it is said that few drops of Amrit (nector) fell from Kalasha when it was being carried by Jayant. It is also said that Raja Shveta had performed 'Tapa' and received blessings from Brahma, since then the Kund is known as 'Bhahma-kund'. Raja Bhartrihari had also performed austerities at this very place and later on Raja Vikramaditya got ghats and pauries constructed here. It is also said that the foot mark of God Vishnu is imprinted on a stone let into the upper wall of the Pauri. The temple of Ganga, Man Sing-Ki-Chhatri, Haricharan temple and Birla tower are also situated around this ghat. The Arti of Ganga which is performed after sun-set everyday is a delightful scene.

(b) *Bhim Goda-Tank* : This place is 2.5 km from the Tourist Office at Hardwar on the way to Rishikesh. It is said that when Pandavas, on their way towards Himalaya, were passing through Harwar, Bhim made this tank with a blow of his knee.

(c) *Parmarth Ashram* : It is only 4 km from Tourist Office on the way to Rishikesh and is a branch of Parmarth Niketan (Daivi-Sampad Mandal Organisation) of Rishikesh. This Ashram is full of beautiful images of Goddess and other deities.

(d) *Sapta Rishi Ashram and Sapt Sarover* : It is 6 km from Tourist Bureau. According to the legendary belief the holy Ganga had to split herself into seven currents here with a view to please seven 'Rishis' worshipping a different spots.

(e) *Daksh Prajapati Temple and Sati Kund at Kankhal* : It is 4 km from Hardwar. There is mythological story about the origin

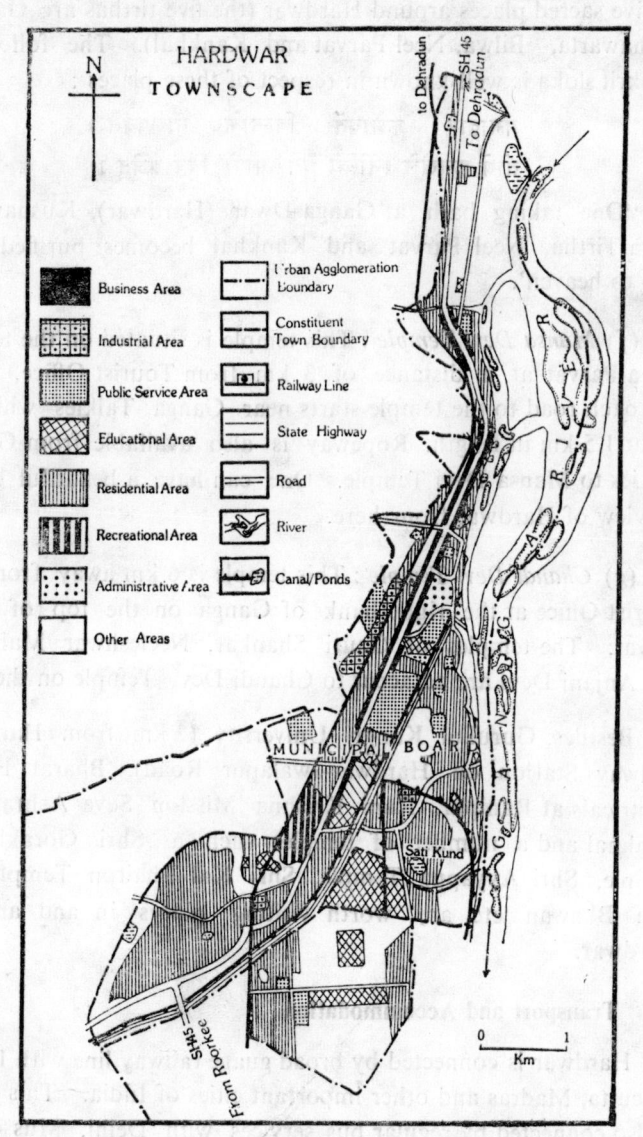

Fig. 5.5

of this place. Here Daksh Prajapati, father of Sati (Lord Shiva's wife) performed a 'yagya' and did not invite Lord Shiva and Sati. Feeling insulted Sati burnt herself in 'Yagya Kund'. It is one of the five sacred places around Hardwar (the five tirthas are Ganga, Kushawarta, Bilwa, Neel Parvat and Kankhal). The following Sanskrit sloka is well-known in respect of these places :

गंगाद्वारे कुशावर्ते बिल्वाके नीलपर्वते ।
तीर्थे कनुखले स्नात्वा धूत पापो दिवं व्रजेत् ॥

"One taking bath at Ganga-Dwar (Hardwar), Kushawart, Bilwa Tirtha, Neel Parvat and Kankhal becomes purified and goes to heaven'.

(f) *Mansa Devi Temple* : This temple is situated on the top of Bilwa Parvat at a distance of 3 km from Tourist Office. The approach road to the temple starts near Ganga Talkies which is about 1.5 km in length. Ropeway is also available from Ganga Talkies to Mansa Devi Temple. One can have a beautiful bird's eye view of Hardwar from here.

(g) *Chandi Devi Temple* : This temple is 6 km away from the Tourist Office at the right bank of Ganga on the top of Neel Parvat. The temples of Gauri Shankar, Neeleshwar Mahadev and Anjani Devi are adjacent to Chandi Devi Temple on the hill.

Besides, Gurukul Kangri University (3 km from Hardwar Railway Station on Hardwar-Jwalapur Road), Bharat Heavy Electricals at Ranipur, Ram Krishna Mission Seva Ashram at Kankhal and a number of temples such as Shri Gorakhnath Temple, Shri Ayyappa Temple, Shri Kal Bhairon Temple, Sri Gita Bhawan etc. are worth visiting places in and around Hardwar.

(iii) **Transport and Accommodation**

Hardwar is connected by broad guage railway line with Delhi, Culcutta, Madras and other important cities of India. This town is also connected by regular bus services with Delhi, Mussoorie, Rishikesh, Dehra Dun and other tourist centres in Garhwal Himalaya. The nearest airport is Jeolly Grant, from where Vayudoot flight is available twice a day for Delhi.

For internal transport taxies, tongas, tricycles, rickshaw and local bus services are easily available. Several travel agencies such as M/s India Tourist Service, M/s Badrinath Tourist Service etc. are also there to arrange conducted tour from Hardwar to other tourist centres in Garhwal Himalaya.

Accommodation does not create any problem in Hardwar in the normal condition as there are scores of dharmshalas, tourists lodges and Government guest houses. Dharamshalas are in good conditions and few of them provide free accommodation and food facilities to the piglrims. The rate charge of hotels ranges between Rs. 15 to Rs. 75 for single room and Rs. 15 to Rs. 110 for double bed room, while rate charge of tourist bungalows ranges between Rs. 20 to Rs. 45 for single bed room and Rs. 25 to Rs. 65 for double bed room. Rate charges of hotels are a bit high during season.

(iv) Tourist Trends and Analyses

Hardwar itself is an ideal religious and recreational centre serving as a gateway to Himalayan shrines. That's why it recives tourists and pilgrims round the year. But this town has two popular seasons-the first tourist season is Summer from May 15 to June 20 and the second is Autumn (September 15 to the last week of October), Summer season has greater magnitude attracting about 70% of total tourists/pilgrims. In Autumn tourists mostly from East and South India visit Hardwar and other Himalayan shrines.

TABLE 5.17

Tourist Arrivals in Hardwar

Sl. No.	Years	Tourist Arrivals (No.)	Variation %
1.	1979	2489142	—
2.	1980	2907295	+ 16.8
3.	1981	3237737	+ 11.4
4.	1982	3345617	+ 3.3
5.	1983	3350000	+ 0.13

For collecting detailed, accurate and valid informations about general characteristics of tourists visiting Hardwar, a questionnaire was prepared and got fill up by the individual tourists as it has been done in the case of other centres also. The survey has been done in two seasons, first time in September-October, 1985 and second time during Kumb fair i. e. in April, 1986. The questionnaire was got filled up by distributing it in selected hotels, dharmshalas and guest houses. Some tourists were personally interrogated for in depth interviews. During October, 1985 about 120 tourists were contacted while during Kumbh fair another 180 tourists were interrogated. Special attention was given to tourists' free time and tension-free mood. Some salient aspects of tourist behaviour at Hardwar are discussed below (vide Fig. 5.6):

(a) Profession of Tourists

As far as profession-wise distribution of tourists in Hardwar is concerned, the highest percentage is constituted by servicemen (52.5%) but the survey which was done during Kumbh fair reveals that fairly high percentage of tourists was related to other professions, like farmiag, self-business etc. The next category was of businessmen in both the surveys.

TABLE 5.18

Professions of Tourists

Sl. No.	Profession	1985 Actual No. of Tourists	Percentage	1986 Actual No. of Tourists	Percentage
1.	Service	63	52.5	17	9.4
2.	Business	30	25.0	28	15.6
3.	Education	12	10.0	20	11.1
4.	Others	15	12.5	115	63.9

(b) Purpose of Visit

Religious feelings were the most dominant feature behind their purpose of visit to this town in both the surveys. But in

1986 survey percentage of religious people increased quite remarkably due to 'Kumbh fair'. To take a holy dip in the river

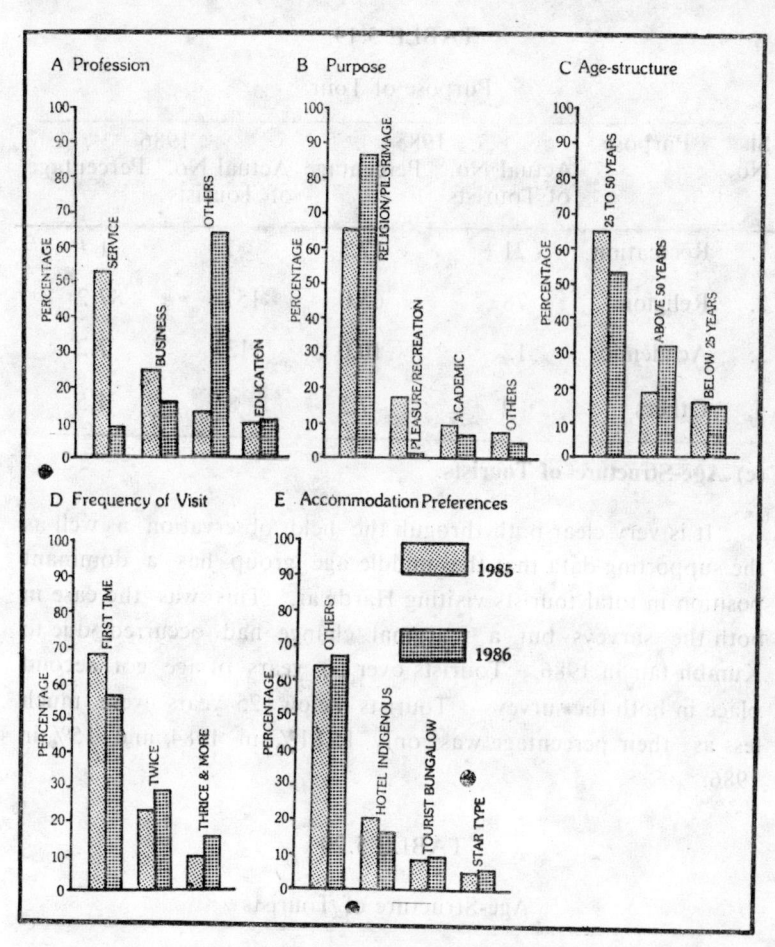

Fig. 5.6 Tourist Trends in Hardwar

Ganga seemed to be the matter of prime concern to almost every tourist. Their percentage was 87.2. A considerable number of tourists came for recreational purposes also. Some of tourists had come for academic purpose but their percentage was not very significant. In 1985 survey about 7.5 percent of tourists were related with some other purposes such as business, official tour etc. In 1986 survey some marked changes were observed due to Kumbh fair.

TABLE 5.19

Purpose of Tour

Sl. No.	Purpose	1985 Actual No. of Tourists	Percentage	1986 Actual No. of Tourists	Percentage
1.	Recreation	21	17.5	2	1.1
2.	Religion	78	65.0	157	87.2
3.	Academic	12	10.0	13	7.2
4.	Others	9	7.5	8	4.5

(c) **Age-Structure of Tourists**

It is very clear both throguh the field observation as well as the supporting data that the middle age group has a dominant position in total tourists visiting Hardwar. This was the case in both the surveys but a marginal change had occurred due to Kumbh fair in 1986. Tourists over 50 years of age got second place in both the surveys. Tourists below 25 years were much less as their percentage was only 15.81% in 1984 and 15% in 1986.

TABLE 5.20

Age-Structure of Tourists

Sl. No.	Age-Group	1985 Actual No. of Tourists	Percentage	1986 Actual No. of Tourists	Percentage
1.	Below 25 years	19	15.8	27	15
2.	25 to 50 years	78	65.0	96	53.3
3.	Above 50 years	23	19.2	57	31.7

(d) Previous Experiences

When tourists were asked about their previous experiences of this town it was found that majority of them (67%) had come for the first time but this percentage decreased in 1986 (55.6%). The slight increase in the number of tourists coming twice and thrice clearly indicates that religion-conscious people often visit Hardwar on pious occasions.

TABLE 5.21

Frequency of Visit

Sl. No.	Frequency	1985 Actual No. of Tourists	Percentage	1986 Actual No. of Tourists	Percentage
1.	For the First Time	81	67.5	100	55.6
2.	Twice	27	22.5	52	28.9
3.	Thrice or more	12	10.0	28	15.5

(e) Accommodation Preference

During the first survey it was observed that the higher percentage of tourists liked other types of accommodation other than luxury hotel-indigenous type of hotel or tourist bungalow. Their percentage was 64.2 and it did not change much during Kumbh fair also. About 20% of tourists were interested in indigenous type of hotel but their percentage decreased in 1986. Very few tourists have shown their likeness for star type luxury hotels.

(f) Tourists' Opinion and Comments

Majority of tourists were almost satisfied with their visit of Hardwar, though few cases of cheating by tonga and rickshaw walas were also mentioned. About the availability and quality of food etc. tourists had varied opinions. Non-availability of good and cheap restaurants were markedly felt mostly at the

TABLE 5.22

Preference for Accommodation Types

Sl. No.	Accommodation types	1985 Actual No. of Tourists	Pecentage	1986 Actual No. of Tourists	Percentage
1.	Hotel Star Type	7	5.8	11	6.1
2.	Hotel Indigenous Type	25	20.8	31	17.2
3.	Tourist Bungalow	11	9.2	18	10.0
4.	Other Types of accommodation	77	64.2	120	66.7

recreation and pilgrimage sites. The general opinion of the tourists about the local people was quite satisfactory and tourists found them very co-operative, hospitable and cheerful.

RISHIKESH

(i) Introduction

Rishikesh occupies an important place among all the pilgrimage centres of U. P. Himalaya as it is the gateway for the pilgrimage to all the inner Himalayan shrines i.e., Badrinath, Kedarnath, Yamunotri, Gangotri etc. It could also be described as a vast sanctuary for sages and saints. At the same time it provides ample opportunity of visiting other recreational centres as Dehra-Dun, Musssoorie, Chakrata and Rishikesh itself.

As regards the origin of this town, it is said that Raibhya, a great Rishi did hard penances here and God appeared before him by the name of 'Harishikesh' and the area was hence forth called by this name. Another story that is famous about Rishikeh is that Bharat-brother of Lord Ram—performed severe penance here and later on a temple in the name of Bharat was constructed at

The Temple Near Lakshman Jhoola where Idols of All Himalayan Gods are Housed together

this very place. The present town of Rishikesh has developed around this temple.

The town of Rishikesh is situated on the right bank of the river Ganga at an elevation of 356 m above sea level. The total area of this town is about 2.59 sq. km with a population of about 29,145 (1981). The town is surrounded at least on three sides by beautiful mountain ranges and lush green forests. The locational beauty of this town itself is a charm and thus major resource of tourism.

(ii) Tourism Nuclei in and around Rishikesh

There are a number of temples and places of interests at Rishikesh. Few of them are as follows :

(*a*) *Bharat Temple* : It is an old temple encircled by massive walls, dedicated to Lord Bharat. This temple is situated in the heart of the main town.

(*b*) *Triveni Ghat* : It seems to be the holiest place at Rishikesh. It is said that here Ganga, Yamuna and Saraswati flow together. It is sacred place where 'Pinddan' and 'Shraddh' are performed. Several temples are located at and around this Ghat.

(*c*) *Gita Bhawan* : This beautiful temple conjugated with group of buildings is about 8 km away from the main town on the left bank of Ganga. 'Slokas' of Gita and Ramayana are written on the walls of this temple. This Bhawan is managed by the trustees affiliated to Gita Press of Gorakhpur.

(*d*) *Swarg Ashram* : It is situated 8 km away from the main town on the left bank of the Ganga. This Ashram is surrounded by dense forest and the temple is dedicated to Shri Badrinath. Badrinath-bound tourists use to visit this temple before proceeding further.

(*e*) *Neel Kanth Mahadev Temple* : This temple is about 12 km away from Laxman* Jhoola at an elevation of 1650 m above

---

* Normally spelt as Lakshman.

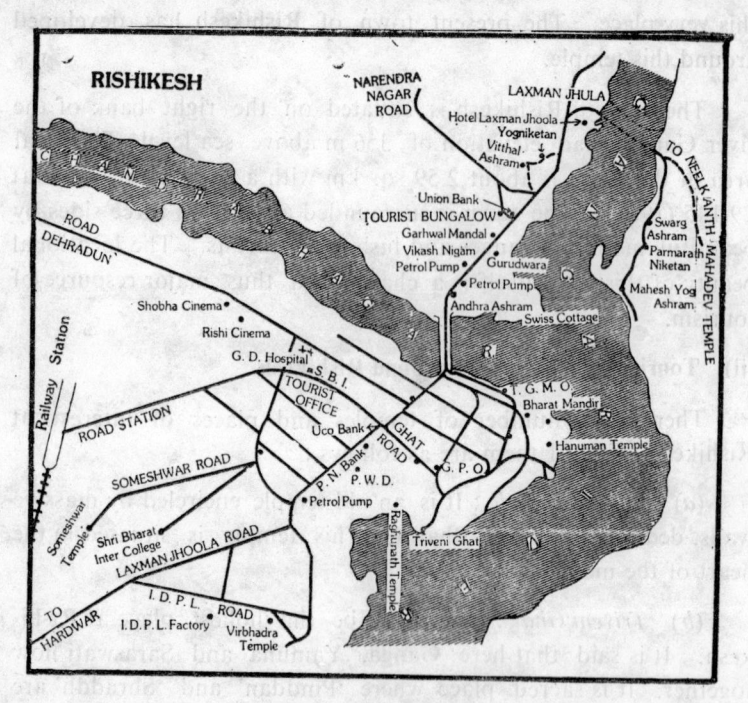

Fig. 5.7

sea level. It is dedicated to Lord Shankar; while going upto Neel khand one can have a wide angled view of Himalayan peaks, Bhabhar forests and plains below.

(*f*) *Laxman Jhoola* : It is one of major attractions at Rishikesh. There was a hanging jute rope bridge over Ganga since 1889. It was in 1939 that the hanging jute rope was replaced by the iron rope. The total span of this bridge is about 140 m. This bridge has been named after Laxman as it is believed that he had visited this place. Shri Raghunath ji's temple is a place of attraction near Laxman Jhoola. Walking over this rope bridge it is quite fascinating to see the narrow stream of Ganga coming out of the high mountain walls on its both sides.

(*g*) *Laxman Temple* : This temple, dedicated to Laxman, the younger brother of Lord Rama, is situated 6.4 km away from the

Lakshaman Jhoola— The Legendary Swinging Bridge at Rishikesh

main town. It is said that Laxman did penance at this very place.

(*h*) *Pushkar Temple* : This temple is situated on the right bank of river Chandrabhaga, about 1.6 km away from the main town. It is a newly constructed temple as an associate of Pushkar Temple at Ajmer (Rajasthan).

(*i*) *Rishi Kund and Raghunath Temple* : It is a popular bathing ghat among pilgrims on the right bank of the river Ganga. About this place it is said that here Lord Rama had taken his bath in holy water of river Ganga.

(*j*) *Shatrughan Temple at Muni-ki-Reti* : This place is about 4.3 km away from Rishikesh. There is a temple dedicated to Shatrughan—the younger brother of Lord Rama.

Apart from these pilgrim centres, Rishikesh has a number of academic and cultural institutions such as Academy of Meditation, Shankaracharya Nagar and Kailash Ashram attracting number of tourists. The 'yoga' centres of Rishikesh have enhanced the significance of the place. Home tourists and foreign tourists from all parts of the world come here to have training in yoga and meditation. The Antibiotics Projects at Birbhadra (6.4 km from Rishikesh) is also worth visiting.

(iii) **Townscape**

The location of Rishikesh is at the meeting point of two rivers Ganga and Chandrabhaga in a traingular shape (Fig. 5.7). The entire town is surrounded by dense forest and mountain ranges almost from all sides. The innermost part of the town is formed by the hotels, banks, hospitals, restaurants and Govt. officies all coping with the needs of tourists. All the religious spots and temples are situated along both the banks of the river Ganga and Chandrabhaga. A number of dharamshalas, tourist bungalows, hotels and some temples are situated on the left side, parallel to Ganga. The area between Rishikesh railway station and Ganga-

Charadrabhaga and around Laxman Jhoola are very conjusted. The entire town is filled with religious fervour.

(iv) Transport Network and Accommodation Facilities

Rishikesh is one of the most easily accessible tourist centres of U. P. Himalaya as both external and internal transport facilities are exceptionally good. This town is directly connected with Hardwar by railway which is further connected with all the major cities of India as-Delhi, Lucknow, Varanasi, Calcutta etc.

TABLE 5.23

Package Tour from Rishikesh

Sl. No.	Name of Tour	Frequencies in a week
1.	Rishikesh, Kedarnath, Badrinath (8 days)	6
2.	Rishikesh, Pauri, Kedarnath, Badrinath (8 days)	6
3.	Rishikesh, Badrinath (4 days)	1
4.	Rishikesh, Yamunotri, Gaumukh (10 days)	1
5.	Rishikesh, Yamunotri, Gangotri, Kedarnath, Badrinath (14 days)	2
6.	Delhi, Kedarnath, Badrinath (8 days)	1
7.	Rishikesh, Valley of Flowers, Hemkund, Badrinath (8 days)	2

The town is also connected with good motorable roads and U.P.S.R.T.C. provides excellent bus services. There are a number of travel agencies which arrange conducted tours for other Himalayan shrines. Among them Tehri Garhwal Motors Union Pvt. Ltd. provides good transport facilities. Garhwal Mandal Vikas Nigam (Muni-ki-Reti) provides package tours to the tourists and pilgrims in season.

Garhwal Mandal Vikas Nigam also arranges trekking tour as mentioned below :

TABLE 5.24

Trekking Tour from Rishikesh

Sl. No.	Trek	No. of Days	Month
1.	Panch Kedar	14 days	May to October
2.	Roop Kund	10 days	June to Sept.
3.	Khatling Glacier	10 days	June to Sept.
4.	Har-ki-Doon	12 days	June to October
5.	Nanda Devi Sanctuary	10 days	June to October
6.	Gaumkh, Tapovan Nandan Van	12 days	June to October
7.	Kauri Paas	10 days	June to October
8.	Valley of Flowers, Hemkund	7 days	Mid-July to Mid-August
9.	Dodital	5 days	March to November
10.	Nag Tibba	8 days	Nov. to March
11.	Chardham	14 days	Alpine Style

Between Hardwar and Rishikesh no less than 17 buses are available in a single day. From here tourists can visit the entire Garhwal Himalaya. For internal transport, city buses, taxies, auto-rickshaws, tongas are easily available at fair rates. The nearest airfield from Rishikesh is Jeolly Grant.

Rishikesh has plenty of hotels, dharamshalas and other accommodation facilities. There are three western type luxury hotels—Hotel Inderlok, Laxman Jhoola and Basera, with 109 rooms and the total bed capacity of 194. Rate charge of these hotels ranges between Rs. 20 to Rs. 40 for single bed room, Rs. 45 to Rs. 75 for simple double bed room and Rs. 50 to Rs. 145 for air-conditioned double bed room. These hotels provide all the possible facilities. Apart from these, there are over 10 Indian type ordinary hotels where rate-charge is comparatively lower. It ranges between Rs. 15 to Rs. 25 for single bed room and Rs. 25 to Rs. 35 for double bed room. A tourist bungalow with 46 rooms and 146 bed capacity is also there managed by G.M.V.N. It's rate charge ranges between Rs. 15 to Rs. 25 for single bed room and Rs. 25 to Rs. 30 for duoble bed room and Rs. 35 to Rs. 40 for four bed room. There are about 30 dharamshalas and some inspection houses of P. W. D., Forest and other departments.

(v) Tourist Trends and Analyses

Rishikesh draws a large number of tourists all through the year but higher percentage of tourists use to come in the months of May and June during summer season or in the months of September and October during post rainy season. Being the gateway of all Himalayan shrines and a place of pilgrimage itself, Rishikesh draws millions of tourits every year. Also being a big centre of 'yoga' learning it draws tourists from all over India as well as other countries who come here to have a lesson in yoga.

Generally Rishikesh also has two popular tourist seasons : (i) Summer cycle-May and June, (ii) Autumn cycle-August to Ist half of November. In the survey it was observed that the second cycle mostly belonged to Bengali tourists.

During survey period 65 tourists interrogated personally. Some of the trends of tourist behaviour are as follows (vide Fig. 5.8) :

Tourism in Garhwal Region

TABLE 5.25
Tourist Arrivals in Rishikesh

Sl. No.	Year	Tourists Arrival (No.)	Variation (%)
1.	1981	2127649	—
2.	1982	2167494	+ 1.9
3.	1983	2201132	+ 1.6
4.	1984	2148476	− 2.4
5.	1985	2374203	+10.5

(a) Profession and Purpose-wise Distribution of Tourists

As far as profession-wise distribution of tourists is concernd the higher percentage was recorded of professions other than Government service, such as-doctors, lawyers, farmers, etc. Their percentage was 35.4. Next category was of businessmen, their percentage was 29.2, third category was of servicemen, having their share of 27.7 percent in total arrivals. Tourists of educational group had very low percentage of 7.7.

TABLE 5.26
Tourists' Professions

Sl. No.	Profession	Actual Number of Tourists	Percentage
1.	Service	18	27.7
2.	Education	5	7.7
3.	Business	19	29.2
4.	Others	23	35.4

Majority of tourists (77%) come to Rishikesh as a part of their pilgrimage. Only 10 percent tourists come here for recreation. A very low percentage of tourists (7.7) visit the place for academic purpose.

(b) Age-Structure of Tourists

The middle-aged tourists were in dominant position in the total arrivals at Rishikesh. Their percentage was 61.5. Tourists over 50 years of age were in the second position with the per-

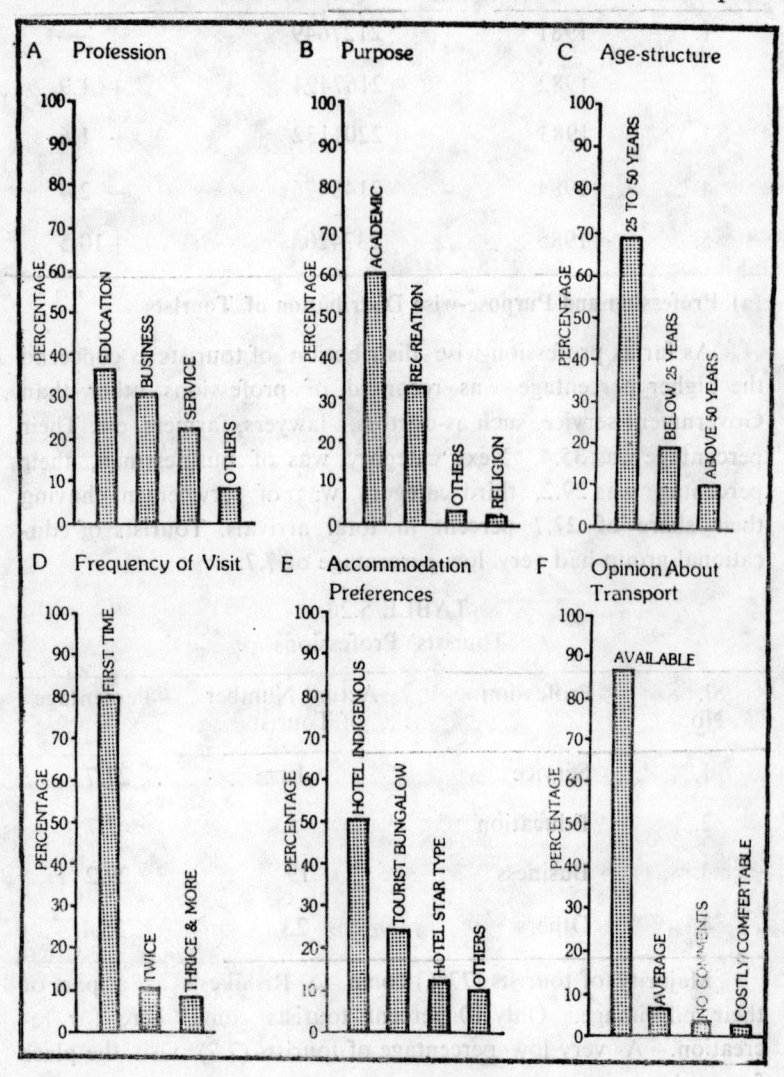

Fig. 5.8 Tourist Trends in Rishikesh

TABLE 5.27
Purpose of Visit

Sl. No.	Purpose	Actual Number of Tourists	Percentage
1.	Recreation	7	10.8
2.	Religion	50	76.9
3.	Academic	5	7.7
4.	Others	3	4.6

centage of 38.8. Only 7.7 percent tourists were below 25 years and mostly they came to give company to the older members of the family as well as for recreation.

TABLE 5.28
Tourists' Age-Group

Sl. No.	Age-Group	Actual Number of Tourists	Percentage
1.	Below 25 years	5	7.7
2.	25 to 50 years	40	61.5
3.	Above 50 years	20	30.8

(c) **Previous Experiences**

When tourists were asked about their previous experiences of this town, if they had any, over 76.9 percent of them admitted

TABLE 5.29
Frequency of Tourist Visit

Sl. No.	Frequency	Actual Number of Tourists	Percentage
1.	For the First time	50	76.9
2.	Twice	12	18.5
3.	Thrice or more	3	4.6

that it was their maiden visit to this town. About 18.5 percent tourists replied that they visited this town once before and it was their second trip of Rishikesh. A fairly low percentage of tourists (4.6) visited this town more than two or three times and they were mostly businesfmen.

(d) Accommodation Preference

In total survey it was noticed that majority of tourists were interested in dharamshalas and other types of accommodation rather than hotels. Their percentage was 61.5. About 18 percent tourists had shown their interest in indigenous type of hotels or tourist bungalows. About 12 percent tourists gave their preference for indigenous type of hotels in the absence of tourist bungalows. Only 7.7 percent tourists of higher income group showed their special attraction for star type luxury hotels as they were comparatively neat and clean and provided all the needed facilities.

TABLE 5.30

Accommodation Preferences

Sl. No.	Type of Accommodation	Actual Number of Tourists	Percentage
1.	Hotel Star Type	5	7.7
2.	Hotel Indigenous Type	12	18.4
3.	Tourist Bungalow	8	12.3
4.	Others	40	61.5

(e) Tourists' Opinion and Comments

Majority of tourists (about 84 percent) were found satisfied with the transport facilities provided at Rishikesh. They regarded it of high standard and exceptionally good. A very low percentage of tourists (9.2) found it of average standard, while other 6 percent of tourists had the idea that it was comparatively expensive. Most of them suggested that the frequency of buses should be improved in order to provide better services to the tourists in peak season. Attention should also be given towards the maintenance of buses.

TABLE 5.31

Tourist Opinion about Transport

Sl. No.	Opinion	Actual Number of Tourists	Percentage
1.	Available	55	84.6
2.	Average	6	9.2
3.	Costly and comfortable	4	6.2

Tourists were almost satisfied with the accommodation facilities available at Rishikesh. They have found it neat, clean and somewhat cheap in comparison to other tourist places. However, a considerable number of tourists complained about the non-availability of desired food stuffs. Although hotels and restaurants were in good number, the quality and variety of cuisine was not much satisfactory. When tourists were asked to express their opinion about the behaviour of local people, a number of them complained about their non-co-operative nature and non-availability of required informations. Tourists were not very happy with the behaviour of Tourist Bureau Staff.

Majority of tourists were full of suggestions for the development of the town and its tourism trade. They suggested that the condition of the roads should be improved. Cheap and good hotels should be constructed by the Government agencies. Guides should be made available at every important place of tourist interest at reasonable charge. Efforts should be made in order to keep all the bathing ghats neat and clean round the clock. At present they are not as they should be. Parking facility also needs some attention.

BADRINATH

(i) Location and History

Badrinath has been the principal seat of religion and pilgrimage since long. The town of Badrinath (32° 44′ N lat. and 79° 30′ E long.) is situated on the confluence of the river Rishi Ganga and Alaknanda at an elevation of 3122 m above the sea level in the northern part of Chamoli district in Garhwal region of Uttar Pradesh. The population of this town is 2576 (1981). The evolution of Badrinath as a pilgrim centre has a long pre-historic and historic records. Once upon a time this sanctified spot was covered with wild berries locally known as 'Badri', which later on gave it the name Badrivan. It is fully exemplified in the text of Skand Purana which is as follows :

अहं कैलास पार्श्वे वे बदरी वन मंडिते ।
देशे वसामि नित्यं वे कण्वगोत्र समुद्भवः ॥
तत्र वे तन्नहाक्षेत्रं बदरीवन संज्ञितम् ।
गंगाद्वारात्पूर्वभागे त्रिशंद्योजनसंमिते ॥

The site is flanked by Nar and Narayan mountain ranges on its both the sides standing like two sentinels over the Badrinath valley, and fully backed by the towering Neelkanth peak.

In Mahabharat time this place attracted Lord Krishna and Arjun who had come here to wash away their sin, to attain 'Moksha' and get beyond the wheel of 'Samsara'. This place also inspired many sages like Gautam, Kapil and Kasyap etc. There are also a number of references to this place and its surroundings in the works of the great Sanskrit poet and dramatist Kalidasa. It entered in its golden era sometime in the last leg of ihe 8th century A. D. when the great thinker, philosopher and social reformer Adi Shankaracharya covering a long way from Kerala to Himalaya established a temple here and rechristened the name Badrinath (Badrinath Puri) from Badrivan. The temple has seen many vicissitudes. It was in 1939 that an act 'Sri Badrinath Temple Act 1939' was passed by the then

Badrinath Temple (Chamoli)

Government of United Provinces. Since then the Badrinath temple is managed and supervised by the head priest (Rawal Sahib) with the help of twelve members.

The temple of Badrinath is dedicated to the Lord Vishnu. To the left of Maha Vishnu are Nar and Narayan performing Dhanurasana and Padmasana respectively. The idol of Uddhava stands in front of the Lord flanked by the silver images of Garuna and Narad. The shrine reflects complete peace and serenity. It is one of the four Dhams (Charodhams), the other three being Rameshwaram, Dwarka and Jagannath Puri. According to Hindu mythology no pilgrimage would be complete unless a pilgrim pays a visit io Badrinath temple. There is a tank of hot water named 'Tapt Kund' just in the front of the Badrinath temple on the bank of Alaknanda river. Mana is last Indian village on China border-4 km north-west from Badrinath. Mana is famous for its tremendous waterfall of Vasudhara and mythological Vyas Gupha. It is an age-old saying that the Vedas were first completed here together by Maharshi Vyas and later on divided into four separate parts with different names. The various *Puranas* were also completed here.

(ii) Transport and Accommodation

Badrinath has somewhat good transport facilities. The town is connected by motorable roads with Rishikesh and Kotdwara. The nearest rail head is Rishikesh (295 km) and Kotdwara (329 km). From there U.P.S.R.T.C. and G.M.O.U.Ltd. buses and private taxies are available up to Badrinath. From Joshimath to Badrinath there is one way traffic. For Badrinath internal transport is not of much significance. However, ponies are available at considerable rates.

According to general survey some 1600 to 1800 tourists/pilgrims visit Badrinath per day. But in the months of May and June this figure goes upto 3000. The total accommodation capacity of the town is for about 2800 to 3000 tourists/pilgrims. As such the town hardly faces any accommodation problem either

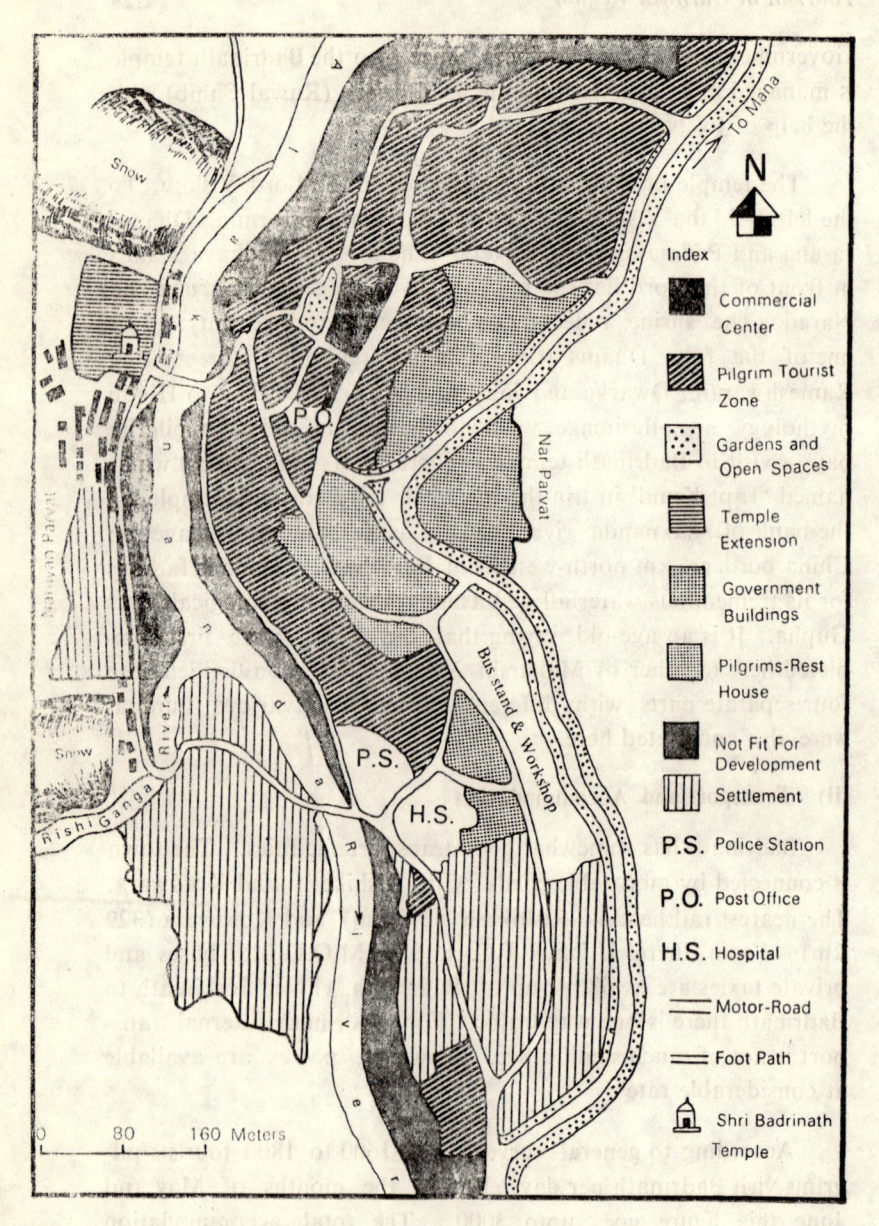

Fig. 5.9 Badrinath Functional Morphology

in general season or in the peak season. There are about 30 dharamshalas, two touist bungalows and two Temple Committee guest houses which provide simple accommodation facilities.

The rate charge of tourist bungalow ranges from Rs. 10 to Rs. 25 for single bed room and Rs. 20 to Rs. 45 for double bed room. For Temple Committee guest house it ranges between Rs. 10 to Rs. 20 for single bed room and Rs. 15 to Rs. 25 for double bed room, for dharamshalas there are either no charges or charges are only nominal.

As for as catering and cuisine facilities are concerned, they are simply average in conformity with the demand of religious tourists.

(ii) Tourist Trends

Although Badrinath is the sanctum sanctorum of Hindus, people of other faith also come here for the fruition of all their earthly desires and for peace of soul and mind. In Badrinath Hindu devotees came from almost all parts of India.

The temple opens in the first week of May and is closed in the first week of November due to severe winter. May and June are the peak seasons, when maximum number of tourists/pilgrims visit this town. The second peak season is from September to October.

For collecting accurate and direct informations the questionnaire was filled in two ways—some were kept at selected hotels, Dak bungalows, tourist bungalows, etc. and some by the individual tourists personally contacted for the in-depth interviews. Every care was taken in the entire process of survey not to disturb the tourists while they were at work. They were contacted only in their leisure time. This helped a lot in the mutual understanding and in clear expressions about the problems. In all 90 tourists were interviewed for understanding the characteristics of all sorts

TABLE 5.32
Tourist Arrivals in Badrinath

Sl. No.	Years	Tourist Arrivals (No.)	Variation in percentage
1.	1979	177616	
2.	1980	234431	+ 31.98
3.	1981	214280	− 8.6
4.	1982	177842	− 17.0
5.	1983	227395	+ 27.9
6.	1984	225200	− 0.9
7.	1985	251867	+ 11.8

Source : Badrinath-Kedarnath Temple Committee Office, Badrinath.

of tourist behaviour. Some of the major aspects of tourism at Badrinath are here analysed (vide Fig. 5.10) :

(a) **Profession of Tourists**

As regards the profession-wise distribution of tourists visiting Badrinath and its environs, the servicemen constituted the highest percentage (54.4). The next category was of businessmen, their share being 33.3 percent. The third category of tourists to this

TABLE 5.33
Professions of Tourists

Sl. No.	Profession	Actual Number of Tourists	Percentage
1.	Service	49	54.4
2.	Business	20	33.3
3.	Education	4	4.4
4.	Others	17	18.9

Tourism in Garhwal Region

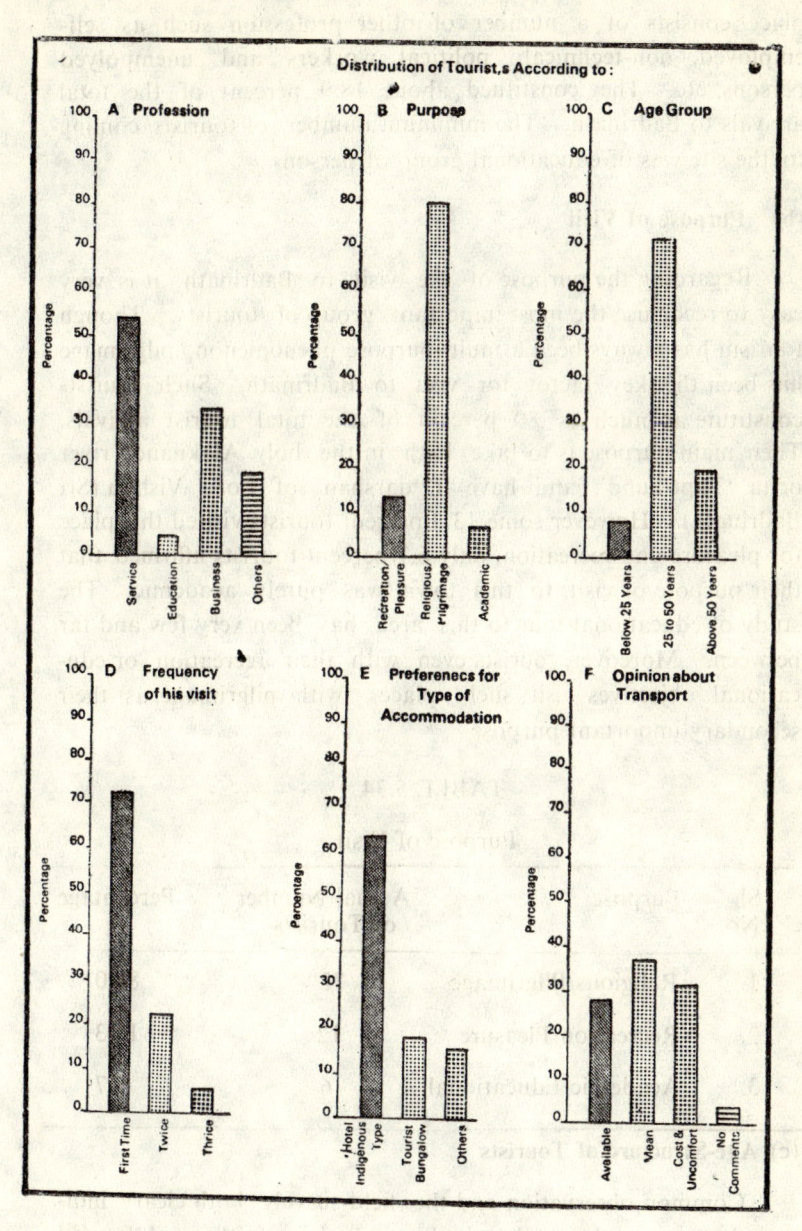

Fig. 5.10

place consists of a number of other profession such as self-employed, non-technical, political workers and unempolyed persons, etc. They constitued about 18.9 percent of the total arrivals to Badrinath. The minimum number of tourists coming to the site was of educational group of persons.

(b) Purpose of Visit

Regarding the purpose of the visit to Badrinath, it is very easy to recognise the most important group of tourists. Though tourism has always been a multi-purpose phenomenon, pilgrimage has been the key factor for visit to Badrinath. Such tourists constitute as much as 80 percent of the total tourist arrivals. Their main purpose is to take bath in the holy Alaknanda river or in 'Tapt-kund', and have a 'darshan' of Lord Vishnu (Sri Badrinath). However some 13.3 percent tourists visited this place for pleasure and recreation, only 6.7 percent tourists affirmed that their purpose of visit to this town was purely academic. The study of educational tour to this area has been very few and far between. Moreover, tourists even with their recreation or educational objectives visit such places with pilgrimage as their secondary important purpose.

TABLE 5.34

Purpose of Visit

Sl. No.	Purpose	Actual Number of Tourists	Percentage
1.	Religious/Pilgrimage	72	80.0
2.	Recreation/Pleasure	12	13.3
3.	Academic/Educational	6	6.7

(c) Age-Structure of Tourists

Common observation and the field-survely both cleary indicate that among the total arrivals to Badrinath, the middle-aged persons in the age-group of 25 to 50 years had dominating position, their percentage being as high as 72.2. They were followed by the persons of the age-group above 50 years. The tourists below 25 years of age were lesser in number. Most of them had to come to Badrinath mainly to render all sorts of support and help to their elders. This group consisted of both males and females.

TABLE 5.35

Distribution of Tourists by Age-Group

Sl. No.	Age-Group	Actual Number of Tourists	Percentage
1.	Below 25 years	7	7.8
2.	25 to 50 years	65	72.2
3.	Above 50 years	18	20.0

(d) Previous Experience

A detailed knowledge was gained about the previous experiences of the visit to this area. About 72 percent tourists paid their visit for the first time. They had no chance to visit this town ever before. More than 20 percent of the tourists indicated that they had come to this region second time. Tourists having visited this Himalayan region thrice or more were very few, constituting only little more than 5 percent of the total arrivals. Only religious tourists felt some sense of attachment with this pious land.

TABLE 5.36

Frequency of Tourist Visit

Sl. No.	Frequency	Actual Number of Tourists	Percentage
1.	For the First Time	65	72.2
2.	Twice	20	22.2
3.	Thrice and more	5	5.6

(e) Tourists' Opinion and Comments

According to the data collected through questionnair and schedule, it was gathered that higher percentage of tourists preferred to indigenouse type of hotels. However, some of them indicated their preference for tourist bungalow first and only in the absence of tourist bungalow they would be going for indigenous type of hotels. About 18 percent of the total arrivals seeking accommodation etc., indicated their choice only in the favour of tourist bungalow. Tourists seeking shelter in various 'dharamshalas' and similar other types of accommodation constituted only 16.7 percent of the total pilgrims.

Some searching questions were also put to them about their comments on the qualitative character of the various types of accommodation. Some 15 percent of the tourists were of the opinion that for the betterment of tourism in the region, accommodation facilities should be further improved. Majority of the tourists did not point to any problem regarding accommodation. They were of the view that the present position of accommodation was more or less satisfactory.

Star-type hotel is non-existant in this area. Actually presently there is no need for the same as such, none of the tourists indicated his choice or even the necessity of such hotels. Regarding the accommodation facilities available at this town, majority of the tourists replied in affirmative. They indicated that facilities were good and not very costly. Moreover some of the tourists

TABLE 5.37
Accommodation Types and Tourist Preferences

Sl. No.	Types of Accommodation	Actual Number of Tourists	Percentge
1.	Hotel-Indigenous Type	58	64.4
2.	Tourist Bungalow	17	18.9
3.	Others	15	16.7

complained about the bad conditions of many dharamshalas. Only very few of dharamshalas such as Birla Dharmshala, Temple Committee guest house, Parmarath Nikatan etc., were in good shape.

Facilities of fooding and catering etc. are not up to the satisfaction of a good number of tourists, mostly they replied in negative.

About transport facilities majority of the tourists expressed that roads and services were of the average standard, which should be improved and U.P.S.R.T.C. buses should be provided for seasonal tourists. A good number of tourists reacted that transport was costly and somewhat uncomfortable. Some of the tourists made no comments about such facilities at all. Majority of the tourists indicated their choice for more cosy and comfortable travel. They suggested that some luxury and A/C buses should also be made available for seasonal tourists and pilgrimage to Badrinath. They opined that the present condition of buses was not very good and that should be improved.

A considerable number of tourists strongly showed their discontentment about the behaviour of the 'Pujari' of Badrinath temple. They affirmed that the Puja system in the temple was very bad. Only money-holders could touch the front of the temple's door. Although it is true that special Puja system is fixed (as

TABLE 5.38

Tourist Opinion about Transport Facilities

Sl. No.	Items	Actual Number of Tourists	Percentage
1.	Available	25	27.8
2.	Average	33	36.7
3.	Costly and uncomfortable	28	31.1
4.	No comments	4	4.4

mentioned in Badrinath Temple Committee Bulletin), yet the system should be made equal to that of Shri Kedarnath Temple. Regarding the suggestions from them about the development of tourism in this town, majority of the tourists felt that good restaurants and hotels should be opened for tourists and pilgrims. Transport facilities should also be improved.

Majority of the tourists expressed overall satisfaction over the assistance and facilities provided in Badrinath. Tourists making complaints about the non-co operative attitude of the official staff were small in number.

KEDARNATH

(i) Evolution of Kedarnath as a Holy Place

The famous Himalayan shrine of Kedarnath is situated on the right bank of the river Mandakini between Badrinath and Gangotri in Chamoli district. The distance between Badrinath and Kedarnath is only 42 km.

Kedarnath is one of the most holy places to Hindus and it occupies a supreme place among Himalayan shrines. The temple of Sri Kedarnath is one of the twelve Jyotirlingas* of Lord Shiva and also one of the famous Panch Kedars. It lies in a cup-shaped valley between lofty peaks of Himalayas.

This temple is dedicated to Lord Sadashiva (the sub-terranean form of Lord Shiva). The form of Shiva which has been worshipped here, is rather peculiar as it is neither an idol nor a Lingam but it is a triangular from of a huge stone symbolising the God.

---

* सौराष्ट्रे सोमनाथं च श्री शैले मल्लिकार्जुनम् ।
उज्जयिन्तां महाकालमोंकारं परमेश्वरम् ।
केदारं हिमवत्पृष्ठे डाकिन्यां श्रीमशंकरम् ।
वाराणस्यां च विश्वेशं त्र्यम्बकं गौतमीतटे ।
वैद्यनाथं चिताभूमौ नागेशं दारुकावने ।
सेतुबंधे च रामेशं घुश्मेशं च शिवालये ॥

Shri Kedarnath Temple

Gorgeous View of Snowy Mountain Near Kedarnath

It is believed that this is the hinder part of the devine buffalo, whose front part is at Kathamndu in Nepal being called there as Pasupswatiara. Four other parts of that buffalo are worshipped at four different places in Garhwal region, namely the arms are at Tungnath—5 km from Chopta on Gopeshwar-Okhimath road; the mouth is at Rudranath—28 km from Mandal on Gopeshwar-Okhimath road via Anusuya Devi Nala; the belly is at Madhyamaheshwar 25 km from Nala near Guptkashi; and hairs are at Kalpeshwar on Joshimath on—Gulab Koti road, 9 km from Helong on foot. These five places are known as 'Panch Kedars' (vide Fig. 3.1). Among these the Shrine of Kedarnath is considered to be most sacred and important. The images of Parvati, five Pandavas with their mother Kunti, Draupadi, Sri Krishna and Ganpati are also carved out on the inside wall of the temple of Shri Kedarnath. On the south of this temple, there is a temple of 'Bhairava', while the Samadhi of Adi Shankracharya, the founder of monism—the Vedanta School of Hindu Philosophy—is on right side behind the temple. From this place a path goes towards north upto Swarg-Rohini (path of heaven). It is said that along with very path Pandavas went for their last journey for self immolation. It is believed that before starting for their last journey, Pandavas performed here a grand 'yagya' and for its proof pilgrims can see here barley grains even at present time.

To further add charms to this Himalayan shrine there are two beautiful lakes at Kedarnath. One lake named 'Choravadi Tal' is about 2 km up from Kedarnath. Right now it is known as Gandhi Sarovar because Mahatma Gandhi's ashes had been immersed here in 1950 (4 Jan.). It also happens to be the river Mandakini's origin place. The other lake is about 8 km away from Kedarnath known as Vasuki Tal. A number of small lakes are also there in and around Kedarnath-Gaurikund (14 km south from Kedarnath last bus station, it is a hot water tank), Rudra Kund, Saraswati Kund, Brahma Kund etc. During winter from November upto April this place remains almost snow-covered. That's why May-June and Sept.-Oct. are the best seasons for Kedarnath. The winter seat of Sri Kedarnath is Okhimath.

The main attractions at Kedarnath are the temple of Sri Kedarnath, holy tanks and 'samadhi' of Shankaracharya. It is an ancient belief that the famous temple of Sri Kedarnath was constructed by five Pandavas for the atonement of their sins after the epic war of Mahabharata. However in modern times, it is believed that this temple was reconstructed by Shankaracharya during the 8th century A. D. In the inner part of this temple a 'Jyoti' has been lighting for hundreds of years known as 'AKHAND JYOTI'. A traditional story is also famous about this Jyoti. It is said that this flame was lighted to mark the occasion of the marriage of Shiva and Parvati, since then it has been lighting continuously. Pilgrims use to smear holy ashes of this Jyoti on their forehead.

Kedarnath attracts thousands of tourists every year. Not only pilgrims but fun-loving tourists too come here to enjoy the devine beauty of mountains and to have a fascinating view of the gigantic Himalayas.

(ii) Transport Accessibility and Accommodation

The nearest rail head Rishikesh is 295 km away from Kedarnath. From Rishikesh tourists have to continue their journey for Kedarnath by bus on road upto Gauri Kund. Efficient bus service and private taxies are available from Rishikesh upto Gauri Kund. From Gauri Kund upto Kedarnath one has to go 14 km on foot (Fig. 5.12 A). Jangal Chatti—3 km from Gauri Kund, is the first stoppage. Tourists use to take their tea/refreshment here. Next stoppage is at a small town of Rambara. Generally pilgrims use this place for their night halt. And in the next morning they start for Kedarnath—8 km from this place. From Kedarnath Vasukital is about 8 km on steep trek route. This lake is of about 1 km radius. The lake filled with the crystal clear water is surrounded by snow covered peaks. From here tourists can enjoy the panoramic view of Chaukhamba peaks.

Accommodation is a great problem at Kedarnath. There are very few dharamshalas and lodges, Traveller's lodge, Temple

TABLE 5.39

Distance and Height Variation from Gaurikund to Kedarnath

Sl. No.	Place	Altitude (m)	Distance on foot (km)
1.	Gauri Kund	1981	—
2.	Jangal Chatti	2010	3
3.	Rambara	2700	6
4.	Kedarnath	3583	14
5.	Vasuki Tal*	4135	20

Committee guest house, Birla guest house. There is a hotel-Himlock, comparatively good, managed by I.T.D.C. Guest houses of P.W.D. and Forest department also provide some accommodations. The rate charge of hotel Himlock ranges from Rs. 25 to Rs. 40 for double bed room and guest house charges range between Rs. 15 to Rs. 20 for a room. Dharamshalas are available either on donation system or at very low charges.

A post office is also there at Kedarnath which provides postal facilities including booking of trunk calls. There are no other facilities available at Kedarnath.

(i ii) **Tourist Trends**

Kedarnath has two popular seasons like other hill stations of U. P. Himalaya and tourists/pilgrims mostly come during these seasons. The Ist season is during May-June while the 2nd season is from August to October.

The temple of Shri Kedarnath opens in the first week of May and closes in the last week of October or Ist week of November every year.

---

* From Kedarnath to Vasukital guide's company is most essential as the route is quite rough and risky. From Gauri Kund to Kedarnath horse, pony, dandy are available.

TABLE 5.40

Tourist Arrivals in Kedarnath

Sl. No.	Year	Tourist Arrivals (No.) Home	Foreign	Total Number Tourists	Variation in percentage
1.	1978	56827	—	56827	—
2.	1979	60839	—	60839	+ 7.1
3.	1980	80588	211	80799	+ 32.8
4.	1981	97070	132	97202	+ 20.3
5.	1982	71875	99	71974	− 25.9
6.	1983	81689	89	81778	+ 13.6
7.	1984	113243	80	113323	+ 38.6
8.	1985	99728	75	99803	− 11.9

Source : Badrinath-Kedarnath Temple Committee Office, Kedarnath.

The table 5.40 reveals that arrivals of foreign tourists have decreased since 1980 while arrivals of home tourists have markedly increased. Maximum number of tourists come in the months of May and June. Tourists from Bengal, Gujrat and Rajasthan use to come during Autumn i.e. in the months of August, September and October.

In order to obtain the detailed informations about distinct features of tourists' characteristics, 92 tourists were interrogated personally, all the informations were gathered either in or around the temple or at their halting places. Kedarnath is basically a religious centre, so all tourism related with it and its surroundings is theocratic in nature.

(a) **Profession of Tourists**

As far as profession-wise distribution of tourists is concerned, the servicemen constituted the major portion of it, their share being over 67 per cent. The next category was of businessmen,

Tourism in Garhwal Region 243

their share being over 19 per cent. The third category was of educational group, mostly teachers and students and thier percentage was about 7. Rest of the tourists were found to be concerned with a number of other professions such as—doctors, lawyers, farmers etc.

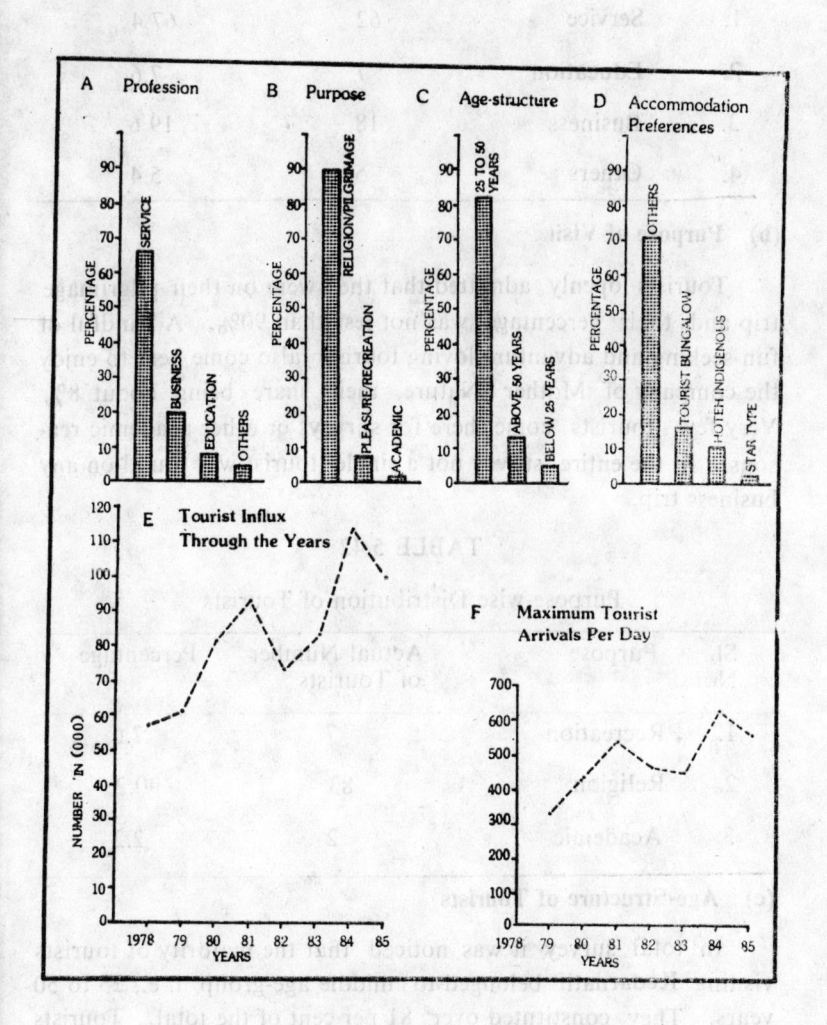

Fig. 5.11 Tourist Trends in Kedarnath

TABLE 5.41

Profession-wise Distribution of Tourists

Sl. No.	Profession	Actual Number of Tourists	Percentage
1.	Service	62	67.4
2.	Education	7	7.6
3.	Business	18	19.6
4.	Others	5	5.4

(b) Purpose of Visit

Tourists openly admitted that they were on their pilgrimage trip and their percentage was not less than 90%. A handful of fun-seeking and adventure-loving tourists also come here to enjoy the company of Mother Nature, their share being about 8%. Very few tourists come here for surveys or other academic reasons. In the entire survey not a single tourist was found on any business trip.

TABLE 5.42

Purpose-wise Distribution of Tourists

Sl. No.	Purpose	Actual Number of Tourists	Percentage
1.	Recreation	7	7.6
2.	Religion	83	90.2
3.	Academic	2	2.2

(c) Age-Structure of Tourists

In total survey it was noticed that the majority of tourists visiting Kedarnath belonged to middle age-group i. e., 25 to 50 years. They constituted over 81 per cent of the total. Tourists above 50 years of age were in the second position, their percentage was over 13. Very low percentage of tourists were below 25 years of age.

TABLE 5.43

Age-Structure of Tourists

Sl. No.	Age-Group	Actual Number of Tourists	Percentage
1.	Below 25 years	5	5.4
2.	25 to 50 years	75	81.5
3.	Above 50 years	12	13.1

This is quite natural in all religious tourism. Somewhat risky and strenuous journey and severe weather conditions come in the way. Only men and women with religious fervour dare take up such hazarduous journey.

(d) **Previous Experience**

Having been asked out their previous experience of this place, over 69 per cent tourists admitted that it was their first visit to Kedaenath. About 25 per cent tourists replied that they visited this town once before, while only 5.4 per cent tourists visited the place more than twice. When these tourists were asked about the reason behind their several visits of Kedarnath, they admitted that the holy temple of Sri Kedarnath attracted them again and again. They wanted to get 'Moksha' after doing 'Tirtha Yatra.'

TABLE 5.44

Frequency of Visit

Sl. No.	Freqeuncy	Actual Number of Tourists	Percentage
1.	For the first time	64	69.6
2.	Twice	23	25.0
3.	Thrice or more	5	5.4

(e) Accommodation Preference

In total survey it has been observed that the greater number of tourists preferred to stay at dharamshalas or lodges. Their percentage was 70.7. About 16 per cent tourists have shown their special likeness for tourist bungalows. Hotels of any types are not available at Kedarnath.

TABLE 5.45

Preference for Accommodation Types

Sl. No.	Type of Accommodation	Actual Number of Tourists	Percentage
1.	Hotel Star Type	2	2.3
2.	Hotel Indigenous	10	10.8
3.	Tourist Bungalow	15	16.3
4.	Other types	65	70.7

As it has been said earlier that accommodation facilities are not sufficient at Kedarnath so majority of tourists do not like to stay here, they rather want to return the same day. Most of them like to stay at Rambara instead of Kedarnath. Although there are no star type or indigenous type hotels at Rambara, yet there are many dharamshalas, B. K. T. C. guest house and G. M. V. N. travellers' lodge.

(f) Tourists' Opinion and Comments

Majority of tourists visiting Kedarnath did not make any complaint about accommodation, transport or food available at Kedarnath although there were many problems such as troublesome journey of 14 km on foot through trek route and lack of good accommodation facilities etc. Tourist can travel on horse or 'palki.' When tourists were asked for their opinion about local people and dharamshalas etc. majority of them came with positive statements. Few tourists, however, have complained against the non-co-operative attitude of local people and the members of the temple committee or priests of the temple.

Pilgrims and tourists gave many suggestions about the development of the town. Majority of pilgrims expressed that trek route between Gauri Kund to Kedarnath sould be improved. They also said that Government accommodation facilities should be made available at Gauri Kund as well as at Kedarnath. Apart from these first-aid facilities including O_2 bottles should be made available at every 5 km between Gauri Kund to Kedarnath. A large number of tourists have the opinion that if it is possible, the Government should make every effort of developing ropeway system for Kedarnath as well as between four Himalayan shrines i. e. Gangotri, Yamunotri, Badrinath and Kedarnath.

Local people felt the need of developing 'MANDNI'—a beautiful valley near Kedarnath as on additional recreational spot.

OTHER PILGRIMAGE RECREATIONAL AREAS

Apart from the places of tourists' interest and holy shrines of Badrinath and Kedarnath described above, Garhwal has much more to offer. The valleys, slopes and ridges of the Himalaya are every where dotted with innumerable shrines, caves and natural scenic spots bringing the mountains close to the soul hungering for beauty and peace, and questioning for Spirit Infinite. Some of them considered to be important both from religious and scenic point of view are taken here for discussion :
(i) **Gangotri**

Gangotri is situated (30°58'10"N Lat. and 78°54'30"E Long.) at an elevation of 3140 m from mean sea level, on the right bank of the river Bhagirathi in Uttar Kashi district.

Himalayan Environment and Tourism

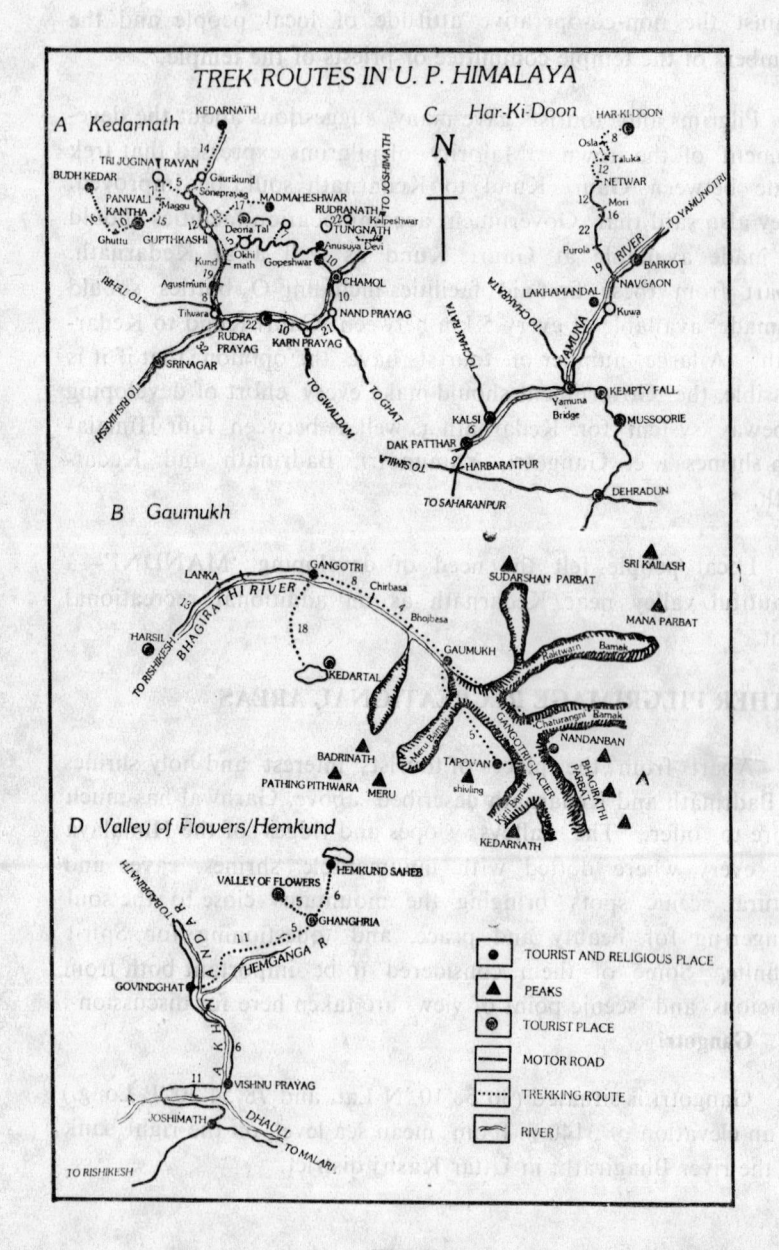

Fig. 5.12

There is a temple dedicated to the Goddess Ganga at Gangotri.* Exactly near this temple there is a sacred stone. It is said that Raja Bhagirath used to worship Lord Shiva at this place and it was here that Ganga came down from heaven to the earth first time. It is believed that near Shri Kanth Parvat Bhagirath had been doing all his efforts for 5500 years to bring down Ganga from heaven. Later on after the great war of Mahabharta, Pandavas came here and performed the grand 'Deva Yagya' to atone the death of their Kinsmen. Says the Mahabharata "To repeat her name brings purity, to see her secures prosperity, to bathe in or drink her waters saves seven generations of our race......There is no place of pilgrimage like the Ganga."

Gangotri is a very small village. A handful of Pandas, shopkeepers, Yogis and Sanayasis stay there. The entire village is full of giant deodar and other coniferous trees. The temple of Goddess Ganga was constructed by the Gorkha Commander Amar Singh Thapa (1803-1814) when Garhwal was under the Gorkha rule. But this temple was destroyed due to glacial activities. So later on, it was reconstructed by the Maharaja of Jaipur. Gangotri albeit a small place has the rare distinction of being an improtant religious centre since long. The temple remains open from May to October, during the rest of the period Gangotri is covered with snow.

Transport, Accessibility and Accommodation

Gangotri is not an easily accessible place as the last railway station is Rishikesh (250 km) from Gangotri. From Rishikesh G.M.O.U.Ltd. and T.G.M.O.U. Ltd. buses and private taxies are available upto Uttarkashi. After the construction of a bridge over the river Jadh recently, tourists can easily reach Gangotri

---

*The Bhagirathi—a huge and forceful river—gushing out of the glacier flows for a while in a northwardly direction and hence the place is called Gangotri (Ganga turned North). In common sense the place is taken to mean the descending point of Ganga.

from Uttar Kashi by Bus or Jeep. Apart from these external transport facilities, Gangotri does not have any internal transport facilities and tourists have to move on foot only.

Though accommodation is not a problem at Gangotri, it does not have good accommodation. In all there are three tourist bungalows of which two with capacity of 50 and 8 bed respectively are managed by Tourism Development Corporation. Another one with capacity of 48 beds is managed by Regional Development Corporation. Besides these accommodations there are many dharamshalas managed by a number of Ashrams. Some Sadhu and Pandas also give shelter to the tourists on simple charges. There are only one hotel and two simple restaurants. Food and other things are very expensive. So government should make effort to provide good hotels and restaurants for tourists.

In total survey exactly one hundred tourists were interrogated of which 92 tourists came simply for religious purpose. About 7 enthusiastic tourists were on their way of expedition to Tapovan, Nandanvan etc. Only one tourist confessed that he was there only to enjoy the natural beauty of glorious mountains. About 18 tourists expressed their wish to have a look at Gaumukh.*

(ii) **Yamunotri**

Yamunotri is an important pilgrim centre in U. P. Himalaya along with Kedarnath, Badrinath and Gangotri. The location of Yamunotri is in the western part of the great peak of Bander

---

*Gaumukh (4255 m) is only 18 km away from Gangotri and this distance has to be covered on foot. The Gaumukh glacier which lies at an altitude of 4138.6 m starting beyond Chaukhamba cluster of snow peaks, in the neighbour-hood of Badrinath, extends as far as Gaumukh. Only hardy pilgrims visit Gaumukh. There is not any clear path leading to Gaumukh and people have to find their way with the assistance of stones arranged on boulders. Accommodation is available at Bhojbasa-14 km away from Gangotri. In Gaumukh there are no accommodations or shops.

The Temple of Gangaji at Gangotri

punch (6315 m) which has the rare distinction of being snow-covered round the year.

It is said that Rishi Asti had his hermitage here and all through his life he bathed both in Ganga and Yamuna. During old age when Rishi became unable to go to Gangotri a small stream of Ganga emerged from the rocks before him at Yamunotri. At this place there is a temple at an altitude of 3322 m dedicated the Goddess Yamuna. Around this temple there are many hot water springs, where water gushes out of the mountain cavities at boiling point forming pools. Surya Kund is most significant among all these pools. Pilgrims and tourists used to dip a handful of rice or potatoes tied loosely in a piece of cloth in the hot water of this pool and take this packed rice with them back home as 'Prasad.'

A rock, named 'Divya Shila,' is there near Surya-Kund which is worshipped before entering the main temple of Yamunotri. The location of this place is in Utter Kashi district at an altitude of 4421 m from the mean sea level. The temple of Goddess Yamuna was constructed by Sudarshan Shah in 1839.

Transport and Accommodation

Rishikesh is the nearest rail head from Yamunotri and connected with some important towns of India. From Rishikesh tourists have to go by bus or private taxi up to Hanuman Chatti (3040 m above sea level) which happens to be the last bus terminus. From here upto Yamunotri there is 13 km trek route. Jankibai Chatti-another place worth visting is 6 km away from Hanuman Chatti. Here too are many sulphur springs. It is about 7 km away from Yamunotri.

Required accommodation facilities are available at every place. At Janakibai there are Chatti, travellers' lodge and P.W.D. Inspection Honses, while at Yamunotri there is a Forest Rest House and many dharamshalas. At Yamunotri tourists have to face catering problem immensely and it is essential to open good restaurants for pilgrims there.

(iii) Hemkund Lokpal

Hemkund Lokpal 'Where the Guru sought his Creater' is an important pilgrim centre of Sikhs and it is known as their "sanctum sanctorum".

The location of this place is in Chamoli district at an altitude of 4633 m above sea level and it is 20 km away from Govind Ghat.

According to Guru Granth Sahib the last Sikh Guru Govind Singh had come here to meditate and seek peace for his tortured soul. Millenia before, Rishi Medhasa of Durga Sapta Shati to Markandeya Purana had come here for penance and King Pandu of Hastinapur had also come here to practise Yoga.

In 1930 Havaldar Sohan Singh discovered this lake first time and identified that this very lake had been referred to in Guru Granth Sahib.

This lake is surrounded by seven snow-covered peaks with green velvety grass. It's water is crystal clear and very sweet in taste. A Gurudwara (Hemkund Sahib) is situated by the lake side and it draws not only Sikh pilgrims but other pilgrims also from all over India.

(iv) Valley of Flowers

(a) Evoluation and Characteristics of 'Nature Garden'

The world famous Valley of Flowers* is nature's rock garden situated in the upper reaches of Bhyunder Ganga in the far interior of Garhwal Himalaya in Chamoli district (30°7'N lat. and 79°7'E long.). Its maximum height above the mean sea level is 3650 m with an area covering about 8750 hectares.

---

*The famed Valley of Flowers has been lately listed as 'Pushpavati Biosphere Reserve.'

This park is 312 km from Rishikesh rail head on Hardwar-Badrinath highway. The distance from Rishikesh to Badrinath can be overcome by bus or taxi, from there upto the 'Valley of Flowers' is a 19 km trek (vide Fig. 5.12 D). After crossing the suspension bridge over the Alakhnanda river at Govindghat, a zig-zag bridle path along Bhyunder Ganga leads to Ghagharia. It is the last station for tourists because from there the 'Valley of Flowers' is only 4 km with no accommodation and tea stall whatsoever.

This valley was discovered by F. S. Smythe in 1931, when he was returning from his successful expedition of Mt. Kamet. The valley is full of wild flowers of which at least 1000 varieties were recognised. Smythe collected some 250 varieties of flowers with the help of the famous English botanist, R. L. Holdsworth. The beauty and the serine atmosphere attracted Smythe so much so that he writes "a peacefulness so perfect that something within me seems to strain upward as though to catch the notes of an immortal harmony...some presence, some all prevading beauty separated from me only to be my own 'muddy vesture of decay' (Smythe, F. S., 1932, p. 287).

During monsoon period (starting from mid-June) the entire valley becomes one of the nature's finest garden, when countless flowers bloom in succession. Many a flowers are so ephemeral that their fragrance and sweetness can be perceived only by the mountain itself, people can only imagine about them. Some of the important flowers that are found in this valley are—primulas, pink, androsaces, saxi frages, yellow potentiallas, snow white anemores, golden lily like nomochairs, blue corydalis, wild roses and many other flowering shrubs. The best season to pay visits to this valley is from mid-July to mid of August (depending on monsoon), when the flowers of this valley are in full of pagentry. The valley remains in bloom for a little more than three months while the floral composition keeps changing every few days. By mid October the hue starts changing and the autumn bids farewell to flowers in the valley and the entire vegetation remains dormant for about next six months. The smiling Valley of Flowers which some time before had presented a beautiful rock garden, now becomes quite barren and snow-bound.

(b) Tourist Trends

In all 120 tourists were interviewed for understanding the characteristics of all sorts of tourists' behaviour. The salient aspects are here analysed :

1. Profession of Tourists

As regards the profession-wise distribution of tourists visiting the Valley of Flowers, the servicemen constituted the highest percentage (49.1). The next category was of educational group, its share being 20 per cent. The third category of tourists of this place consists of a number other professions such as—doctors, non-technical, political workers and unemployed persons etc. They constituted about 18.4 percent of the total arrivals of the Valley of Flowers. The minimum number of tourists (12.5%) coming to the site was of businessmen.

2. Purpose of Visit and Age-Structure of tourists

Regarding the purpose of the visits to the Valley of Flowers, it is very easy to recognise that recreation/pleasure was the key factor. Such tourists constitute as much as 95 per cent of the total tourist arrivals whose main purpose was recreation or pleasure. Only 4 per cent tourists affirmed that their purpose of visit to this peak was academic. Common observations and the field survey both clearly indicate that more than 97 percent tourists were in the age-group of 25 to 50 years.

3. Tourists' Opinion and Comments

A considerable number of tourists opined that tea stalls with O_2 bottle should be made available on every 4 or 5 km between Govindghat to Valley of Flowers. Majority of tourists also suggested some luxury and A/C buses should also be made available for tourists from Rishikesh to Govindghat. This park was closed between 1982-83 for tourists due to excessive grazing and biotic pressure. In 1983 the park was constituted into a National Park and now tourists have to seek permission before entering this park. A number of tourists were interrogated for knowing their opinion about this restriction. However, majority of them expressed that as the process of taking permission is very easy, the question of making complaints does not arise.

The Valley of Flowers as a centre of recreation and researches needs a remodelling of the trek route. Tea stalls on every 4 km and some more accommodation facilities between Govindghat and the Valley of Flowers are needed for better accessibility to the site.

6

Impact of Tourism, Its Problems and Planning

TOURISM AS A MULTI-DIMENSIONAL PROCESS OF DEVELOPMENT AND CHANGE

Tourism has become one of the most important phenomena of man's spatial behaviour in modern time. Increasing pleasure travel tends to beget a number of changes in human life every where in the world. Tourists bring money and ideas with them which further cause numerous changes in every sphere of life. Economic transformation through tourism has now normally been accepted by all and accordingly tourism has been recognised as an industry. It increases employment and income potential in almost every sector of economy at national, regional and local level. The impact of tourism in international development and trade has also been fully accepted. However, money-making is not and has never been the better part of tourism. The social and cultural aspects of tourism, though less perceptible has more far-reaching consequences than economic and others. The perception of social change is intimately related to human values. Socio-cultural transformation through tourism is rather gradual and its real evaluation involves a considerable span of time.

For a country like ours endowed both with huge natural wealth and human resource, tourism has a special significance for it can help largely in the economic development particularly of backward areas. The significance of tourism as a foreign exchange earner has become all the more important in the context of the country's trade deficit. It brings in a number of other benefits too like international understanding and co-operation. In the case of India with its size and diversity tourism may generate a sound and healthy feeling of national integration. The ecological and environmental changes that may be brought by increasing tourist phenomenon needs to be taken in the right perspective from the very beginning. Thus tourism works in a number of ways and its impact are numerous and varied. Here an attempt has been made to analyse the multifaceted impacts of tourism by putting them into three distinct groups :

(i) Economic impact,

(ii) Socio-cultural interaction, and

(iii) Ecological-environmental changes.

(i) Economic Impact

Recreational travel induces growth on three levels-national, regional and local, but the quantam of this growth will be different from level to level. These include increases in employment and income in several sectors of economy, development of infrastructure and a number of industries which are only due to tourism. Thus tourism may pave the way for total development of the region which could not be developed otherwise. Such benefits of tourism may sometimes be offset by various operational costs and socio-cultural problems. However, the growth generated will compensate more than loss in the long run.

There has been a progressive rise in the number of tourists comming to the Hill Region of Uttar Pradesh for the last few years and the increase in tourist activities has definitely an impact on the economy of the region. However, relevant data for analysing this aspect at this stage are not available. As such mention about such activities would be made mainly in general terms.

(a) Tourism Related Industries and Employment Potential

Tourism as an industry has peculiar features, apart from its job generating capacity. It is not a single industry but a loose confederation of a number of other industries. Tourism is a smokeless industry. It is not mainly agriculturally or industrially productive activity, it is usually classsfied in the tertiary sector, which is in the main a service sector (Wahab Abdul, S. E. 1971, p. 23). It has been commented that tourism does not produce goods but services. But at the same time goods sometimes shade off into services and 'services' into 'goods' and the time between them may be hard to find. To some, it is a market and to other an industry, geographers name it a 'landscape industry (Singh, T. V., 1982, p. xiv), because the products of tourism are made of natural beauty, dramatic landscape and cultural heritage etc. The development of various segments of tourist industry depends upon the importance and popularity of tourist places. Popular tourist places attract comparatively more tourists and a number of industries and crafts naturally, develop at those places to produce goods and services to suit to the tourists' interest, for example, the world-famed Taj Mahal in Agra attracts a vast number of tourists and miniature model of marble Taj is in great demand, as such marble related industries have developed in considerable number in and around Agra.

In 1984 the Government of Uttar Pradesh declared tourism as an industry in order to give tourism a special boost by making a number of concessions for its growth. The nature of tourist industry manifests itself in a number of related trades such as transport, accommodation, entertainment, souvenir and shopping etc. The origin, growth and the development of sub-sectors depend upon the stage and status of tourism development in the region. The number of tourist arrivals is directly related to the development of various components of this industry.

Transport as it has already been said is the life line of tourist movement in any region. Various types of circulatory systems are required according to the terrain of the region, rail, roads of various types, trek route, rope-ways all require a huge labour force for their construction and up-keep. As tourism has stepped in the hill region only just recently, road carving, cutting and building, rock-blasting and site-clearing activities are in their full gear and they give employment to thousands of labourers both skilled and unskilled, who would have otherwise been unemployed and ready to flee the region in search of jobs. Thus road-construction itself is responsible for employing persons and checking labour migration.

Provision of better and comfortable accommodations is considered to be the main thrust of modern tourism industry. Rather it is the heart core of present-day tourism. A brief discussion of various types of accommodations available at selected places of U. P. Himalaya will definitely show the employment potential of this sector. Mainly four types of accommodations are available in Himalayan towns : 1. Classified hotels (star type), 2. Hotels indigenous, 3. Tourist bungalows and other stateowned establishments, 4. Other types specially tent houses and dharamshalas etc.

In the category of classified hotels normally we include star type hotels and hotels of western style. In a rough estimate there are nearly 70 to 80 such hotels with a total of 2000 bed capacity. Such hotels are located mainly in Nainital, Mussoorie, Dehra Dun, Almora and Ranikhet. Because of comparatively high rate charges these hotels serve mainly either foreign tourists or elite class domestic tourists of India. In field survey it was observed that the average number of persons employed in each such hotel ranged from fifteen to twenty. However, the employees herein are mostly seasonal and average paid.

Indigenous types of hotels are mostly used by domestic tourists. These hotels are of mixed type, some are good and even excellent but majority of them are in bad shape. Hardly they provide all necessary facilities, neither they have good staff nor maintenance. Their employment potential too is very weak. Employees are comparatively low paid. Having sprung up in response to local economic needs of the region, they have no tourist-service out-look and suffer from commercial overtones which often hurts tourism industry.

In U. P. Himalaya there are some good establishments in Nainital, Mussoorie, Dehra Dun and Ranikhet etc. Here many hotels are suitable for medium class of international tourists. These hotels adequately make up by introducing 'Indian atmosphere' which international tourists often seek.

The third category of accommodations consists of various types of Government houses, i.e. tourist bungalows, circuit house, inspection house, dak bungalows and guest houses of different departments. Barring tourist bungalows, accommodation capacity of these establishments is somewhat limited. They are mostly used by Government officials, as they are not very popular as tourists lodges. The persons employed here are Government servants, hence the employees are regular and comparatively better paid.

As regards the other categories of accommodations, dharamshalas predominate in religious/pilgrimage zone of Himalaya. Hardwar, Rishikesh, Badrinath Kedarnath, Gangotri, Yamunotri and many other centres of pilgrimage have a number of dharamshalas of various categories. Some of them provide most of basic facilities on meagre and nominal charges. Some dharamshalas provide free fooding and lodging such as Baba Kamli Wala's dharamshalas, Parmarath Niketan etc. Lal Bihari Baba Ka Ashram is the unique establishment on Gangotri-Gaumukh route, it provides free food and accommodation for all types of tourists-pilgrims, saints and expeditionists. It has been doing it for the last twenty years or so. As these dharamshalas are erected mostly with religious and philonthropic zeal, their motive is not income raising. As such their labour employment potential is also very weak.

Souvenir industry is the special category of industries developed and catered at tourist places to provide goods and items of tourist interest. It includes those articles and goods which are very typical and somewhat specialised for the region. These items are in great demand by the tourists and pilgrims comming from out side. Normally tourists in the hill region of Uttar Pradesh spend 15 to 20 per cent of the total expenditure on shopping. As regards shopping pattern, only those items are in demand which help to retain the memorable visit of the particular tourist spots. Such items are kept as show pieces by tourist after their return.

The U. P. Himalaya as our country as a whole has a rich potential in her wonderful and fascinating hand-made goods. All tourists domestic or foreigner buy not only artistic creations but carry with them a symbol of Himalayan culture and tradition. The handicrafts of U. P. Himalaya have a special significance in this regard and very much bare the stamp of tourism geography. Many of the items are the direct products of peculiar Himalayan environment. Different types of grasses, bamboo, wood, stones provide sufficient raw materials for a number of fashionable items. Artistic candles of different shape, size and colour produced at Nainital ; various types of wooden goods like walking stick, wooden cases for keys and mirrors, wooden model of Taj Mahal, lakes boats and bamboo basket at Hardwar ; fancy carpet and woollen cloths and caps produced at Nainital, Mussoorie and Dehra Dun ; copper ware in Almora and Kimkhob at some places of Garhwal region are some of the items earnestly demanded by the pilgrims and tourists. Some tribal dresses and costumes have great appeal for the feminine heart. It is often observed about a tourist in Kumaun that before packing he hurriedly purchases a shawl for his wife, an Almora tweed for himself, a pair of skates for his kids, a few decoration pieces made of pine cones for his drawing room and handful of picture postcard for his friends. Thus he goes back with a belief that he has seen, known and enjoyed enough of Himalaya.

TABLE 6.1

Tourist Expenditure Pattern

	Items	Expenditure (in per cent)
1.	Hotel and catering	45.0
2.	Internal transport	25.0
3.	Shopping	15.0
4.	Entertainments	7.5
5.	Miscellaneous	7.5

Thus we can conclude that tourism industry proves to be a somewhat labour intensive activity which consumes various type of labour force in different capacities and in turn supplies commodities in the form of goods and services to the tourists. A large number of seasonal workers become able to seek employments in towns of the hill region in providing various types of services to the tourists/pilgrims. Such people normally belong to the interior part of the hills and are mostly semi-skilled. On account of a number of constraints on agricultural activities these people are always in search of jobs to earn their livelihood. As such they become easily available to render such services as masons, carpenters, porters, rickshaw pullars, hotel guides, waiters, tourist guides, jobs in conducted tours, boatmen, pony owners, dandi carriers etc. If such job opportunities are made available even in smaller and subsidiary tourist resorts in the interior parts of Himalaya, these can well sustain the hill economy to a large extent.

(b) Income Aspects and Multiplier Effect

Tourism is a big source of income, which comes in many ways. On a large scale, tourism circulates existing wealth among social groups and geographic regions. Like a primary activity such as mining or agriculture or secondary activity such as manufacturing, tourism does not create truly new wealth. This effect is most clearly seen in the transfer of money from one region to another as tourists travel. However, to make any evaluation of the wealth that tourism adds to the economy, it becomes necessary to estimate the number and expenditure of all tourists. Their expenditures are normally expressed in terms of various sectors of tourism industry regarding accommodation, cuisine, transportation and entertainments etc. The money spent by the tourists goes to the local business in number of ways. This money in turn is spent on salaries and on meeting the demands of the tourists such as food, drink, entertainment etc. Each time a tourist makes an expenditure, a ripple of additional spending is sent through the economy. This ripple is called a multiplier (Smith Stephen, 1983, p. 171). The multiplier describes the additional spending or job creation caused by a given level of tourist spending. In other words expenditure incurred by the tousists supports not only the tourist industry directly but indirectly also supports a number of other activities which produce goods and services for the tourist industry. In this way money spent by tourists may be said to be used several times and spread into various sectors of economy. As many times the money changes hands it provides new income. This short of impact is called 'the multiplier effects' by the economists (Robinson, H., 1976, p. 126). However, the multiplier effect is some times reduced to a considerable extent because of various sorts of leakages in the form of import of foreign goods, interest on foreign investments etc.

Such income is of special significance in a marginal area such as hill region of Uttar Pradesh which is relatively isolated, economically underdeveloped and have an acute unemployment problem. This income mechanism may help to redress the economic imbalance in the region. Through the income realised from tourism a series of new resorts may be developed to bring prosperity to this region which has traditionally been under-developed. The real estimate of tourism multiplier is a difficult task. A number of authors have worked out various methods to deduce the multiplier effect of tourism in different regions. But their results quite vary. In an U. S. Govt. survey report the multiplier effect of money spent by tourists has been said to be ranging between 3.2 to 4.4 times, depending upon leakage. Peters comments that even for those economy where there is a high import and leakage contents, it is hard to visualise a multiplier of less than 2 (Peters, M., 1969, p. 241). However, any method to quantify the multiplier effect should use reliable and refined data and a normally accepted theoretical basis. For an effective multiplier effect in the hill region indigenous market should be fully developed.

(c) Infrastructure and Regional Development

Tourism is one of the best course to initiate and generate infrastructural development and improvement. This development is the primary component for the beginning of tourism in any region. The construction and psovision of road, rail lines airports, electricity and gas supplies, sanitation, water supply and a number of many other things are undertaken to attract and facilitate tourists from outside. These changes also benefit the residents of the region itself by providing them amenities which till now they had not enjoyed. Besides, the development of infrastructure prepares the basis for diversification of other economic activities. Taking the help of these external economy, varieties of industries may be established which may not be directly linked with tourism. Thus the expenditure of tourists directly or indirectly is a stimulating force to give birth to a number of other economic activities.

So far as our study region is concerned, tourism decidedly opened a new vista for the total development of the region. With the beginning of tourism in the modern sense this hill region has been totally exposed to outside world. All sorts of means of transport and communication, facilities for drinking water, electricity generation are being developed at a large scale. If these expansions are large enough, economy of scale may be possible. Thus the road network, a power plant or an industry may be built or set up at a lower cost per unit than would have been possible without tourism.

Thus the regional development is a natural corollary of the development of tourism in the region. In a number of studies tourism has been regarded as a process, as via media to initiate development in many regions otherwise backward. Tourism is not only a source of earning money and foreign exchange but it also plays a key role in the establishment of a number of industries having potentials for development of a region.

With the advent of tourism, the hill region of Uttar Pradesh has come into the main focus and now there is a serious thinking for its planned regional development. As such besides tourism a number of environmentally suitable economic activities such as small-scale industries, horticulture, roads, rope ways and means of communication and hydel plants etc. are being developed at an accelerated pace. A number of Hill Industrial Estates have been established at various places to promote resource-based and demand-based small industries in the region. These would certainly provide some employment avenues for hill people and thus would help in checking their migration to the plains.

(ii) **Socio-Cultural Interaction**

Tourism impacts as mentioned are broadly defined into three categories—economic, social and environmental/physical. Generally economic impact is regarded as positive, it broadens and diversifies the economic base, increase income and provides employment etc. as stated above. But however, social or environmental impacts are not always positive, instead they become even negative. It is in this respect that tourism has become somewhat controversial among a number of social scientists. If some social scientists see good future in tourism and consider it as an omnibus for international understanding, brotherhood and co-operation ; contrary to it, for some tourism only favours a very small mostly non autochthon group, leading to neo-colonialism, xenophobia, demonstration, acculturations effect (Singh, T. V. et. al., 1982 ; p. xvi).

Tourists not only bring money to a region, they may also bring a strong visible life-style with them. Their dress and address, food habits and merry making manners—all bring some newness and uniqueness in the region of their travel. Their lifestyles sometimes give pleasure to the residents of the locality and tempt them to adopt the same life style. But sometimes it causes cultural shock which may prove an antithesis to the very spirit of tourism.

Tourists visiting countries especially of backward economy leave behind them a life style and spending pattern which have many demonstrative effects. The residents of host countries are tempted to follow the same pattern without giving much thought to it. It normally yields to negative results. Numesous cases of social hybridization can be seen at almost all the places of tourist attractions. A new generation is being emerged out of this process. Jafari (1974 : The Socio-Economic Costs of Tourism to Developing Countries) has called such social hybrid as marginal man. Marginal man is a resident of host country who has accepted the values and life style of tourists and tries to achieve them. He is caught between the two cultures and lies on their interface. A number of vices like prostitution, gambling, drinking, smoking, drug addicting and juvenile deliquency may be attributed to foreign tourists. The pouring in of a number of tourists from foreign countries specially the harbingers of new culture 'Hippies' have very seriour impact on social life—in Varanasi, Puskar (Rajasthan) and in Hardwar, Rishikesh, Dehra Dun etc. The traditionally religious atmosphere of these regions is being distributed by such encroachments. The tremendous influx

Impact of Tourism

of visitors during the summer season result in overcrowding, traffic congestion, noise and inflated prices of goods and services specially in Nainital, Dehra Dun and Mussoorie.

Relationships among social groups also change as a result of tourism development. Tourism may generate cultural awakening, sometimes it becomes a psychological case for social tension. Thus, and in many other ways tourism acts and interacts with established cultural setting and brings changes both positive and negative. Foreign tourism has badly disturbed the culture, manner and behaviour pattern of workers engaged in a number of informal sectors of our economy. We observe empirically a number of changes in behaviour of men engaged in service sectors also. In Varanasi normally rickshaw pullers, tonga-walas, boatmen, dealers in beads and 'malas' and other businessmen take full advantage of the strangers leaving aside all the norms of Indian culture. In hill areas specially in Nainital and Mussoorie all the men or workers engaged directly or indirectly in different sectors of tourism activities take full advantage of tourists comming from outside. Gradually and gradually they are leaving aside the simplicity and humility of their behaviour—a unique feature of hill people. Modern tourism has made them cunning and clever.

Tourism brings a number of positive cultural and social changes too. Culture consciousness, cultural re-awakening, cultural-social rennovation and preservation are good symptoms of modern tourism. It has resulted in the restoration of architectural monuments, buildings and preservation of important landscape. Without tourists these may have been allowed to slowly decay without notice. U. P. Himalaya is the best example of this cultural process. Here every pilgrimage centre, scenic spot and historical, religious-cultural centre is being remodelled and refashioned to give them a newer and fresher look. So that they may attract large number of tourists. Cultural rennovation increased tourism and economic growth generation has now become a cyclic process for most of the regions. Hill people have become fully conscious of this culture and they are preserving it to harvest money and thereby push their economy far ahead.

Further, in order to develop tourism and attract tourists from outside the culture of the land is often commercialised. Religious beliefs, traditional dress, secular celebration and other mores of life are reduced to tourist communities in the search for a marketable tourist product. It ultimately results in the loss of self-respect among the residents, it becomes an insult to them and many sorts of voilence may spark off.

Xenophobia, the fear of strangers can also result from some typical social changes due to the occurrence of the foreign tourists which are not easily acceptable to the residents. Overcrowding in market, on roadways and at recreational spots may slowly increase the level of frustation among local residents. More often xenophobia can result from a sense of loss of control over the state of affairs. Some time the local residents feel that they are no longer as free or as important as once they were. They find somewhat helpless in managing the affairs. However, this sort of problem is not easily descernible in the hill region of Uttar Pradesh and the whole issue needs a purely clinical approach for its thorough investigation. These negative impacts of tourism development have begun to surface in academics only within the last decade. Only some less developed countries have provided such symptoms where cultural transformation has occurred to a considerable extent as a result of tourists influx from western countries.

iii Ecological—Environmental Changes

Tourism has generated a lot of controversy and debate over its role as an agent of change and development in the physical/natural scenario of the tourist destination. Modern society has becoming day by day more ecology and eco-system conscious. Environmental quality and control have assumed the top most priority in almost all national planning. Conservation and preservation of all sorts of biome and natural resources have become the slogans of present day environmentalists. A number of humanists and sociologists like Elzeard Bouffier of France, Toyohiko Kagawa of Japan, Sundar Lal Bahuguna (India) have made their life mission to make the public environmentally conscious.

It is in these contexts that the role of tourism has to be fully appreciated. Himalaya one of the most fragile mountains needs some special attention. Here environment should be given first priority. It is not so much the number of tourists that will prove a danger, it would be the failure to provide drainage, disposal of garbage, supply of water, power and communication etc. Due to the wanton encroachment by man the degradation of the eco-system and environment shall ultimately destroy the scenic beauty. In U. P. part of Himalaya soils, bio-mass-flora and fauna and water etc., have suffered a great loss due to heavy and unplanned encroachment upto the far interior. Flora and fauna have been badly affected due to a number of projects to flourish tourism in the region. The Ramganga dam has submerged a vast area falling under the natural habitat of tiger and other animals. Controversial Tehri Dam and Jamrani Dam may be cited other examples.

Increasing construction at Gangotri is causing great loss to a number of plant species like chir, fir, silver birch (Bhojpatra) etc. Heavy human use of open space adversely affect the biomass. Trampling directly kills plants, it causes soil compaction, increased use of an area changes the micro climate and water balance and thus kills plants. Increasing use of wood as fuel and timber in a number of industrial products (including souvenir industry) also leads to felling and cutting of trees. These initial changes in the local biotic community can lead to the eventual loss of other species. Plants are also lost by plucking of wild flowers and leaves by wanderers. A number of rare plants in the Valley of Flowers are being exhausted by this very habit of a number of tourists.

Wild life species are also badly affected by the proximity of human beings. Musk deer—a rare Indian species is almost vanishing due to excessive human interference and deforestation. In addition to the physical loss of animals human pressure increase the incidence of disease. Over harvesting of fish is special problem in Ramganga and Alaknanda near Tehri. Contamination due to washing, bathing, drinking and sewage treatment is also on increase at different watering places in Himalaya.

A closer analysis of the alleged anti-environmental character of tourism clearly shows that it has been rather over emphasised. Tourism phenomenon should not be considered as an anti-thesis to environmental ethics, rather it is a complementary and supporting idea of the ecological maintenance. Clare A. Gunn in one of his papers has beautifully presented the symbosis of the forces of tourism, recreation and conservation. "It seems quite obvious that much of conservation ideology and practice fosters tourism and recreation. Conservation, as a social value is supported by the popularisation of the landscape by tourism and recreation interests. Conservation, in the sense of efficiency, is fostered by the geographic clustering tendencies of business enterprise, especially at transportation node. Conservation, in its concern over aesthetics, plays directly into the hands of recreation and tourism, especially in support of protecting and making accessible both vast and intimate areas of outstanding scenic beauty. Conservation of plant and animal life is providing basic appeal to society to view and understand biology. Concerns over species elimination and pollution are highly complementary to the interests of tourism and recreation. Certainly, conservation in the sense of cultural and heritage protection, restoration and interpretation, heightens people's interest—hence complements this form of recreation and tourism" (Clare A. Gunn in Singh, T. V., 1982, p. 17).

TOURISM IN THE HILLS—RETROSPECT AND PROSPECT

A cursary glance over what has been said and analysed throughout the works gives an insight into the real nature of pilgrimage and tourism in the Hill Region of Uttar Pradesh. Its tourism history is as old as the human occupance of the region itself. However, the nature and format of tourism have changed markedly. In the days gone by it flourished in the guise of pilgrimage. Most of the sacred places associated with ancient religious beliefs are situated in the lower and upper Himalayas. The theomorphic manifestation of Godhood in these hills, coupled with the sylvan beauty, inspired the hoary bands of pilgrims to scale the Himalayas throughout the history. This phenomenon has been playing a pivotal role in designing the socio-cultural fabric of this region. It is interesting to note that most of the important townships of Kumaun and Garhwal regions are situated on ancient highways which led either to Kedarnath or Badrinath or Pasupatinath Temple in Nepal.

Skipping the interim period when we jump directly to the post-independence era, a marked change is noticed in the concept of tourism. Religious motives are no more the prime consideration for touring the hills. Sight-seeing, change of climate, enjoying holidays etc. are some of the new dimensions which have added themselves to the earlier cause. It is in these contexts that tourism has assumed a new shape in Himalayan region. Perhaps no region in the world but the U. P. Himalaya can claim that once started in the hoary past, the sprit of tourism never ended here—the only place which kept the lamp of tourism burning though with flames of varying colour and magnitude. But inspite of its long historical records tourism was never given due attention as it meritted. This was always overlooked. Even the Indian people know very little about the whole region except that some shrines devoted to Hindu pilgrimage are situated here. Whatever has been done in the name of development of modern tourism in this region during the last two decades has not adequately been publicised or efficiently planned.

(i) **Some Problems**

The hill region of Uttar Pradesh has so long been neglected and beset with so many problems of complex nature that development of tourism is not an easy job here. But one thing is clear that if tourism is one developed on scientific lines it will prove an immensely valuable asset for the region as a whole.

For the proper development of tourism phenomenon, the basic problems which have gripped the region severely are to be first identified so that some rational measures may be suggested for their proper eradication and improvement. Some of the problems that need special attention in the development of tourism may be diagnosed as follows :

1. The greatest of the problems that this region has to face in terms of tourism development is the shortage of easy and safe transport. The difficulties of access are severe and facilities are almost negligible, leaving this part of the land still primitive. Roads are quite insufficient and have been constructed haphazardly. Road construction has been done in a most unplanned way in the hill region and consequently most of the roads are wrongly aligned. Unnecessary cutting and broadening have increased erosion and allied problems. The opening of roads to many new areas and the interior parts of Himalayas holds a still greater promise for tourism in these areas.

2. The problem relating to accommodations—their quality, number and distributional pattern etc. is also very serious in the region. Mostly good hotels or hotels of western style owned or managed by Govt. or other private agencies are concentrated only at certain selected spots like Nainital, Dehra Dun, Mussoorie etc. They are somewhat costly and cater to the needs of the high-ups of the society. They provide all sorts of facilities of lodging and cuisine etc. Even these hotels become awefully short during the peak season. For low middle class tourists accommodation facilities are there but such hotels are rather ill-equipped and ill maintained. Moreover such hotels seldom provide fooding facilities. In peak season they present acute problems as they become markedly short in comparison to demand. Common or low paid tourits mostly visit centres of pilgrimage rather than scenic spots. At

these religious places in the name of accommodation for them there are only dharamshalas-most of which are in bad shape. At peak season a number of pilgrims/tourists are forced to sleep in the open specially at Hardwar and Rishikesh. At scenic spots there are hardly sufficient accommodations for such tourists even if they wish to visit these places. Further almost all accountable hotels are concentrated at certain selected places. On the contrary, there is no proper and regular arrangement to accommodate tourists at places like Kausani, Mukteshwar, Baijnath, Devaprayag etc. So inspite of their attractions and importance all these places do not pull tourists in considerable number. Moreover, this sort of distribution of hotels breeds regional imbalance and can easily be accounted for the lopsided growth of tourism as an industry. The hotel charges too specially in Nainital, Mussoorie, Dehra Dun etc. are sky rocketing and fluctuate with the seasonal rush.

3. The third serious but hardly carefully attended to problem is of food, cuisine and drinking water. Food available for general tourists is mostly costly and is not always palatable too. For such tourists the question of varieties of food items hardly arises. Common tourists have to pay a large sum on this very item and even then they hardly feel satisfied. Non-availability of drinking water is an acute problem at almost all the hill stations. It is easier to get cold drink here than to have a glass of simple water. As we proceed further in the interior of Himalay, the dimension of water problem becomes greater. It is in this context there is a proverbial saying that the sons and water of the hills do not come to the use of hills (Pahar Ka Putra aur pahar ka pani pahar ke kam nahi ata hai). Mostly sons of the soil migrate to the plains in search of better avenues and hill water discharges itself unto the plains.

4. Another problem of high magnitude is the assembly and organization of basic amenities and utilities in the hills. Water (for general use), electricity, hospitals, post-telegraph-telephone offices, banks, chemists and druggists and general merchandise etc. play a big role in the development of tourism. Except at

bigger places these facilities are quite short and meagre or sometimes absent at a number of places, specially in the interior of the region.

Facilities for entertainments like theaters, museums, clubs, libraries souvenir shop, books and newspaper stalls are markedly lacking at a number of tourist sports. These are the basic requirements of modern tourism. They should be made available to the tourists so that they may enjoy their stay and spend the same with fun and frolic, otherwise evening in the hills would be sheer dull and boring.

5. Ignorance of the region and about a number of its places important both from religious and scenic point of view is also of major concern. The most pious and the best scenic spots of Himalaya are perhaps least advertised or publicised. Apart from the places of historical and architectural importance, the scenic beauty of the hills too has not been exposed fully. There are scores of beatiful spots but most of them are either unidentified or still neglected. No publicity has so far been given to the architectural and incongraphic wealth of the hill region, which can become the most favoured haunts for many. What to speak more, it was observed that some of the tourist bungalows lying between Uttarkashi and Gangotri remain vacant as few people know about them.

6. Lack of tourism consiousness among the people is also a major problem, without which scientific development of tourism is an impossibility. The irony of the trade is that tourism is still considered to be a luxury or hobby confined to only a privileged few. We have not still been able to feel at home with tourism and do not regard it as a real source of education, knowledge, co-operation and brotherhood.

7. Though the process of tourism development has been initiated by a number of agencies at local, regional and state level, yet the rate of growth is still very slow. Desired results could not

be achieved for want of rational policy, planning and programming. Lack of systematic organization and co-operation among various agencies like-U. P. State Tourism Development Corporation, Hill Development Board, Kumaun and Garhwal Mandal Vikas Nigam etc. are mainly responsible for the bad shape of things in the region.

8. A number of other major and minor problems also come in the way of tourism development in the region. The system of toll taxes at the entry-point to the towns is both irksome and time-consuming. Lack of open space for parking specially at Hardwar, Reshikesh and Mussoorie creates serious problems. Hardwar being a break of bulk point becomes conjested because of vehicular traffic.

9. The last but not the least serious problem is that of environmental degradation and ecological imbalance created or liabale to be created by the infrastructural development whatsoever in the region in the name of tourism. Whatever has been done or planned to be done in the Himalaya poses a number of problems to its soil, water, climate and regional bio-mass. Silting of the lake at Nainital impairing its beauty and sanitation may be a pointer.

(ii) Planning Measures

A closer analysis of the above and many other problems clearly show that they need some special attention and effort on our part for their eradication and improvement. Tourism, a flourishing trade in the hills no doubt offers some hope but it is a capital intensive process and simultaneously needs co-ordinated development and appropriate planning. Only then it can claim any significant contribution to the regional economy. Tourism is a proposition that should be promoted on priority basis and it is high time to workout a proper strategy for its planned development. Tourism is the only hope for mountainous area where there is not much land fit for agriculture due to predominance of slope, thin soil, erosion and several other constraints. Possibilities of development of mining or industries or equally limited due to inadequate surveys and prospecting of the potential. Horticulture, floriculture or tree culture (forestry) also can not become profitable business for these areas unless basic infrastructural facilities are developed to some considerable extent.

Any planning for tourism development should be considered as an integral part of the overall national plan for economic development. The success of tourism development depends very largely upon appropriate facilities being available at the right place at the right time and these can only be provided by adequate research into 'national tourist assets'. Peters has attributed an important role to tourism research in its future development. Tourism planning means an integrated development of tourism resources and tourist activities to derive the optimum benefits in terms of social, economic and ecological objectives on the one hand and satisfaction of the tourists on the other. Any integrated approach to tourism development needs careful planning based on detailed survey of the tourism potential base area and studies of future customers based on surveys and forecasts. In order to achieve the desired goals some immediate, short-term, long-term and perspective projects should be prepared. A number of authors have given their own models of tourism development in different situations. But in each such Tourism Complex Planning Model survey for making an inventory of the recreational resources, development of infrastructure and tourist facilities, scaling and ordering of tourist places at different territorial levels (micro, messo, macro), linkage in between them and lastly their integration into a complete whole etc. are some of the basic premises.

In order to develop tourism in the region, a number of measures that may be taken up in a planned and coherent way are summarised as follows :

1. A detailed survey of the entire hill region should be planned to make a classified inventory of all present and possible

tourism-recreation-pilgrimage resources and spots. A Tourism Planning Atlas of the hill region based on micro research and survey using even the remote sensing technology should be prepared by an apex national organization on scientific lines. This would certainly pave the way for all further development of tourism trade and industry.

2. The second point of focus is necessarily the basic infrastructure specially transport and accommodation required for the development of tourism as an industry in the hills.

(a) Road-system is the life line for any region but that is much more significant in a hilly terrain moreover in the context of tourism. Circulation constitutes the back bone of tourist industry. Pucca and metalled roads should be built to all the pivotal points and minor roads should also be made more dependable.

Wherever possible it is better to encourage rope ways or small flying clubs on European lines. Small helipads at some important places would be quite helpful. Trekking should be encouraged to the utmost and these pathways should be made safe for carefree and comfortable journey. Arrangement for mile stones should be made on Gangotri-Gaumukh road to facilitate the trekkers. Travel circuit route already in operation should be popularized.

The bus-service here needs a complete overhaul. More comfortable buses of different sizes should be introduced for major and minor roads. Travel agencies and agents should be all licence holders and duly registered to avoid cheating of tourists. It is often observed that roadways buses are mostly sub-standard not fit to ply on zig-zag hilly roads. They need some better replacement. It was proposed by many that G.N.O.U. Ltd. and K.M.O.U. Ltd. should be given the full responsibility for operating the total transport in the region.

(b) Accommodation is the basic component of tourism industry. Comfortable and somewhat cheap boarding facilities should be made available at all possible spots to suit to the needs and choice of all sorts of tourists and pilgrims. Government must come forward to diversify the hotel industry. While increasing the number of hotels and other lodges in the region we must not think of offering three or five star hospitality. Together with being costly, the erection of these hotels does not suit the regional milieu. The idea of making small cottages and log huts may also be viewed in this context. Mostly dharamshalas have become outdated, they should be rennovated to suit modern tastes and requirements.

3. Fooding which is one of the acute problems is often overlooked. There should be sufficient restaurants which may provide common Indian food at cheap rates. This will cater to the needs of common Indian tourists and pilgrims. Provision should be made to make drinking water available at almost all places in the hill region.

4. Tourism consciousness is a prerequisite condition for tourism development in a region. All possible measures should be taken to educate people about the importance of tourism-its religious, recreational and educative value and encourage them to participate at all levels. It is not only a means of simple religious or recreational satisfaction but also a vehicle of total regional development and better means of national integration. Unless and untill this tourism consciousness is generated especially among the younger and educated people, there is least possibility of transformation of this traditionally religious old people-dominated tourism into a modern and scientific one. Tourism should be considered as an enterprise of the people, by the people for the public good.

5. The hills are not given a proper projection in any planned manner. Therefore, extensive publicity of the regional character should be made through all possible media-booklets, posters, news papers, radio, TV, video and short films etc.

6. Activities focussing regional cultural traits like festivals, fairs, dances, music etc. should be properly patronised and artists should be given proper facilities and subsidies to develop and display their traditional arts. However, every possible care should be taken to preserve native customs and traditions of the local residents.

7. Traditional handicrafts of the hill region should be given proper boost up to enable them to cater to the modern needs and fashions. It is only thus that souvenir market can be fully enriched. Government must come forward with an action plan to provide basic raw materials, necessary capital and marketing facilities to the local crafts men for developing and producing better items of souvenir trade.

8. Tourism in the hill region is concentrated mostly in towns. Hill people who are engaged in production of various types of citrus fruits and vegetables specially potato in the far interior should be linked with tourism trade. Fruits more or less can be made tourism items. Some small industries should be set up in the region for packing fruits and preparing some items from them. These would fetch good money from the tourists. Apple juice industry in Himachal Pradesh has become so much popular only because of incentives given by tourism there.

9. At some selected places of historical and archeological significance like Champawat, Pithoragarh, Baijath, Tehri museums and art galleries should be opened. It would help in preserving the valuable art and culture of the region.

10. Sufficient number of trained guides are essential for the development of tourism in the region. They should be well-behaved and well versed with the geography and culture of the land. A guide training centre may be opened at some appropriate place in the region.

11. There should be a package programme for the improvement of wild life parks and sanctuaries in the hill region.

Rules regarding the protection of the wild life should be made stricter and enforced rigidly.

12. Proper initiative should be taken to popularise winter sports, mountaineering and trekking etc. Provision should be made for oxygen bottles on the way from Gaurikund to Kedarnath and Govind Ghat to Valley of Flowers. Some of the pilgrims/tourists feel uneasy for want of sufficient amount of oxygen there.

13. Tourism should be provided a respectful place in the academic curricula of the universities and collages. Proper incentives be given to the researches on various themes of Indian tourism especially in marginal areas. A National Institute of Tourism Research and Development should be set up in the country with its two major centres each devoted to tourism promotion in the hills and on the coasts.

14. Tourism in Himalaya should be developed on the lines of Alpine countries especially of Switzerland where a perfectly planned tourist industry drawing lakhs of international visitors has become the key stone of national economy.

15. In excuting these planning measures ecology and environment of the hill region should always be taken into consideration. Things should be planned in such a way that everything desired is achieved without damaging even an iota of Himalayan ecology. A balance between tourism-recreation and conservation-ecology should always be the best policy. The quality of Himalayan environment at no cost should be minimised or impaired.

It is thus no exaggeration to say that tourism is the most important of all the resources available to man in this region. Himalaya is a unique repository or store house of all sorts of tourism attractions distributed rather evenly in time-space perspectives, and with rational and careful planning they are sure to bring revolutionary transformation in the economy of the whloe area. Properly planned it would certainly prove a boon to the region.

REFERENCES

Anand, M. M. 1976 : Tourism and Hotel Industry in India, Prentice Hall of India, New Delhi.

Archer, B. H. 1973 : The Impact of Domestic Tourism, University of Wales Press, Bangor.

Atkinson, E. T. 1973 : (Reprint) : The Himalayan Gazetteer, Vol. II, Part I, Cosmo Publication, New Delhi.

Bendra, V. P. 1979 : Tourism in India, Parimal Prakashan, Aurangabad, Maharastra.

Berry, Ramesh 1970 : Story of Doon Valley, Jugal Kishore and Co., Dehra Dun.

Bhardwaj, S. M. 1973 : Hindu Places of Pilgrimage in India—A Study in Cultural Geography, Thomson Press (India) Ltd., Delhi.

Bhatia, A. K. 1983 : Tourism Development—Principles and Practices, Sterling Publishers, New Delhi.

Bhatt, Madanchandra 1973 : Uttar Pradesh, Vol. 1, No. 1 Kumaun University, Nainital.

Blache, P. V. D. 1950 : Principles on Human Geography, M. T. Constable Publishers, London.

Boesh, H. 1964 : A Geography of World Economy, D. Van Nostrand Co.

Bose, A. 1973 : Studies in India's Urbanization, Tata McGraw Hill Publishing Co., Bombay.

Bose, S. C. 1976 : Geography of Himalaya, National Book Trust, Bombay.

Braun-Brumifield, 1964 : The Changing Travel Market, Inc., Ann Arbor, Michigan.

Brown, R. M. 1935 : 'The Business of Recreation,' Geographical Review, Vol. XXV, pp. 467-75.

Bryden, John M. 1973 : Tourism and Development, The University Press, Cambridge.

Burkart, A. J. 1975 : The Management of Tourism, Heinemann, London.

Burton, T. L. (ed.) 1970 : Recreation, Research and Planning, Allen and Unwin, London.

Clawson, M. and Knetsch, J. L. 1976 : Economics of Outdoor Recreation, John Hopkins Press, Baltimore.

Cohen, Erik 1978 : 'The Impact of Tourism on the Physical Environment.' Annals of Tourism Research, Vol. V, No. 2, (April/June) Stout.

Cooper, I. R. 1977 : 'Images of Tourism', New Society, Vol. 41, No. 777, pp. 385-86.

Cosgrove, I. and Jackson, R. 1972 : The Geography of Recreation and Leisure, Hutchinson, London.

Dattar, B. N. 1961 : Himalayan Pilgrimage, Publication Division, New Delhi.

Davis, Kingsley 1962 : Urbanization in India-Past and Future, in Roy Turner (ed.) India's Urban Future, Oxford University Press, Bombay.

Davis, H. D. 1968 : Potentials for Tourism in Developing Countries, Finance and Development, London.

Doswell, Roger 1978 : Case Studies in Tourism, Elden Press, Oxford.

Dower, M. 1970 : "Leisure-Its Impact on Man and the Land," Geography, Vol. 55, pp. 253-60.

References

Fairburn, A. N. 1951 : 'The Grand Tour,' Geographical Magazine, Vol. XXIV, pp. 118-27.

Gearing, C. E. Charles 1976 : Planning for Tourism Development Quantitative Approach, Praeger Publication, New York.

Gilbert, E. W. 1939 : 'The Growth of Inland and Seaside Health Resort,' Scottish Geographical Magazine, January.

Greely, R. B. 1942 : 'Part Time Farming and Recreational Land use in New England,' Economic Geography, Vol. 18, pp. 145-52.

Gupta, S. P. and Krishna, Lal 1974 : Tourism Museum and Monument in India, Oriental Publication, Delhi.

Hastings, J. (ed.) 1967 : Encyclopaedia of Religion and Ethics, Vol. 10, T. and T. Clark, Edinburgh.

Hunziker, W. 1951 : Social Tourism—Its Nature and Problems, Alliance International Tourism, Geneva.

Jafari, J. 1974 : 'The Socio-Economic Costs of Tourism to Developing Countries,' Annals of Tourism Research, pp. 227-62.

Jodh Singh Bagli Negi, T. 1920 (Reprint 1987) : Himalayan Travels, New Gian Offset Printers, New Delhi.

Jones, C. F. and Darkenwald, G. G. 1947 : Economic Geography, Macmillan Company, New York.

Joshi, S. C. Joshi, D. R. and Dani, D. D. 1983 : Kumaun Himalaya, Gynodaya Prakashan, Nainital.

Kaul, R. N. 1985 : Dynamics of Tourism (3 Vols.), Sterling Publishers Pvt. Ltd. New Delhi.

Kaur, J. 1976 : 'Re-evaluating Nainital Tourist Capacity for Diffusion of Planned Tourism Activity in Kumaun Lake Basins', Tourism Recreation and Research, Lucknow, Vol. I, pp.21-26.

Ibid 1978 : 'From Ganga to Gaumukh,' Tourism Recreation and Research, Lucknow, Vol. III, No. 1, pp. 23-30.

Ibid 1979 : Bibliographical Sources for Himalayan Pilgrimages and Tourism Studies : Uttarakhand,' Tourism Recreation and Research, Lucknow, Vol. 4, No. 1.

Khacher, L. K. 1978 : 'The Nanda Devi Sanctuary,' Journal of the Bombay Natural History Society, Vol. 75, No. 3.

Lal, J. S. and Maddie, A. D. 1981 : The Himalaya—Aspect of Change, Oxford University Press, Bombay.

Law, B. C. (ed.) 1968 : The Himalayan Mountain—Its Origin and Geographical Relation, in Mountain and Rivers of India, National Committee for Geography, Calcutta.

Lansing, J. B. and Blood, D. M. 1964 : The Changing Travel Market, University of Michigan.

Leszcayeki, S. 1964 : Applied Geography or Practical Application of Geographical Research, Problem of Applied Geography, III PWN Polish Scientific Publishers.

Lloyed, E. Hudman 1978 : 'Tourism Impact : The Need of Regional Planning', Annals of Tourism Research, 5 : 1 (Jan.-March) Stout.

McIntosh, R. W. 1972 : Tourism-Principles, Practices, Philosophies, Grid, Inc. Columbus, Ohio.

McMurry, K. C. 1930 : 'The Use of Land for Recreation', Annals of the Association of American Geographers, Vol. 20, pp. 7-20.

Medlik, S. 1972 : Profile of the Hotel and Catering Industry, Heinemann, London.

Ibid 1973 : 'Some Tourism Economics', The Cornell Quarterly, Vol. 14, No. 2, August, pp. 2-4.

References

Mercer, D. C. 1970 : 'The Geography of Leisure—A Contemporary Growth Point', Geography, Vol. 55, pp. 261-72.

Mishra, R. P., Sundram, K. V. and Rao, V.L.S.P. 1976 : Regional Development Planning in India—A New Strategy, Vikas Publishing House, New Delhi.

Mitchell, J. C. 1968 : Quoted in Gerald Breeze, Urbanization in Newly Developing Countries, Prentice Hall of India, New Delhi.

Painuli, P. 1967 : A Tourist's View of the Valley of Gods, Vanguared Press, Dehra Dun.

Pandey, B. P. : Kumaun Ka Itihas, Shakti Press, Almora.

Patmore, J. A. 1970 : Land and Leisure, David and Charles.

Peters, M. 1969 : International Tourism, Hutchinson, London.

Poddar, H. P. 1957 : Kalayan-Tirth-Ank, Vol. I, Geeta Press, Gorakhpur.

Preobrazhensky, V. S. and Krivosheyev, V. M. 1982 : Recreational Geography of U.S.S.R. Progress Publishers, Moscow.

Richards, G. 1972 : How Important is Tourism in Real Term ? Catering Times, 3rd August.

Robinson, H. 1976 : A Geography of Tourism, Macdonald and Evans Ltd., London.

Schanche, Don A. 1966 : 'Your Image Not Mine', P. A. T. A. (15th Annual Report), San Francisco.

Sharma, P. Mahadhar 1974 : Tapobhumi Uttarakhand, Matidhar Sharma and Sons, Badrinath, Chamoli.

Sigaux, G. 1966 : History of Tourism, Leisure Art, London.

Singh, C. B. 1982 : Studies of Tourist Places in U. P., Un-published Ph. D. Thesis University of Gorakhpur.

Singh, O. P. (ed.) 1983 : The Himalaya-Nature, Man and Culture, Rajesh Publications, New Delhi.

Singh, P. N. 1985 : Successful Tourism Management, Sterling Publishers, New Delhi.

Singh, R. L. (ed.) 1971 : India-A Regional Geography, National Geographical Society, Varanasi.

Singh, S. N. 1986 : Geography of Tourism and Recreation, Inter India Publication, New Delhi.

Singh, T. V. 1975 : Tourism and Tourist Industry in U. P., New Height, Delhi.

Singh, T. V. and Kaur J. (eds.) 1982 : Studies in Tourism, Wild Life Parks, Conservation, Metropolitan Book Company, Delhi.

Smith, Stephen 1983 : Recreation Geography, Longman Group Ltd., London.

Smythe, F. S. 1932 : Kamet Conquered, Victor Gollancz Ltd., London.

Spate, O.H.K. and Learmonth, A.T.A. 1967 : India and Pakistan, Methuen and Company Ltd., Chaucer Press, Suffolk.

Stedman, G. 1947 : 'Business Aspects of Vacation Travel,' New York State Commercial Review.

Wadia, D. N. 1961 : Geology of India, Macmillan and Co. Ltd., London.

Wahab, S. E. 1971 : An Introduction to Tourism Theory. Travel Research Journal, I.O.V.T.O. Geneva.

Watron. H. G. 1929 : District Gazetteer Dehra Dun, Allahabad.

White, J. 1967 : History of Tourism, Leisure Art, London.

Williams, J. E. and Zelinsky, W. 1970 : 'On Some Patterns of International Tourist Flow', Economic Geography, Oct., pp. 549-67.

Zierer, C. M. 1952 : 'Tourism and Recreation in the West', Geographical Review, Vol. 42, pp. 462-81.

Pamphlets and Booklets

Aggarwal, A. C. 1981 : Tourist Guide to Kumaun Region, Nest and Wings (India), New Delhi.

Aggarwal, A. C. 1984 : Tourist Guide to Garhwal Region, Nest and Wings (India), New Delhi.

Census of India, 1981 : Part XA, Town Directory, Govt. of India Puclication, New Delhi.

Development of Hill Region, VIth Five-Year Plan, Progress Report 1980-81 and Planning 1981-82, U. P. Govt. Publication, Lucknow.

Development of Hill Region, Progress Report 1983-84 and Planning 1984-85, U. P. Govt. Publication, Lucknow.

Jagannath, R. 1985 : Badrinath and Kedarnath, The Heritage, Editorial and Management Office, Chandigarh, July.

Kumaum Mandal Vikas Nigam Ltd., Nainital 1978-79 : VIIIth Annual Report.

Misra, P. K. 1986 : Charms-Natural and Divine, Dec., Times of India, Lucknow.

Sarita 1979 : Tourism Special, Delhi Press, New Delhi, May (I).

Ibid 1987 : Tourism Special, Delhi Press, New Delhi, May (I).

Travel News 1984 : Travel Agent Association of India, Bombay, Feb.

Wama 1985 : Tourism Special, Times of India Publication, New Delhi, May.

APPENDIX-A

DEFINITION OF URBAN AREA AND URBAN AGGLOMERATION

Urban Area

As the concept and criteria of towns have not been static throughout, it becomes very much essential to have a knowledge of their true character for their comparative study and growth analysis.

In census 1981, the definition of 'Urban Area' was same as in 1971. In this census urban area has been defined as follows :

(a) All places with a municipal corporation, municipal board or cantonment board or notified/town area,

(b) All other places which satisfied the following criteria :
   (i) a minimum population of 5,000,
   (ii) a population with a density of at least 400 per sq. km (or 1,000 persons per sq. mile) and
   (iii) at least 75% of the male working population engaged in non-agricultural activities.

Allied agricultural activities such as fishing, logging etc. have been considered agricultural in 1981 census for determining the proportion of engagement of male population in non-agricultural activities for the purpose of declaring a place as town.

Appendix

Urban Agglomeration

The concept of urban agglomeration of the 1971 is also adopted for 1981 census. Very often the growth of towns overlapped the statutory limits of the city or town. Large railway colonies, university campuses, port areas, industrial areas etc. came up outside the limits of the town but they formed continuous growth with the town. These outgrowths may or may not by themselves qualify to be treated as separate towns but these outgrowths deserve to be treated as urban areas. Such a town with their outgrowth areas is treated as one urban unit and called 'Urban Agglomeration; An urban Agglomeration may constitute :

(i) a city with continuous outgrowths (the part of outgrowth being outside the statutory limits but falling within the boundaries of the adjoining village or villages).

(ii) a town with similar outgrowth or two or more adjoining towns with their outgrowth as in (i), *or*

(iii) a city and one or more adjoining towns with their outgrowths all of which form a continuous spread.

APPENDIX B-1

KUMAUN DIVISION
Tourist Centres and Distances in between them

Places From	To	Distance (Km)
(1)	(2)	(3)
Allahabad	Lucknow	201
Lucknow	Tanakpur	385
Tanakpur	Champawat	75
Champawat	Lohaghat	15
Lohaghat	Abott Mount	16
Lohaghat	Pithoragarh	62
Pithoragarh	Munsiari	154
Munsiari	Milam Glacier	54 *trek*
Munsiari	Thal	35
Thal	Chaukori	20
Chaukori	Berinag	13
Berinag	Almora	40
Almora	Jageshwar	34
Almora	Binsar	30
Almora	Bageshwar	90
Bageshwar	Kapkot	15
Kapkot	Pindari Glacier	58 *trek*
Almora	Kausani	53
Almora	Nainital	68
Nainital	Bhimtal	23

Appendix

(1)	(2)	(3)
Nainital	Sat tal	21
Nainital	Naukuchiatal	26
Nainital	Ramgarh	26
Ramgarh	Mukteshwar	26
Nainital	Ranikhet	59
Ranikhet	Marrila *via* Bhatrohjhan	70
Manila	Dhangarhi	50
Dhangarhi	Ramnagar	15
Ramnagar	Kalagarh	25

APPENDIX B-2

GARHWAL DIVISION

Tourist Centres and Distances in between them

Places From	To	Distance (Km)
(1)	(2)	(3)
Rishikesh	Deoprayag	71
Deoprayag	Srinagar	36
Srinagar	Rudraprayag	34
Rudraprayag	Karnprayag	32
Karnprayag	Chamoli	31
Chamoli	Joshimath	51
Joshimath	Govind Ghat	18
Govind Ghat	Badrinath	26
Govind Ghat	Valley of Flowers	19 *trek*
Govind Ghat	Ghangaria	15 *trek*
Ghangaria	Hemkund Sahib	5 *trek*
Joshimath	Chamoli	
Chamoli	Gopeshwar	10
Gopeshwar	Ukimath	69
Ukimath	Guptkashi	10
Guptkashi	Gaurikund	37
Gaurikund	Kedarnath	14 *trek*
Gaurikund	Tilwara	60
Tilwara	Tehri	70
Tehri	Dharasu	42

Appendix

(1)	(2)	(3)
Dharasu	Uttarkashi	28
Uttarkashi	Bhatwari	37
Bhatwari	Sukhi	29
Sukhi	Lanka	29
Lanka	Gangotri	11
Gangotri	Gaumukh	18 *trek*
Gangotri	Dharasu	135
Dharasu	Barkot	6
Barkot	Hanumanchatti	34
Hanumanchatti	Yamunotri	13 *trek*
Barkot	Mussoorie	98
Mussoorie	Chakrata	82
Chakrata	Kalsi	42
Kalsi	Mussoorie	40
Mussoorie	Dehra Dun	36
Dehra Dun	Rishikesh	43
Rishikesh	Hardwar	24
Hardwar	Lucknow	593

APPENDIX-C

PLACES OF TOURIST INTEREST IN THE HILL REGION OF UTTAR PRADESH

Sl. No.	Name of Town	Places of Tourist Interest
1	2	3

1. Uttarkashi

1.	Uttarkashi	1. Temple of Vishwanath, 2. Nehru Institute of mountaineering, 3. Kutti Devi Temple.
2.	Barkot	1. Old Temple, 2. Temple of Goddess Yamuna, 3. Divya Shila, 4. Hot Water Spring in Yamunotri.
3.	Bhatwari	1. Gangotri—Famous Temple of Goddess Gangaji

2. Chamoli

1.	Badrinathpuri	1. Badrinath Temple, 2. Hot Water Spring, 3. Narad Kund, 4. Panchshila, 5. Brahma Kapal, 6. Panchdhara, 7. Sheshnetra, 8. Urvashi Mandir, 9. Charan Paduka, 10. Neelkanth Parwat, 11. Mata Murti.

Appendix

1	2	3
2.	Kedarnath	1. Kedarnath Temple, 2. Adi-Shankracharya's Samadhi, 3. Bhairon Shila, 4. Bhim Cave, 5. Madhu Ganga, 6. Kheer Ganga, 7. Vasuki Tal.
3.	Chamoli Gopeshwar	Shiv Temple and Other Temples.
4.	Joshimath	1. Jagat Guru Shankracharya Temple and Winter Temple of Badrinath Ji.
5.	Karanprayag	1. Pindar and Alaknanda River confluence, 2. Uma and Karna Temple.
6.	Nandprayag	1. Alaknanda and Nandakini River confluence, 2. Gopalji Temple.

3. Tehri Garhwal

1.	Tehri	1. Confluence of Bhagirathi and Bhilangana River, 2. Maneri Dam.
2.	Narendra nagar	1. Panoramic Sun-set view.
3.	Deoprayag	1. Alaknanda and Bhagirathi River confluence, 2. Shiv Temple, 3. Ram Temple

4. Dehra Dun

1.	Dehra Dun	1. Sahastradhara, 2. Robber Cave (Gucchu Pani), 3. Malsi Deer Park, 4. Gandhi Park, 5. Khalanga Fort, 6. Forest Research Institute, 7. Doon

1	2	3
		School, 8. Indian Military Academy, 9. Gurudwara of Guru Ram Rai, 10. Tapkeshwar Temple (Lord Shiva 1699) 11. Laxman Sidh, 12. Tapovan.
2.	Mussoorie	1. Gun Hill (Bunder Punch, Sri Kanta and Gangotri Group 1), 2. Kempty Fall, 3. Municipal Garden, 4. Kathgodam Tibba or Children Lodge.
3.	Rishikesh	1. Bharat Temple, 2. Triveni Ghat, 3. Rishi Kund, 4. Raghunath Temple, 5. Puskar Temple, 6. Venkateshwar Temple, 7. Chandra Mauleswaram Temple 8. Laxman Jhoola, 9. Swarag Ashram, 10. Geeta Bhawan, 11. Parmarath Niketan.
4.	Vikas nagar	1. Dak Pathar.
5.	Chakrata Cantt.	1. Deoban, Tigar Hill, Ashok Edicts at Kalsi.
6.	Virbhadra	1. I.D.P.L. Virbhadra Temple.

5. Garhwal

1.	Srinagar	1. Kameshwar Mahadev Temple and Vishnu Temple.
2.	Rudra prayag	Alaknanda and Mandakini River confluence, Rudranath Ji and Chamundi Temple.

1	2	3
3.	Kotdwara	Sidhbali Temple.
4.	Lansdowne Cantt.	Beautiful scene of Himalaya Nanda Devi.
5.	Pauri	Beautiful scene of Himalayan Range including important Peaks.

6. Pithoragarh

1.	Pithoragarh	It has many Historic Fortifications Dating Back to the Time of Chand Rajas of Kumaun.
2.	Lohaghat	Centre of Historical and Mythological Importance.
3.	Champawat	It was at one time capital of the Chand Rajas.

7. Almora

1.	Almora	Katarmal (Sun Temple), Mohan Joshi Park, Simtola, Kalimath, Kasar Devi Temple, Chitai and Bright end Corner.
2.	Ranikhet Cantt.	Chaubatia, Bhaludam, Upat and Kalika, Mountain Golf Link, Majkhali, Co-operative Drug Factory, Tarikhet.
3.	Bageshwar	Confluence of Saryu and Gomti and Associated with Shiva Pindari Glacier.
4.	Dwarahat	Principal seat of the Katyuri Rajas, cluster of age-old Temple divided into eight distenct group.

1	2	3
		8. Nainital
1.	Nainital	Naina Peak, Laria Kanta, Snow view, Dorothy Seat, Lands End, Hanumangarhi, State Observatory, Kilbury, Khurpa Tal, Jeolikote.
2.	Bhowali	Health Resort and Hill Fruit Mart, T. B. Sanitorium, Ramgarh Pictureque hamlet in the heart of orchard Land.
3.	Bhimtal	Lake resort for boating and picnic at its centre, Sat Tal, Naukuchia Tal, Corbett National Park and Jim Corbett Museum.
		9. Hardwar
1.	Hardwar	Har-ki-Pauri, Canal Centenary Bridge, Bhim goda Tank, Sapt Rishi Ashram, Sadhu-bela, Daksh Mahadev Temple, Mansa Devi Temple, Chandi Devi Temple, Sri Gorakhnath Temple and Cave, Gita Bhavan, Kal Bhairav Temple, Maya Devi Temple, Bhola Giri Ashram, Manokamna Sidh Temple, Ganesh Ghat, Maya Pur, Manokamna Sidh Hanuman Temple, Awdhoot Ashram, Kankhal, Narayan Shila Mayapur & others important Temples, Gurukul Kangari University, Ved Mandir, Musium and Pharmacy.

APPENDIX D-1

SCHEDULE

(Town-Case Profile)

Sl. No.

1. Name of the town　　　　　　Height

2. Division　　　　　District　　　Tahsil

3. Administrative status—
   Municipality/Cantt/Town Area/Notified Area

4. Scenery—
   (a) Rock system
   (b) Land forms
   (c) Water, rivers, lakes, water falls, glaciers etc.

5. Flora and Fauna—
   (a) Forest, grasslands, national park etc.
   (b) Wild life, birds, zoo, games.

6. Climate
   Sunshine, cloud, rain and snow, health resorts, mineral water etc.

7. Culture
   - (a) Sites and areas of archaeological interest
   - (b) Historical buildings/monuments/remains
   - (c) Places of historical significance
   - (d) Museum
   - (e) Modern culture
   - (f) Educational/religious/institution

8. Traditions
   - (a) Regional/local festivals
   - (b) Arts and handicrafts
   - (c) Music-folk lore
   - (d) Native life

9. Entertainments-(Participation and viewing spots)

10. Any other attraction-not available elsewhere

11. Accessibility and ease of transport to the resort and surrounding
    Air, rail, road-bus coach, car etc.
    Pedestrain, animal riding, rope-ways etc.

12. Accommodation to meet the demands of all social levels and pockets
    - (a) Hotels-grade   No.
    - (b) Motels
    - (c) Dak Bungalows
    - (d) Tourist house/bungalows
    - (e) Lodges
    - (f) Others

Appendix

13. Parking facility for visitors and excursionists
14. Open spaces, parks, recreation areas, garden, floral displays
15. Amusement/entertainment facilities—
    Theatres, funfairs, clubs, etc.
16. Game facilities—
    Boating, water skiing, golf, tennis, swimming, hunting etc.
17. Shopping facility-items of interest
18. Catering facilities-restaurant, coffee house, bar etc.
19. Information centres/enquiry offices
20. Any other facility

APPENDIX D-2

QUESTIONNAIRE

(Interviews with the Hotel Management)

Sl. No.

NOTE : Informations collected would be kept secret and it would be used for the research purpose only.

1. Name of the hotel   Type and grade

2. Total No. of employees   A. Permanent   B. Seasonal

3. Total salaries of employees (Rs.)

4. Total annual income (Rs.)

5. Food and cuisine

    (a) (i) Vegetarian, (ii) Non-vegetarian, (iii) Both

    (b) (i) Indian North/South, (ii) Continental, (iii) Chinese, (iv) Others

6. Accommodation

    (a) Total No. of rooms

    (b) Types of rooms

       (i) Single bed room, (ii) Double, (iii) Triple bed room, (iv) Other types

Appendix

8. Whether the tour/visit is
   (i) Recreational
   (ii) Religious
   (iii) Academic
   (iv) Others

9. Places he visits or plans to visit in the Hill Region

10. Kind of accommodation he prefers to
    (i) Hotels (Star system)
    (ii) Hotels Indigenous types
    (iii) Tourist Bungalows
    (iv) Others-tent houses, Dharamshalas etc.

11. Duration of his stay

12. In what proportion he spends on
    (i) Transport
    (ii) Accommodation
    (ii) Food etc.
    (iv) Amenities
    (v) Recreation
    (vi) Shopping

13. His holiday habits

14. Frequency of his visiting the place or area
    (i) For the first time
    (ii) Twice
    (iii) Thrice

15. Cuisine of his likeing
    (i) Indian North/South
    (ii) Continental

(iii) Chinese
   (iv) Others

16. Shopping pattern (articles)

17. His opinion about accommodation
    (a) (i) Very comfortable
        (ii) Comfortable
        (iii) Not comfortable
    (b) (i) Costly
        (ii) Average
        (iii) Cheap
    (c) (i) Neat and clean
        (ii) Average
        (iii) Dirty

18. Tourist opinion about transport
    (a) (i) Easily available
        (ii) Not easily available
    (b) (i) Comfortable
        (ii) Not comfortable
    (c) (i) Costly
        (ii) Cheap
        (iii) Average

19. Season he likes to come in

20. Special problems
    (i) Transport
    (ii) Accommodation
    (iii) Cuisine
    (iv) Recreation

Appendix

    (v) Information
    (vi) Guide etc.
    (vii) Others

21. Any suggestion

Place :   Signature
Date :   Name :
                                    Address :